Give Me a Second Chance

Rachel Saginsky

Cover Design: Leah Ben Avraham/Noonim Graphics
Typesetting: Optume Technologies

ISBN: 978-965-7023-32-7

1 3 5 7 9 8 6 4 2

Gefen Publishing House Ltd.
6 Hatzvi Street
Jerusalem 9438614,
Israel
972-2-538-0247
orders@gefenpublishing.com

Gefen Books
c/o Baker & Taylor Publisher Services
30 Amberwood Parkway
Ashland, Ohio 44805
516-593-1234
orders@gefenpublishing.com

www.gefenpublishing.com
Printed in Israel

Library of Congress Control Number: 2020925004

Contents

Preface

In 2016, I wrote a series of articles about women who had spent time incarcerated in Israel's only prison for women, Neve Tirtza. The women I spoke to shared the same message: "We were wrong. We've paid the price. We've changed. And now we're asking for a second chance."

Second chances. We all want them. We all believe in them – to a degree.

God created teshuvah (repentance, or more accurately, return) before creating the world, with the knowledge that we're human and that human beings make mistakes. So God gave us the gift of second chances – the choice to say, "I made a mistake. I'm sorry. I want to change."

Teshuvah is fundamental. But if we are brutally honest with ourselves, most of us find that we believe in it only to a degree. Because when it comes to giving a second chance to someone whose choices have changed the lives of others in ways that can never be repaired, we begin to question the power of teshuvah.

When I met "Racheli" for the first time, I didn't know all of her story. I saw an attractive woman, full of life, light, and laughter. What on earth had she done to end up in prison? As she shared her story, I wondered how she lives with the knowledge of what happened. I wondered from where she draws her strength to forge forward day after day, rebuilding her life.

The novel that you are holding is the answer. It's a novel. But it is based on a true story. Names, identifying details, and the events themselves have been changed. It's a dark novel, and it was hard to write. But I believe that this novel has a mission.

It was written to give hope to all who feel that they have fallen to a place from which they cannot escape. It shows that they can rebuild themselves and fashion a core of inner strength that makes them into people they never dreamed they'd be.

It was written to show the mechanism behind how terrible things can happen. This will bring understanding to anyone living in an ongoing abusive situation.

It was written with the hope that you, dear reader, will find the strength to give a second chance to those who have fallen.

Today, Racheli has rebuilt her relationships with almost all of her children and family members. She has built a strong second marriage. She spends her days helping to look after her grandchildren and working in something she enjoys.

This book is dedicated to the strong: to those who find the strength to rise from the ashes and to those who find the strength to allow others to rise from the ashes.

Acknowledgments

Thank you to the rabbis I consulted who encouraged me to write this story. This quote is an example: "Your intention is to highlight the dangers and praise the determination to overcome the difficulties. Those are definitely holy goals!"

Thank you to everyone who spoke to me to give me a better understanding of the events described in this book. Thank you to "Racheli," her parents and siblings, and her friends. Thank you to the Rabbanit of all the prisoners.

Thank you to everyone who read this novel as it was being written and after it was completed to give me feedback. A special thank-you to the people who went the extra mile to help me. You know who you are.

Thank you to my husband. For being there for me. Always.

Thank you to my superb editor Kezia Raffel Pride for your excellent work. Your eagle eye spotted every inconsistency. Your research skills astounded me. You anchored my imagery.

Thank you to the publisher of Gefen Publishing House, Ilan Greenfield; project manager Daphne Abrahams; cover artist Leah Ben Avraham; and proofreader Ruth Pepperman.

Thank you, Hashem. I pray that I have used the gift of words that You gave me in a way that You would want.

לאדם מערכי לב ומה' מענה לשון

Man can arrange his feelings, but eloquent speech is a gift from Hashem.
– From the Rosh Hashanah Musaf prayers (Proverbs 16:1)

Prologue

Jerusalem, December 2008

A few days after I divorced Daniel, I married Rav Natas. It was a secret marriage, and no one aside from those in our inner circle knew about it. The children and I didn't move into the Rav's house until two months later. Traveling back and forth between the house that Daniel and I had shared for so many years and the Rav's house had exhausted me.

Early one morning, I packed a suitcase for myself and told my eldest daughter, fifteen-year-old Yael, to pack for herself and the children. I looked into ten-year-old Yaakov's room. He had already left the house for yeshivah. I had to remember to call him and tell him to come to the Rav's house. Our new home. Meir, Aharon, and Hillel, my youngest three children, aged seven, five, and three, were still sleeping. When had they gone to bed? I didn't know. Routine and schedules were a thing of the past. Lost in the mists of time. I didn't mind. No, we were involved with something so much bigger than breakfast at seven thirty and bedtime at eight. We were part of the elite. A royal family. Rav Natas was a *tzaddik*, and we had been granted the honor to serve him. In his great wisdom, he was going to purge the evil out of my two youngest sons, Aharon and Hillel.

Suddenly, the house was stifling. Too small for my mission. I strode to the enormous living room windows that faced the street and yanked open the blind. I stepped onto the porch. The Jerusalem air was crispy, sharp as shards of glass, so early in the morning. I breathed in deeply. It was filled with promise. A promise that had nothing to do with Daniel, father of my eight children, and everything to do with Rav Natas. His wife! Like Tiferet, I was now also his wife. I was going to help him, this hidden miracle worker, to do great things. I spun around and headed back into the house. I could hear Yael banging open closet doors. Slamming drawers as she looked for pajamas, sweaters, socks. If I had spent more time on the porch, instead of rushing ahead like I always did, maybe I would have noticed the geraniums that were wilting, the pots filled with crinkled, brown leaves. Maybe I would have smelled the rot in the air.

I drove quickly. By now, I could have driven to the Rav's house with my eyes closed. But maybe it was simply that the Rav was guiding my car toward him with his spiritual powers. I pulled into a parking spot alongside the building where Rav Natas lived. I was finally home. I turned around to face the three boys strapped in the back seat. Hillel was sleeping again. I shook him awake. Had he been sleeping for long? I had to wash his hands when we got in. "Be good children," I told them. "Try to behave like Yehoshua." I wanted my sons to make the Rav proud. Just like his son Yehoshua did. Hillel rubbed his eyes. "Don't touch your eyes before I wash your hands," I said sharply. The Rav was so careful about things like that. Now that we were in his house, our new home, we would have to be more stringent. Suddenly I couldn't wait. I had to see him. "Bring the luggage in," I told Yael. I slammed the door and ran into the building and up to the first floor.

Tiferet, the Rav's first wife, opened the door. White blobs of something stained the front of her robe. Black bags, swollen like miniature eggplants, hung under her eyes. She didn't invite me in. I didn't expect it. After all, we were two wives sharing one husband.

"Where's the Rav?" I asked.

"Gone to the mikveh," she said. "We didn't sleep all night. He went before sunrise, for the *neitz* minyan."

I didn't ask when he would be back. We never knew. The ways of the *tzaddik* were hidden.

"The Rav has given you the room near the bathroom," she said. She stared at the children standing behind me, but made no move to welcome them. "The children can share the beds."

"Where are Shimmy and Avner?" I asked. I hadn't seen my two eldest sons in days.

Tiferet shrugged. "At the mikveh. Maybe. We need to clean the walls today."

I peered into the semi-darkness behind her shoulder. The walls. I would scour off every scuff mark, every fingerprint. The Rav would be proud of me.

The children spent the day in their room. I wished Yaakov were at the mikveh with the Rav, but Tiferet wasn't even sure that the group had gone to a mikveh. And there were hundreds of mikvehs in Jerusalem. Maybe they had gone up north, to the graves of holy rabbis. Maybe they had gone to Netivot.

Yael unpacked the suitcases and repacked them, stacking every child's clothes in neat piles. "Hillel doesn't have socks," she said when I stopped my scrubbing for long enough to peep in.

I shrugged. I had given her plenty of time to pack.

Hillel pulled at my skirt.

"Wanna eat something," Aharon said.

I shrugged again. Aharon was always hungry. It wasn't good to be so hungry all the time. It meant there was something evil lurking inside him. The Rav had told us so, just over two months ago, the last time he had come to our house, when Daniel and I were still married. "Later," I said. "You'll eat later."

The morning passed. The afternoon passed. And still the Rav had not come home. In the early evening, I lay on my bed. My shoulders ached from scrubbing the walls, and the skin on the edge of my right thumb had split. A tiny papercut that burned like fire every time I knocked it. I closed my eyes. I heard Aharon going to the bathroom. He was drinking water from the *netilat yadayim* cup.

I must have fallen asleep, because I woke with a start when Hillel banged into my side. And then I heard him. The Rav was back. I jumped up. I had to wash my hands. Fast...before he saw the impurity that had settled on them as I slept. I ran to the sink outside the bathroom, but the *netilat yadayim* cup was gone. I remembered Aharon drinking. I turned on the faucet and washed my hands without a cup.

The Rav was in the living room, sitting at the head of the table. The lapels of his black, shiny frock were perfectly pressed, like the closed wings of a beetle. Yigal stood on his right, Eran on his left.

I stood at the end of the table. Waiting for him to notice me. He didn't look at me. It was the impurity on my hands. I was sure of it. Then he looked up. Even from the end of the table, I could see the gold flecks in his eyes flashing. My heart beat faster. He knew. Like he knew everything else. Fear coiled around and around me, squeezing out the breath inside me.

"Bring the food," he said. "Today is a *hillula*. We must honor the *tzaddik*."

I wanted to hurry to the kitchen, to have the honor of serving the Rav his meal, but my legs were glued to the floor tiles. Because Tiferet was the wife who always cooked at the Rav's house. Sheets of fire flickered over the Rav's eyes. He was in a different place. Seeing things that we could not see. How lucky I was to be part of his greatness.

Tiferet brought out platters of chicken and roast potatoes. Peas in red tomato sauce, spiced with cumin. I could smell the spice. It tickled my nostrils, reminding me that I hadn't eaten all day. I ground my teeth together. Food! How could I think of food when there was such spiritual greatness around me? I had to focus on the darkness, on the evil that we were purging out of the world.

To understand how it happened, you have to suspend normal thinking. Normal things happen within a range that is normal. But to understand this story, you have to leave behind everything that is on the spectrum of normal. Leave behind every single thing that is right and correct, delete them completely, and enter an abnormal world. Here, you do not feel anything normal. Not one sole aspect of life is normal.

PART ONE

The difficulty in life is the choice.
– George Moore, *The Bending of the Bough*

CHAPTER ONE

A Child's Glimpse

Moshav Ayin Yaffa, 1975

Yossi was way ahead of me on the dusty track to the paddock. Jogging along, hurrying to reach Champion's enclosure and squeeze in a ride before the van that took the boys to the yeshiva arrived. I'd heard him leave the house, and I'd slid out of bed right away, careful not to wake Faygie. But I'd wasted minutes finding a pair of pants to wear instead of the skirt that Ima had laid out for me the night before. By the time I'd found the pants, tiptoed past Ayelet's room, and run around to the back of the house, Yossi had reached the eucalyptus tree. I knew that I could catch up to him. I was a good runner. The sun was low on the horizon, but it was already too warm. The air hung still and heavy over the cotton fields that stretched all the way to the hills that surrounded the moshav. "Yossi," I yelled. "Wait for me."

Yossi was too far ahead. He didn't hear me and didn't turn around.

I began to run. My bare feet hit the ground, sending up puffs of red dust. "Yossi!"

He had reached the paddock. Champion walked toward him, his tail swishing.

I reached the fence.

And then Yossi swung around. In the sunlight, his hair burned red, like Abba's. His eyes narrowed. "Go back home, Racheli," he said. "Ima or the girls will take you to *gan*."

I didn't move.

"No," I said. I bit my lip. I didn't want Yossi to be mad at me, but I also didn't want to go to *gan*, to play with Lego and puzzles, to sit at a table and eat my sandwich.

Yossi patted Champion's hard flank. "You don't have sandals," he said.

I shrugged. "I want to ride."

"No. I'm riding today."

I climbed onto the fence and sat balancing on the top bar. "I want to ride to *gan*," I said.

"It's too early."

"I'll wait for Morah Chagit."

Yossi looked at his watch. "Just for today."

I jumped off the fence and ran to the horse. I rubbed Champion's muzzle. The hair was short. Bristly against my palm. I pushed my face against his muzzle and breathed in the musty smell. Yossi fetched the saddle from the shack at the corner of the paddock. He threw it over Champion and buckled the strap.

"You're five now. You have to wear a skirt," Yossi said.

I put my foot into the stirrup and waited for him to push me up. "Soon," I said. I didn't want to argue. I hated arguing with anyone. I could never find the right words. It was much easier to agree.

Yossi opened the gate. He held tight onto the lead rope that he had attached to the halter, and we walked out. High above, a group of three birds was drifting in circles on a gust of wind that we couldn't feel. We passed the eucalyptus tree and turned off the trail.

We stopped in front of the *gan*. It would be at least half an hour until Morah Chagit arrived. I slid off Champion and grinned at Yossi.

Yossi was already riding away when in the distance, I spotted Asaf. He was always the first in the *gan* on the moshav. Well, today, I'd beaten him. He pulled a leaf off the tree in front of the *gan* and stood in front of me. I didn't tell Asaf that trees have feelings too and that it hurts them when you pull off their leaves. Even though I knew it was true because Abba had told me so. Abba knew everything.

"Someone is coming to *gan* today," Asaf said.

"Who?"

Asaf shrugged. "I heard Morah Chagit telling my mother when she came to borrow a cup of rice last night. I didn't hear who." He bent to pick up a stray building block and hurled it far, far away. Much further than I could throw.

I remember that morning in *gan* clearly. It stands out in my mind like a single fluffy cloud in a summer sky. That was the day that a Chabad rabbi came to our *gan* and taught us new songs that I had never heard before. More than that, it was the day that I learned that I was a soldier in the army of Hashem.

Our home was what you'd call a Modern Orthodox home. When my American parents made aliyah to Israel, they came with five children ranging in age from fourteen to five. I was the youngest. Abba's daughter, seventeen-year-old Gila, from his first marriage, stayed behind in New York with her mother. It was the early seventies, and like so many Jews the world over, they were riding the wave of euphoria after the victory of the Six-Day War. With little more than fervent idealism and no knowledge of cotton farming, my parents moved into the prefabricated house with walls that we could whisper through, allotted to them by the Sochnut (Jewish Agency). Together, my parents studied the black and white pamphlets that the Sochnut had given them, and then they became cotton farmers. I often wonder if this idealism was genetic and if my life would have been different if I hadn't inherited it.

Yiddishkeit was a framework for our lives. Home was a haven where the technical details of halachah were followed with little questioning. Judaism was about what you do and what you don't do. There was a way to do things, and we did them without questioning. Every morning, no matter how early I woke up, Abba was always sitting at his desk with an open Gemara, learning. I was sure that this was what an angel looked like.

Although we had a framework of halachah, there wasn't much in the way of building a personal relationship with Hashem. I don't remember ever sitting in the yard and just talking to Hashem like I would talk to a friend. I don't remember being told that if I needed something, I could turn to Hashem, because He was looking after me. There were no stories of *tzaddikim* or Chassidic tales to fuel my active imagination. In spite of all of this, I was always thirsting for something, and anytime I could find something more spiritual, I would cling to it. That's probably why Shabbat was the best day of the week. Abba would sit at the head of the table and sing so many beautiful songs. Since I was the youngest, I always got to sit on his lap.

As I grew up, I began to realize that there were some things that other people did and we didn't do. But that was fine, because in our house, Abba decided what we had to do. Abba knew everything. He even knew when the cotton bolls would crack open and show their white fluff. And he was always right.

I knew Ima thought Abba was always right, because she never argued with him. One time she did disagree, but he explained to her why she shouldn't. "If a brain surgeon were to invite you to watch him performing an operation, would you question him when he was about to make the incision?" he told her. "Would you suggest that he make the incision horizontal instead of vertical? You make good chicken soup. When I want to know how to make chicken soup, I'll come into the kitchen and ask you. But there are some things that you know less about."

Ima was quiet after that.

Later that evening, when she sat knitting on the porch, I asked Ima if it was true that Abba knew more about things than she did.

"Abba knows about lots of things," Ima said, her knitting needles clacking together.

"More than you, Ima?" I pressed.

"Racheli, it's best not to argue with your husband. Bumps in the road are a part of any marriage."

And then the night air was still except for the sound of crickets chirping, and Ima's knitting needles going clickety-clack.

***

Today, I no longer remember the name of the rabbi who came to our *gan* that morning. Maybe I didn't know it even back then. But I do remember that he had a short black beard and eyes that sparkled when he smiled, which was most of the time.

We sang songs that I hadn't heard before. Lively, happy tunes, over and over again, until I felt like I was floating high, high up in the sky, with the clouds. And he told us that we were soldiers. "Each and every one of you is a soldier in the army of Hashem, and each and every one of you can do mitzvot that will put bricks in the walls of the Beit Hamikdash," he said.

I flew home that day, eager to tell Ima that I was a soldier in the army of Hashem. That I was putting bricks in the walls of the Beit Hamikdash. The table was laid and lunch was ready when I raced in. Abba was talking on the phone. Four deep lines, like the furrows carved by a plough, were etched onto his forehead. "The plastic piping for the drip irrigation system hasn't arrived," Abba said. "I need it this week."

I stood close to Abba, hopping from leg to leg, waiting to tell him that I was a soldier in the army of Hashem. He was holding the phone tightly. Finally, long after I was sure that I was going to pop, Abba put down the phone. "Daven, Rita," Abba said to Ima. "There's some sort of problem with the supplier."

I had waited too long. I moved so I was standing right in front of Abba, my nose in line with the buckle of his belt. "Abba, I'm a soldier in the army of Hashem," I said.

Abba smiled, patted me on the head, and said, "Make sure you're the best soldier." Then he sat down at the table.

As soon as I had finished eating, I ran to the paddock, to Champion. The smell of Champion always comforted me. In the summer, it was a dusty, peppery smell that floated around in a cloud of chaff. In the winter, it was a damp smell of soaked straw and wet manure. It would be hours until Faygie and Ayelet came home from school on the nearby moshav. Faygie was seven years older than me, and Ayelet nine years older than me, so I didn't spend much time with them. The boys, eleven-year-old Yossi and ten-year-old Dov, were closer in age to me.

That evening, I sat next to Ima on the porch outside. She was knitting a scarf in the dim light that came through the living room window. I snuggled up to her and sniffed in the soft smell of rose hand cream that she always used. The words I had wanted to say flew away into the dark night. The feelings I wanted to share melted like shadows in a hazy dream. I was left with a flat, frustrated feeling that I wasn't even sure was really there. I certainly didn't know how to tell Ima about it. I wasn't sure how to put my feelings into words. And anyway, Ima was knitting. The days slipped by, and I forgot about being a soldier in the army of Hashem. Almost.

But I was driven to reach for everything spiritual. Like a missile honing in on its target, I charged after the mystical, the transcendent, what I thought was the divine. And I didn't realize when I was veering off course.

CHAPTER TWO

Always Moving

Jerusalem, 1976

The summer I turned six, we moved to Jerusalem. Abba had found an office job that suited him better than the mud and water of the cotton fields. Within a few weeks, we had packed up our lives and settled into a two-story house in the suburbs of Jerusalem. Instead of Champion and open cotton fields, we had a pretty garden, behind which was an empty lot. The empty lot became my place of refuge. Here, I could mourn over the moshav that we left behind. Cry over Champion – now in someone else's care – and the open spaces that had let my mind breathe. But best of all, here, I could put on my head the *kippah* that I snuck out of Dov's drawer, and I could sing "Anim Zemirot" just like I heard it in shul. Something inside me lifted when I sang this song. Even though I didn't understand most of the words. Some deep part of me knew that Hashem was listening to me.

When I sang *ki elecha nafshi taarog*, I thought it meant that my soul would die for Hashem. I didn't like to think of dying. But I liked to think of loving Hashem. I sang *v'shimcha achabed*...I will honor Your name. I knew how to honor my parents. I had to listen to them. That meant that I had to listen to Hashem. I decided that I would always listen to Hashem. I would always do what Hashem wanted me to do. Something inside me rose high and floated away on the wind with my voice. After that first time, I often pulled the *kippah* out from behind the foot of my bed and came to the hill to sing.

***

There was one tiny pinpoint of light in our move to the city. Now that we were here, I began to attend the same school as Yossi and Dov. Every day, twice a day, we traveled by bus to school. There were clear-cut rules: I wasn't allowed to sit next to Yossi and Dov, and I had to sit next to Faygie or Ayelet; I wasn't allowed to go play with the boys during recess; I wasn't even allowed to say that I was their sister. But rules are made to be broken, and older brothers are there to look out for their baby sister.

I didn't settle into my new school easily. Part of the problem was that we lived in a neighborhood that was far away from the school and also far away from where most of my classmates lived. I had lost my friends from the moshav, and play dates didn't happen. I knew that the other girls met up in the afternoons outside their apartment buildings. I knew that Malkie was in charge of the jump rope, and she decided what games to play and who would go first. No one invited me to come home with them after school. They had their friends, and they didn't need a newcomer. I knew this without being told. Just as I knew that if I told Faygie or Ayelet that no one was inviting me to their house, they would tell me to invite the girls to my house. But I was afraid to do that because maybe the girls wouldn't want to come.

So I found other things to do. I brought home stray animals. A turtle, a kitten, a dog. One day, I found a chameleon and put him in a box under my bed. But Faygie found the box and threw it into the garden even though I told her that chameleons eat mosquitoes. I put the kitten in a corner under the stairs that led to the second floor. But Ayelet said she had allergies to cats, and Abba made me leave the kitten by the garbage dumpster, where she would have plenty of food. I wanted to tell them that a kitten needed to be hugged and kissed, but I didn't. Besides, I was afraid Ima would shout about the kitten's germs. And I knew that I had to listen to Abba.

I couldn't shine in class, but I learned to make up for it by doing well in other areas. I became very competitive at school. I was the winner when it came to any game we played in recess. Capture the flag, jump rope, hopscotch, cops and robbers. Whatever it was, I played to win. And if anyone dared to question me, I'd run to the boys' side of the school, to Yossi.

Only when I'd received Yossi's promise to "beat her up" did I run back to the girls' side of the school.

I don't remember if Yossi ever made good on his promise. But I do remember that the threat that my big brother was going to come and take care of everything was usually enough to make the other girls relent. The knowledge that Yossi would take care of everything made everything right. My brothers, I knew, were people I could rely on.

***

At the end of third grade, my half sister Gila, Abba's daughter from his first marriage, came to spend the summer with us. Gila lived with her Ima in New York. I wasn't sure why she didn't live in Israel. It was so much more fun in Israel. Gila brought presents for all of us. Clothes, mostly. Socks. Sweatshirts. Thick, woolen sweaters. I didn't know what Ayelet would do with another sweater. Her closet was packed with sweaters. Gila brought tuna for Ima. Mouthwash for everyone. After she unpacked, she zipped her suitcase closed and pushed it far under her bed. But I had already seen the stash of M&M's and Reese's Peanut Butter Cups in there. I decided that her hair was auburn. Like the highlights in my own hair. It was because her father was my father. I wondered if we were alike in any other way.

The morning after Gila arrived, I peeked into Ayelet's bedroom. Gila was curled under her blanket, like the black and white kitten that I kept in a shoebox under the rosemary bush in the farthest corner of the garden, where it wouldn't make Ayelet's allergies flare up. I was very quiet, but Ayelet opened her eyes anyway. She flung back an arm, making her bracelets jingle. The blanket was spread out wide. I ran to Ayelet and snuggled in the warmth. Her hair was soft against my cheek. As soft as the fuzz on Champion's muzzle.

"So what do you do all day?" Gila asked us when we were all finally dressed and dipping cookies into hot chocolate.

"Ayelet and I hang out. Go shopping. Racheli roams the countryside like a vagrant," said Faygie.

Gila was already standing up. "Hiking? Walks in nature?" She spread her arms wide. "I love the outdoors. Let's go!"

I ran to the front door, before Faygie could make Gila change her mind. Gila stopped in the garden. She picked a yellow flower and stuck it into the elastic that held my ponytail. Then she gave me a bag that she was holding. It rustled and crunched. As if there were packets of M&M's and Reese's Peanut Butter Cups in there. I took Gila to my kitten.

"She doesn't have a name yet." I draped the kitten over my shoulder and nestled her against my neck where it was warm.

"Kitty," Gila said. "All cats like that name." She took Kitty and put her on her own shoulder. "Now take me on a hike," she said. "I hate shopping."

***

On the school bus and during recess, I sometimes saw Faygie and Ayelet. They were popular girls who talked a lot and made the other girls listen to them. So I began to copy them. I learned to talk a lot – to chatter brightly. I discovered that I had a good sense of humor and that I could make the girls laugh. And I was a good actress. I was always in charge of the skits that we put on. Finally, I had found a niche. And I made friends.

Now that I had a niche and friends, I also learned how to fight back without relying on my brothers. One day, on the bus ride home, I stuck my head out the window. The wind blew through my hair. I felt it being tugged gently backwards by the wind. And then the bus driver yelled at me to pull in my head. I didn't listen, and he yelled louder. I yelled back. I told him that I could put my head where I want. And I stuck my hand out the window. The driver slowed down. He was going to stop the bus. Everyone on the bus was staring at me. I pulled in my hand and muttered, "Who's he to tell me what to do? Why should I listen to him anyway? Who cares what he says?"

I waited for Yossi and Dov to stand up for me. I waited for Faygie and Ayelet to tell the driver that I could put my head where I wanted. But they didn't say anything. They were busy with their friends. All the kids on the bus went back to whatever they were doing. But I didn't. I stared out the window at the people on the streets. I checked that the driver wasn't watching me, and I stuck my hand out the window. No one could tell me what to do.

I didn't tell Ima what had happened. How angry and hurt I was that no one came to my rescue. I didn't talk about my feelings, because I was starting to feel no one listened to feelings.

CHAPTER THREE

Hello, America

1983, New York

When I was twelve years old, the emphysemic lungs and resulting chronic bronchitis of my grandmother called my parents back to the States. It was a good time to go back, as far as they were concerned. Ayelet was married and had a baby girl. Faygie had just married. And there were plenty of yeshivahs good enough for Yossi and Dov. In a year or two, they'd be old enough to come back to Israel alone to learn. I was devastated. Like any kid my age would have been. But what I thought or felt didn't really matter. We had to go back.

We moved into a large house with a large yard, but these didn't make the move any easier. Instead of the cotton fields, instead of the wild hill behind our house in Jerusalem, we had streets filled with houses built with Lego-like precision. Since we lived in Queens and all my classmates lived in Flatbush, once again, I didn't have any friends close by.

But I had Gila. Now that we were living in New York, Gila moved into our house. She was twenty-four and single. Gila worked in an advertising agency and was busy all week, but Sundays were our days. On lazy Sundays, we would go to Central Park. Mostly we went on miles of hikes around Long Island. We hiked to haunted lighthouses, across foot bridges, beside gurgling swamps and salt marshes. I learned to tell apart red cedars, sassafras, black oak, and shadbush. I learned the hard way to watch out for briars and poison ivy. Soon I could spot red-tailed hawks, seagulls, and osprey before Gila could. My favorite hike was to the seals at Oyster Pond. Sometimes we traveled further to the Appalachian Trail near Bellvale Mountain.

Despite Gila's friendship, I was still lonely. My parents had sent me to a girls' yeshiva elementary school that had a high school as well. This way, when I graduated, I'd just continue on into the high school. It was a very Zionistic school, which helped me feel more at home. Many of our teachers spoke to the students in Hebrew so that they would learn the language and feel like Israelis. On Israeli Independence Day, we would march in the Israel Day Parade.

But it still took a while for me to fit in with the girls. They had been together since first grade, formed their cliques, and weren't eager to make room for a newcomer in seventh grade. The girls laughed at my Israeli accent every time I tried to join in their games. I stopped chattering, joking, making everyone laugh. Instead, I took a ball to school and played by myself in the yard. Bang. Bounce. Bang.

Suddenly Suri grabbed my ball. "Give it back," I yelled. I'd never been shy.

"And what if I don't?"

"I'll beat you up." My ball was all that I had, and I was still a tough Israeli.

Suri hugged my ball tight against her chest. Her ponytail swung back and forth as she hopped around. I lunged. My fist flew through the air and stopped when it hit her jaw. She screamed. The girls around us yelled. A teacher came and yelled something about not doing things like that here.

"You'll spend the rest of the day in the principal's office," she said.

Deep creases ran down either side of her nose to the corners of her mouth. I was angry. Far angrier than I'd ever been. She couldn't tell me what to do. The bus driver hadn't told me that to do. I'd stuck my hand out the window when he wasn't looking. I wanted to walk away and go home, but some part of me knew that what I'd done wasn't okay. So I followed the teacher to the principal's office and spent the rest of the day counting the tiles on the floor.

That night, I told Ima that I wanted to go back to Israel. But I didn't tell her about my ball. Ima stopped filling the salt shaker and didn't answer.

"It's not bad here," Ayelet said. She had dropped by and was chopping up a salad for supper.

The tomatoes in America didn't taste as sweet as the tomatoes in Israel.

"You'll get used to it, you'll see," she said. And then she came over and gave me a hug.

I was in seventh grade already, but I let her hug me. I snuggled up to her and smelled that Ayelet smell. She was a mother already...maybe that was why her hugs felt so good. I wanted to tell her that, but the words stuck on the tip of my tongue like a hair.

"What about Bubby?" Dov asked. "Who'll look after her if we go back?"

I didn't want to think about Bubby alone, but I couldn't live here. "I hate it here. I want to go home," I said.

"This is home. You can't hate it," Ima said. She lifted the lid off a huge pot, and I smelled the meatballs.

"I hate the kids at school," I said. "They hate my accent. They say mean things."

"So say mean things back to them," said Yossi.

Ima put back the lid on the pot of meatballs. She straightened my collar. "Be nice to the girls, and they'll like you," she said.

I sat down at the table and stared at my plate. White meatballs were swimming in red slop on top of my mashed potatoes. I liked meatballs made from ground beef. Not these ground chicken ball things. "Yuck." I pushed my plate away.

"You have to eat your meatballs." Ayelet was wearing Ima's apron and waving a ladle in the air. Red sauce splatted onto the floor.

"Chicken balls are healthier than meatballs," Yossi said. "Chicken balls have less cholesterol than meat balls. You'll be healthy at eighty."

I didn't care about my cholesterol. Eighty was too far away to think about. Who knew if I would live to be that old?

"I hate chicken balls," I repeated.

I threw the chicken balls in the garbage when Ayelet turned her back. Then I got my ball and went into the yard. I bounced the ball hard against the stones in the driveway. I was upset. I bounced hard, and with every bounce I drove a dangerous lesson deeper inside me: I couldn't be upset; I had to push my yucky feelings to the side. I hurled the ball at the hoop that Abba had put up for the boys. The ball rolled around the edge and slipped into the net below. I was good at basketball. I was good at making people laugh. I caught the ball and hurled it again. I thought that maybe Ima was right. I needed to be nice to the girls so that they would like me.

The next day, Riki told us about the pizza party that they had had for supper.

"Chicken balls. We had chicken balls," I said. I didn't think anyone heard me, but Shulamis had.

"Dummies eat chicken balls," she said. "We eat meatballs. Every Wednesday."

I wanted to punch her, but I didn't want the teacher to yell at me again, like she had the day before. "Chicken balls are healthier," I said. "You should tell your mom to make chicken balls, or else you'll die before you reach eighty."

Shulamis stuck her tongue out at me.

"Chicken balls are healthier," I said again. I hated chicken balls. But Yossi said they were better than meatballs, and so I told Shulamis that she had to eat chicken balls. We raced each other back into class when the bell rang at the end of recess. I flopped into my chair and thought about chicken balls. I'd told Shulamis exactly what I thought. Except that it wasn't really what I thought…it was what Yossi thought.

I knew it was right to follow people who know better, because Ima did that. Like the time we had a young couple, Shoshi and Ben, over for Shabbat lunch. I was helping my sisters clear the table when the discussion turned to the different outlooks of two groups of Jews. Ima said something about it, and Abba said, "Rita, I'm not sure you know enough about this."

Shoshi blinked. Ben turned to Ima, leaning forward slightly. But Ima just cut another slice of apple pie. Dropped a scoop of vanilla ice cream on top. And then she pressed the spoon hard against the crust of the apple pie and watched it crack. But she didn't say a word.

It was best to keep silent.

***

By the time I was fourteen years old, I had once again found my niche in my circle of friends. I'd lost my Israeli accent and instead had a thick Brooklyn one. I always helped organize color war and pep rallies. I took part in so many activities. I was an actress, singer, dancer. I was in charge of extracurricular events, even though I wasn't a senior, probably because my sense of fun was contagious. I wasn't a particularly studious student. Many times I left class for a walk in the halls. On one of these walks, I saw Estie, one of my favorite classmates. We decided to have a water fight with the fire extinguisher. Needless to say, we were called to the principal's office.

Outside school, when the family went on vacation, sometimes to Emerald Hills, a bungalow colony in the Catskill Mountains, sometimes further afield, I learned how to ski and how to waterski. I went rappelling and canoeing with the boys while Faygie and Ayelet wandered through the malls pushing their baby carriages. I loved singing and made sure that I attended any and all of the Miami Boys Choir performances. I also went to the Mordechai Ben David shows. The positive energy that I felt at these musical events mirrored my own endless energy. I was so busy, so satisfied, that I barely felt the little hole that had begun to quarry itself somewhere in the middle of my chest. The little hole that was filled with half thoughts and feelings that didn't have a clear color. I began to look for things to stuff into the hole. To fill up the emptiness. An emptiness that I wasn't absolutely sure was there. That undefined hole was there, unsettling me, making itself felt.

And that was why I signed up for a marathon with Yossi and Dov. We were going to raise money for a children's shelter. For weeks, we trained together in the evenings. Twenty-six miles. It wasn't forever, I could do it. I bought new pink Adidas sneakers for the big day. I was excited to be part of something big. I looked forward to being in a crowd: the more, the merrier. I was excited to be part of a group with a common goal. Early Sunday morning, a reef of clouds spilled onto the sea of people with yellow numbers on their chests. Ima and Abba were there to see us off. I ran alongside Yossi and Dov until my heart was thumping like a drum and my chest was on fire. Then I slowed down. But it was okay because I was still in the front of the runners. Everyone, Yossi and Dov, Ima and Abba, and even Ayelet and Faygie were going to be proud of me. I was making the whole family happy.

We were running and running, but a little voice inside me wanted to know where we were running to. Run, rabbit – run, rabbit – Run! Run! Run! I ran until I'd eaten up the twenty-six miles. Ima hugged me at the finish line. Ayelet poured a bottle of water over my head. And when it was over, when everyone had stopped smiling and telling me that I'd done a great job, I wondered why I had run. I didn't know why my legs felt like they had been pumping at emptiness. I had thought that I was part of something bigger and better, but it had come to an end.

***

It was Israel Independence Day when I fought a new battle. Hila had invited me to her house for a meal. I liked Hila. She was Israeli, but her parents had moved to New York many years before. Her father had a dry-cleaning company that everyone used. Hila's uncle, Shammai, had come to New York to raise money for an agricultural school in the Jezreel Valley. He had thick, muscly arms, tanned as brown as the wooden table. At the meal, we spoke about Israel.

"An armchair Zionist, that's what you've turned into," Shammai said to Hila's father. "I've never seen a Golani soldier become as soft as you." He poked at the middle of a wedge of homemade bread. "Like this," he said.

Hila's father laughed. "Shout like that, and you'll go home with an empty wallet," he said.

Shammai pulled off a piece of bread and rolled it into a doughy ball.

I did the same.

"It's easier when the bank account is full," Hila's mother said. "And here, with a full bank account, we can be more religious."

I knew all the answers in this debate. It was one that my father and brothers rehashed every time Faygie said that she would never go back to Israel. "Of course we need to live in Israel. It's the Holy Land," I said. I knew what to say because my father and my brothers had said all of these words. Countless times. "It's a mitzvah to settle the land," I said.

Hila's mother sighed.

She was probably thinking of her relatives back in Israel. I tried to remember what else my father said. "People don't go because they're scared. They have their comforts here," I said. I could parrot my father's words perfectly.

"When you have to feed a family, you'll understand better," Hila's father said.

I repeated my father's words. Dov's words. Yossi's words.

Hila scratched a pattern in the tablecloth with the tip of her fork. "It's okay here," she said.

I didn't wonder if Hila and her family were right. Because whatever Abba and Yossi and Dov said had to be right. And I couldn't trust myself to weigh the sides because I'd never done that.

Besides, I loved Israel, and I knew that one day, I would go back to live there.

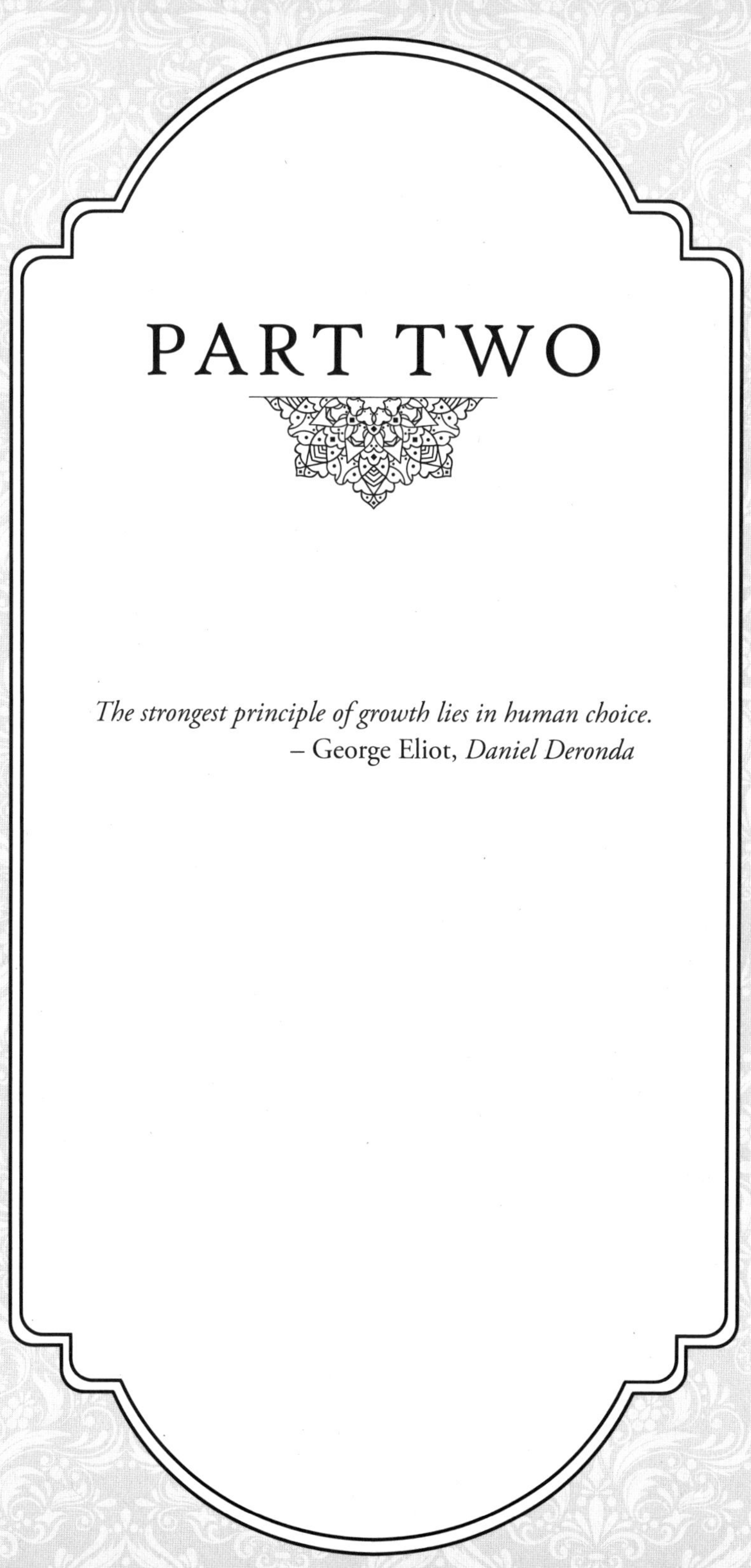

PART TWO

The strongest principle of growth lies in human choice.
– George Eliot, *Daniel Deronda*

CHAPTER FOUR

Who Will Be My Husband?

1985

I was fifteen when Bubby died in her sleep. I used to walk over to her house on Shabbat, and we would sing Shabbat songs together, with all sorts of harmonies, for hours. After Bubby died, we stayed in America even though she'd been the reason we had come. It didn't make sense to me, but I thought it wouldn't be right to ask, so I didn't.

The year Bubby died was the year I first stared in the bathroom mirror and realized that my bangs curled up instead of lying flat on my forehead. Daniel Kole, Yossi's friend, was in the yard. I could hear the shouting, the basketball banging against the backboard. I wanted to run out to join them. But first, I wet my bangs. I brushed them hard against my forehead and felt the bristles of the brush scrape my skin. I practiced my best smile to show off my perfectly white, perfectly straight teeth. Something inside me stirred. Daniel was very tall. He had light green eyes that sparkled when he smiled. What was stirring inside me? Was it excitement? Was it fear of rejection? I didn't know. I was fifteen, and I still hadn't learned to analyze what I was feeling. In that dark, murky hole in my chest, many half thoughts swam around. Feelings were something that happened to you and that you didn't tell anyone about. No one listened to feelings anyway. I gave my bangs one more brush and ran into the yard.

Daniel was much taller than Yossi, but Yossi was a better player. Yossi hurled the ball into the basket. Before either of them had a chance to reach the ball, I had it in my hands. I dribbled and threw. A perfect shot. When I turned around, Yossi was whistling, his hands on his hips. I'd given him a good reason to be proud of me. Daniel was kicking hard at a knot of grass. He didn't look up, even though he must have seen my shot. I threw the ball at him and it hit his shoulder, right above the lettering on his sweatshirt. Daniel caught the ball and swung his body to block me. Soon the three of us were horsing around, and I forgot that I wanted Daniel to notice my straight bangs and my white teeth. But I didn't forget Daniel's hesitant smile.

Like all teenagers, my siblings and I were always busy nursing new friendships and burying old ones. In our Modern Orthodox crowd, boys and girls mixed freely. Daniel drifted in and out of our lives like so many other buddies and acquaintances. Like ships that pass each other in the night, sometimes we simply exchanged looks, sometimes we stopped to speak. I was always on the lookout for him. Maybe he'd be at this barbeque. Maybe at this Chanukah party. Maybe at a concert at the Young Israel shul.

Part of me felt sorry for Daniel. His father had died of a heart attack many years earlier, and he was an only child. I tried to imagine his quiet house, but I quickly gave up. Anyway, there was so much more than pity involved – Daniel was the first boy I tried to impress. Something about Daniel pulled me toward him. Sometimes I wondered what it would be like to marry the first boy you have a crush on. That's what a childhood sweetheart was all about. It sounded like something out of a fairy tale. I wanted so much to be the princess in that fairy tale.

***

By the time I was sixteen, I had realized that dating wasn't something I could shine at. It was a mystery that hovered just beyond my fingertips. Perrie, Sara, Robyn…like pretty spring butterflies, the girls in my class fluttered around and drew their admirers with a skill that eluded me. In the pizza shops, at the bowling alley, in the park, Perrie, Sara, and Robyn always had boys who teased them, who joked around with them. Even Hila, who still spoke with an Israeli accent when she got mad and had acne scars on her cheeks, had her admirers. But I didn't.

I knew that I was a popular girl. My hair was thick and wavy and had the same auburn highlights that I'd had as a kid in Israel. My sense of humor and adventure meant that I had lots of friends. But when we hung out together, not a single boy searched for me and only for me. I davened about it once or twice. Asked Hashem to make my hair thicker, wavier, my skin flawless. But davening didn't take away the heavy feeling in my chest, the question. It mixed in with all the other jumbled feelings in the center of my chest. Sort of like the chocolate streak in a marble cake. Except that here, in my chest, there were lots of marbled streaks. What was wrong with me?

Then, I got my driving license and a car. An Audi. Not all of the kids in my crowd had a car, so I knew that I was lucky. One Sunday afternoon in April, right after Pesach, I took a group of girls to the Brooklyn Botanic Gardens to see the cherry blossoms. It was a warm day filled with yellow sunlight and pink blossoms that drifted like half-formed dreams in the cool breeze. There, on the lime-green lawn, we met a group of guys that we knew from our summer vacations in the country. They were from Long Island Yeshiva and had arrived on the subway a few minutes before we had.

"Hey, Racheli, hand over your keys," Avi joked. His *kippah* had flipped over in the wind, and he rubbed it back into place.

"Audis are junk," Reuven said.

I knew that he wanted to stay in the park. I had seen the way that he looked at Perrie. "Audis are the best," I said. Abba had told me.

"The keys..." Avi was still waiting.

I didn't want to give him my car, but I didn't want him to be mad at me. "Be back in an hour," I said, throwing him the keys.

Perrie was pulling apart the petals of a blossom that Reuven had given her. She didn't want the boys to go. "If you want to know who Racheli has a crush on, watch who she gives her car keys to," she said. She shifted the strap of her pocketbook so that it was more comfortable on her shoulder.

I didn't have a pocketbook. I had a pouch that snapped closed around my waist. I shoved at Perrie and I laughed, but inside I wasn't laughing. I knew that boys could be more than friends. Like Perrie and Reuven. But no boy was ever more than just my buddy.

That evening, after I had dropped off everyone outside their homes, I drove to the mall. I walked around the stores until I found a pocketbook that was the same color as Perrie's. I was too tough. Too loud. And I didn't know how to giggle. I stared at my reflection in the smudgy glass of the ice cream parlor. Sometimes, I imagined that I was a silvery sparkler...a spider's burst of light and fire. Everyone wants to hold a sparkler, but no one hugs a sparkler. I was still too Israeli even though I had been in New York for four years. I swung my new pocketbook over my shoulder like I'd watched Perrie doing. I couldn't stop talking loudly, joking, making everyone laugh. Because if I did, someone might notice that wobbly space inside of me. That space that wasn't sure who Racheli was. That little hole filled with half thoughts and feelings that didn't have a clear color.

***

I was studying at Stern College to be a gym teacher when I noticed Daniel at the Chanukah party on the Yeshiva University campus. I hadn't seen him for a while. Maybe even for two years. He was standing at the edge of the crowd. He was still taller than the other boys. His bangs kept falling into his green eyes, and he pushed them back with his hand, quickly, impatiently, as if he had more important things to do than worry about a haircut. I remembered how we played basketball in our yard. I wonder if he remembered too. I walked up and down trying to look busy until Daniel saw me. He waved…it was a salute of sorts. And then he smiled. He came toward me, and we started talking, as if we'd seen each other just the other day. He was studying sociology at YU. He didn't say much, but I could sense that he was enjoying my company. He didn't look beyond my shoulder when I cracked one joke after the other. He didn't begin shuffling his feet when I told him how I'd been rappelling with Yossi and Dov in the summer. When he saluted and drifted away, I felt like he had taken a sliver of my heart.

The next time I met Daniel, we were on a family ski trip in Vermont. He came over to our campfire at night even though he was staying in another hotel with his friends. Mrs. Kole, his mother, was a quiet woman, everyone said, who rarely went on vacation. Daniel talked with Yossi and Dov and then came to sit next to me. Again, he didn't say much, but finally…finally I knew what it felt like when someone seeks you out.

The next day, we went skiing together. I liked the narrow trails with trees crowding along the edge, but Daniel preferred the wide, mellow runs. "The fresh powder opens up your mind," he said. I preferred the angles of the narrow trails, but I was so happy to be skiing together that I didn't want to ruin it by telling him straight.

Instead, at the beginning of the run, when I was strapping on my skis, I said, "The narrow trails are fun."

Daniel looked at me.

I stared back. "Exciting. Fun."

Daniel shrugged. "The fresh powder opens up your mind. Can't you feel it?" he asked.

Feel what? The narrow paths pumped adrenaline through me. That's what I felt. But Daniel was adjusting his skis without waiting for my answer, so I didn't answer. All through the ski, with snow laid out like icing on a wedding cake, I tried to feel the fresh powder opening up my mind. By the end of the ski, when we cupped our hands around the hot chocolate, I could pretend that my mind had opened. Even though I still thought that the narrow trails were more fun.

That night, Daniel came again to visit the family. Four or five of his friends came with him. But we sat next to each other in front of the fire. Daniel was here. Next to me. Because that was where he wanted to be. I turned my head, pretending that I was looking for Huvie, my five-year-old niece. But my eyes settled on his profile. His nose was straight. His jaw square. This was probably a strong face. The more I looked at him, the more I felt that empty space in my chest filling up.

Daniel didn't talk much, so we stared at the flickering flames in silence. He got a dry branch from the pile we had collected in the afternoon and plucked off the twigs. We tossed them into the fire one by one. Yossi and Dov were playing chess. Faygie and Ayelet were exchanging recipes. And I was watching orange sparks whir up into the sky. The fire crackled and spat.

Daniel's friends drifted over. One of his friends, Ron, had a guitar. He also had small, sharp teeth. I decided that I didn't like his teeth. Daniel began to sing, and his songs made my heart fly.

Yossi and Dov came over. They began to talk about the future. They were both going to move back to Israel even though none of their friends would do the same. I held my breath. What did Daniel want? He got up and poked deep into the fire with his branch.

"It's good to live in Israel," he said. "Anyone who lives outside of Israel is like an idol worshiper." He pulled out the stick. The tip was glowing red with fire.

Except for Yossi and Dov, no other boy that I knew wanted to move to Israel. Not surprisingly, Daniel and I began to date.

***

"You're different when you're around him," Marcy said. She was blow-drying my hair because tonight I was going bowling with Daniel. I was wearing the new skirt I had bought. It was flowery and billowy. I pushed my bangs back the way Daniel did with his bangs.

Marcy swatted the back of my hand with the warm brush. "You've ruined my work!"

I pulled a face in the mirror.

"I said you're different around him." Marcy pulled hard at my hair.

I shrugged. It wasn't true. I was still loud, funny, and vivacious. But Daniel liked me to be quieter, so when I was around Daniel, I was quieter. Who said I had to be the center of everything all the time? I could be more quiet around Daniel. I kept quiet because I wasn't sure how to tell Marcy what I was thinking and feeling.

I stood up and twirled. My skirt billowed around my legs, like a cloud of flowers. I wondered if Marcy was jealous of me. Daniel was the best-looking boy in our crowd. "I'm not different around Daniel," I said, because I couldn't explain to her why I was. And anyway...who said it wasn't okay to act different with different people?

***

One Sunday afternoon, when it was so hot that the heat shimmered up from the sidewalk, we organized a swimming party at a nearby motel. Mixed swimming was fine in our crowd. Abba had told me. If it was fine with Abba, it was fine with me.

I had forgotten to bring my bathing suit, so I swam with my shorts and T-shirt. Daniel wasn't there at first, and I worried that he wasn't going to come. He'd told me that he didn't like swimming. After ten minutes, I flopped onto the warm paving around the pool. A shallow puddle of water collected under me, and I stirred the water with my finger. Around me the buzz of conversation was like a bee gone mad. I closed my eyes. The sun warmed my skin.

Then I heard Daniel's voice. "Good," he said. "You're not wearing a bathing suit. It's more modest this way."

I'd never worried about being more modest or less modest. And I wasn't sure why wearing shorts and a shirt was better than wearing a bathing suit. But I didn't tell Daniel that I had forgotten my bathing suit. I was happy that he had come to the pool after all. Daniel sat by my side like a statue with a hesitant smile.

I made sure not to laugh too loud and not to talk too much. I tried to shrink into myself so that he would stay by my side, and it worked pretty well. When it was dark and the first stars studded the sky, we packed up.

As we walked toward our cars, I cracked a joke. The bubbles and fizz inside me, on hold all afternoon, just had to get out. Sort of like an uncorked bottle of champagne. I don't remember what I said or what I did, but suddenly everyone was laughing. Avi was laughing so hard he couldn't catch his breath. Ron laughed so hard that I could see every one of his small, sharp teeth. I laughed too. But then I stopped laughing because Daniel was walking away, his shoulders hunched forward, his hands stuffed so deep into his pockets that I was sure he was going to rip them out. I ran after him.

"Daniel…" I shouted. I knew what I'd done wrong.

He slowed down.

"Daniel…" I wasn't sure what to say. How do you say you're sorry for being you?

"It's not good to be so loud," Daniel said.

I stared at him. The wind was blowing his hair into his eyes, but he didn't take his hands out of his pockets. I didn't want to argue, because I wasn't good with words. And I didn't want Daniel to be angry with me.

"You stand out too much," Daniel said.

I didn't know what to answer, so I said nothing.

Daniel started walking again.

I walked beside him. I was upset. Upset that he didn't like my jokes. Upset that I couldn't make everyone laugh anymore. And I was angry with myself for following him. For letting him take me away from the others. What was I supposed to do with so many feelings? I didn't know.

But I did know that I wanted Daniel to stay by my side.

***

One day, in the middle of my last year in college, I went alone to Coney Island. I had come to watch the jet skis. But instead of watching them scoot across the water, I began to turn inwards, to that empty part of me that was filled with thoughts and feelings that I couldn't name. I wondered if I was as happy as I used to be. Two jet skis were skimming across the sea. They were leaping over the waves. Free. I felt like I was losing something of myself. Daniel told me that it wasn't good to have so many friends. One or two was enough. I knew that if I wanted to keep Daniel, I would have to always be quieter. I listened to the far-away roar of the jet skis. I had always covered up the hole inside me with a lot of noise and a lot of motion. Now all that clamor was being muffled. I wondered if it was okay. And then I remembered that I felt good around Daniel. I didn't need to keep going back to these feelings that I couldn't name anyway. I could enjoy being with Daniel.

Six months later, we were engaged. And my friends were not happy.

"You're not marrying him," Perrie told me. It was two weeks after my engagement party. Three of my friends had taken me to a motel for Shabbat.

"We're not sure that this is good for you," Evie said, scooping up a handful of popcorn from the couch between us.

"Every time you get upset with him, he convinces you that he's right," Donna said.

"That's not true," I said. I wished that Evie and Donna hadn't come to this surprise Shabbat. They weren't my closest friends. I didn't need so many friends now. And I didn't care what they thought.

"It's true. He always convinces you that he's right," she insisted. "Like with the barbeque last week in your yard. You were behind it all, and then at the last minute, you backed out and we had to find a new venue…"

"And it was all because Daniel didn't want a barbeque," Donna said.

It had been right after our engagement. I had wanted all my friends to meet Daniel. To see how lucky I was. But Daniel hadn't liked the idea. He'd told me it wasn't right for him to meet all my friends. He'd said that our engagement was a private thing and that we shouldn't flaunt it in front of everyone. I hadn't been sure that he was right, but he hadn't wanted to talk about it more after he'd told me what he thought, so I had told Perrie to find another place for the barbeque because we weren't coming.

"Every time you want something and he doesn't, he makes you change your mind," Donna said.

It wasn't true. Daniel didn't want a videographer at the wedding, but I did, and so we were having one. "Thanks for worrying," I said. "But no thanks. I'm not changing my mind. I'm marrying Daniel."

After Shabbat, I told Daniel what my friends had said.

"If you need to know anything, ask me," he said.

He didn't say anything else. Which was also fine, because I'd already learned that Daniel didn't speak much. Daniel, I realized, was going to be like Abba. He was going to decide things in our house, and that was fine. He would look after me just like Abba looked after our family.

CHAPTER FIVE

Married and Merry

1992

The last four months had been hectic. Both Daniel and I graduated, and three weeks later, we got married. I hadn't had a chance to think about the changes. No time to think about how I felt about leaving home. But I did know that I was happy to be married to Daniel.

On the last day of our *sheva berachot* week, Daniel told me that we were going to Sea World. I spent more time on my makeup that morning, outlining my lips with the plum-colored pencil that Ima had picked out for me and filling them in with a plum-colored lipstick that had the hint of a shimmer. The red in my hair caught the light where my baseball cap didn't quite cover in it. Daniel didn't notice the extra effort, and I could tell that there was something on his mind. It was the way his shoulders hunched forward as he maneuvered the car in the traffic.

In the main lobby, I glanced at the main notice board. If we hurried across to the sea cliffs, we'd make it in time to see the otters being fed. "Let's go, Daniel," I urged him.

Daniel lingered by the wall map.

"Come…"

He was still lingering.

"You'll love their bald heads and whiskers."

Daniel's face lit up with a smile, and then I realized that his eyes were focused on something behind me.

I turned around.

Ron, Daniel's closest buddy, was standing there, blowing his nose into a soggy tissue.

I turned back to Daniel.

Daniel brushed past me. "How's the cold?" he said.

Ron shrugged and scrunched up his tissue.

"Ron's coming with us," Daniel said. "He's not feeling well, and no one's at home."

I stared at Ron. I didn't want him to come with us.

Ron looked away.

"Racheli wants to see the otters eating," Daniel said. "Racheli, lead the way."

I didn't move. I turned my back to Ron so he couldn't see me. "I don't want him to come with us," I mouthed softly. But I could still hear myself, and the sound of my voice made me brave. "It's not…right," I said.

"Not right?" Daniel lifted the corner of his lip. "Ron isn't feeling well…"

A couple with matching T-shirts walked past us. Couples had to be together. Alone. How was I going to tell Daniel that? "If he's sick, he should be at home," I said.

The corner of Daniel's lip was angled into a sneer. "Alone? At home all alone? Who'll take care of him?"

I didn't care who would take care of him. But I didn't want it to be me and Daniel. I also didn't want Daniel to sneer at me. To get mad.

"Don't you want to do something nice and take care of a sick friend?"

Of course I wanted Daniel to think that I was a kind person.

"Ron helped me choose your flowers when we got engaged."

The white roses and white baby's breath zoomed into my mind like a camera shot gone crazy. I'd told Daniel which flowers I liked. And I'd wondered why he hadn't chosen flowers with vibrant, loud colors that shouted about life. Now I knew why.

"Let's go," Daniel said. He walked up to Ron and put a hand on his shoulder.

Ron was blowing his nose again into his sodden tissue. He was coming with us. Even though I didn't want him to. At least Daniel wouldn't be mad at me. I led the way. I tried to ignore the feeling that this wasn't right. Maybe Daniel was right…maybe we needed to look after Ron…to let him share in our happiness… But the entire morning, that feeling, that something that told me it wasn't right, niggled me like a pebble in my sneaker. I didn't ask Ima or Marcy or Perrie or even Gila what they thought because…because Daniel and I were happy. And anyway, who said I was right to be upset?

***

"Migdal Yam," Daniel said one evening about three weeks after the wedding. He hung up his windbreaker on the coat stand that we had bought at a garage sale.

"What?" I was arranging the flowers I had bought on the way home from visiting Ima.

"That's where we're moving to."

I put down the red carnation. I knew we were going to move to Israel. I knew it would be soon. But I didn't know it would be so soon. My breath caught in my throat. I was twenty years old. And I was finally going home. I looked at Daniel's face. His eyes were bright, filled with hope. He was looking into our future.

"You're excited, right?"

I nodded.

"So many Jews make it only after 120…" Daniel said.

We were moving. Leaving my family behind. Daniel was going to be all the family that I would have. "Where's Migdal Yam?" I asked.

"In the south. Everyone says it's the place to be. Somewhere where everyone can make a difference."

I thought about making a difference. "When we lived in Israel, my parents took us a few times on marches when a new settlement was being established in the Shomron," I said.

Daniel shook the coat stand. It wobbled. He looked at the legs, trying to figure out how to balance it. He bent down. "Tell me about it," he said. His voice was muffled.

"I was a kid. I remember walking down some kind of long, dusty track. Following lots of people. Some were carrying Israeli flags. The hills around us were covered with green grass. And then we all sat down on the hill. There were some caravans there. And it began to rain. Just a soft drizzle. Abba said it was a *berachah* from Hashem blessing the new *yishuv*…" I was back there. In Israel.

Daniel straightened up. "Give me a piece of paper."

I folded the paper that the flowers came in into a square.

"We won't be in any caravan, Racheli. We're going to have a real house by the beach. And our kids will play in a yard with grass."

"It's hot in the south. Desert…"

Daniel smiled. "Your parents are helping us."

Suddenly my heart was dancing. My legs needed to dance. To dance and to shout. Israel! I was going back to Israel. With my husband. And we were going to make a difference in the world. Ima and Abba hadn't managed to stay in Israel, but I was going back! Daniel and I were going to be part of a much bigger picture, the return of the Jewish people back to our land. I looked at Daniel. How lucky I was to have him! Daniel and I would manage together.

Daniel was stuffing the piece of paper under one of the legs of the coat stand. "Daniel?" I said.

He straightened up.

"It's about more than just returning to Israel," Daniel said, wiping his hands on his pants. "We're living in the times of Moshiach. The Jews are coming back home, and Moshiach is right around the corner, waiting to bring back every single one of us."

I remembered the rabbi who had come to my *gan* on the moshav. I remembered what he had said. Maybe, maybe I'd see Moshiach at the entrance to Migdal Yam. We'd stand there, Daniel and I, surrounded by all of our kids, waiting to invite him in. "Daniel…" I wanted to tell Daniel all of these things. Tell him that I was proud of him. That maybe a teeny part of me was afraid…no, not afraid…I could never be afraid. Anxious… nervous, maybe. Part of me was anxious, but I knew we'd be okay together. All these feelings were whirling around in me. But they weren't thought-out sentences.

And then Daniel opened a book and sat at the table.

"It's nice when we do things together," I said.

He looked up.

"Like fixing the coat stand."

"We'll take it with us," he said. He licked his thumb and turned a page.

Migdal Yam. A tower by the sea. Daniel and I were going to be a tower, a tower of light for the Jewish people.

***

The next day, when Daniel was out taking care of things we needed to do before we went, I didn't think about packing, and I didn't think about the things we needed to buy. I wanted to work on our wedding photo album.

I had picked up the professional photos from the photographer, and I had already developed all the photos that my friends took with my camera. Now I wanted to put them into an album. I took out the enormous wedding album that Daniel's mother had bought for us. It was silver and white with our names embossed on the cover. I ran my fingers over the thick, smooth pages as I planned the layout.

I started with pictures of the bride. I lingered over the photos. My gown with layers and layers of organza that Ayelet had said were a must-have. Underneath the gown, my sneakers peeked out. I had insisted that I had to be comfortable to dance. Photos of Daniel. Of us together. Of our families. I slipped in a photo of Faygie's eldest daughter, Shira, posing with my bouquet of white and purple on the *kallah* chair. I'd been working for three hours straight when Daniel came home.

"Close your eyes," I said, standing in front of the table with my arms spread to hide my work. "Ta-da! Open." I bowed and swept my arm like an artist unveiling his masterpiece.

Daniel glanced at the mess on the table. Then he flopped onto the couch, laid his head back, and closed his eyes. "There are a million things to get done before we leave," he said.

A million things. I didn't want to hear about a million things. I had spent all morning on our album. "Look at the album," I said.

He opened his eyes. "What album?"

"I worked all morning on our wedding album."

"Who needs pictures? We know that we're married."

"Take a look. It's gorgeous." Of course he'd love it. Men were just different. I was learning that.

But Daniel's eyes were closed again. "My head hurts."

I put the album on his lap.

He opened his eyes and flipped through the first few pages. "I had a look. Nice work," he said. "I wish my dad had been there."

His dad. Daniel never spoke about his dad. Weddings, bar mitzvahs, Seder night. Those were the times when you realized you missed your family. I was lucky to have my family intact around me. I glanced at Daniel. I loved his mother. Had loved her from the minute we met. She was petite, full of energy. Like a bird. And she made the best brownies I'd ever tasted. I'd call her more often when we were in Israel, I decided. Maybe even tell her to come visit.

Daniel's eyes were closed. He'd been running around all day. Getting things ready for us.

***

We were out of milk. Again. I shrugged into my denim jacket, one of the things that still wasn't packed, and shouted to Daniel.

"I'll come with you," he said.

I liked walking next to Daniel. He was much taller than me. Being married was fun. Even just buying milk was fun when you did it together.

In the store across the street, I threw a packet of Oreos and M&M's into our basket. Who knew when I'd have them again?

Daniel laughed at me. "Tuna," he said. "Take tuna as well. And shampoo."

I was already moving toward the canned goods when I realized that he was joking. "You'll get used to things there, Racheli," he said.

Racheli. Daniel had his own way of saying my name. I tipped my head to see him better. There was light dancing in his eyes. I'd never imagined that I could be so happy. Daniel took the basket, and I followed him to the cashier.

Mr. Bornstein was at one of the tills. He had known me since Ima started sending me to the store alone.

"We're moving," I told Mr. Bornstein as I packed our shopping. "To a *yishuv*. To a house with a yard and grass." I told him about Migdal Yam. About how Ima and Abba used to take me to the opening of new settlements. "The Ingathering of the Exiles, you should be part of it too," I said.

Mr. Bornstein handed me the change. Daniel took the shopping and hurried out of the store. He swung the bag back and forth so hard that I was sure all the Oreos would be crushed into powder before we got back.

Something caught in my throat. "Daniel?"

He stopped for a red light and turned to me. "It isn't good to speak so long to another man," he said. "It isn't…modest."

I swallowed. Was he upset with me? He wasn't looking at me. Modest… what was he talking about?

The light changed. I hurried after Daniel. I'd never thought about who I spoke to. I'd never thought about modesty. Except for when Daniel told me that it was good to swim in shorts and a T-shirt.

"You're a married woman now. Don't you want to be more modest?"

"He's an old man," I said. "A family friend."

"It doesn't matter," Daniel said. "You shouldn't talk so much to men."

***

"Ima has booked rooms at the Grand Hall for Shabbat," said Faygie as soon as I picked up the phone. "Suites for the marrieds. Rooms for the singles. It's going to be a perfect Shabbat."

I heard Faygie's baby crying somewhere in the house. Shira was singing.

"She says it's for her birthday, but I think she wants us all together before you and Daniel leave." Faygie paused. I heard her heels click-clacking across the parquet. Then the baby's cries got louder. She had picked him up.

"Mmm," I said. I wished that Ima had never had this idea.

"I need to find them matching outfits. I think I'll go for pastels."

I didn't care what color the outfits were going to be.

"We could go shopping together…you know…a sort of last-time outing before you leave…"

"Maybe…"

"Pastels…or shall I go for more color?"

Pastels or color… Last night, when I told Daniel about Ima's plans for our last Shabbat in New York, he'd been quiet. Quieter than usual. And he hadn't mentioned anything in the morning.

"Pastels are great," I said. I hated pastels. I liked strong colors. Colors that burst with life. Colors that danced. Someone was knocking at my door. "Gotta go," I said.

Gila was standing there with paper bags from the Chinese takeaway.

"Tell me you're done with the packing and ready for a heavenly Shabbat at the Grand Hall," Gila said. She bent back the silver cover of a disposable foil tray, wiggled out a crispy spring roll, and handed it to me.

The door slammed shut. Daniel hung his windbreaker on the coat stand. "Done with the packing and ready for our last Shabbat…at home," he said. The coat stand didn't rock anymore.

Gila sealed the foil tray carefully. She looked at me and licked her fingers slowly.

My eyes swiveled between Daniel and Gila.

"We don't go to hotels," Daniel said.

He was looking at me. "Daniel…" Where were the words to tell him what I wanted? To tell him we had to do this for Ima. I tried again. "Daniel…"

"You go to ski resorts," Gila said. Her voice was dry. As if she was telling Daniel that the sky was blue.

"There are no ski resorts in Israel," Daniel said.

"Nonsense. There's the Hermon." Gila's voice had changed. There was something fiery in it. And Daniel's eyes were hard. I was trapped. Trapped between two people I loved. I felt my heart shrinking. Shrinking and folding in on itself until the blood was no longer pumping through smoothly.

"But the Hermon is beside the point. Ima has booked a Shabbat for the family," Gila said.

"We're not coming," Daniel said.

"You can't be serious." Gila stared at him.

"We are." Daniel was looking at me.

I knew he wanted me to agree, but I couldn't. I wanted to go. But I couldn't insist. Because I also wanted to be a good wife. And I wanted to do what he wanted.

"This is supposed to be fun – a birthday celebration!" Gila waved her hand. Her bracelets jangled. But it wasn't a merry sound.

CHAPTER SIX

My Head Is Still above Water

Migdal Yam, 1992

There wasn't much to unpack into our caravan in Migdal Yam. How much stuff can you bring over with you? But I was okay with living in a caravan for the two months until our house would be ready. *Idealism*… I rolled the word on my tongue. It tasted sweet. It felt good…this belonging to something so much bigger than ourselves.

Despite the fact that our kitchen equipment consisted of plasticware, two pots, and a can opener, home became home the minute Daniel brought home a kitten, a few mornings after our arrival. "All kittens should be called Kitty," I told Daniel, snuggling my neck against the warm fur. The kitten's heart thump-thumped against my neck. Kitty. "Gila said all kittens have to be named Kitty."

Daniel shrugged. "What's for breakfast?"

I shrugged back. I wasn't much of a cook. We'd spent four months living on food from the freezer section of Mr. Bornstein's grocery store and Ima's kitchen.

"My mother made us delicious omelets for breakfast," Daniel said. "I'll show you and Kitty how."

His mother. I watched Daniel making omelets and thought about how I should call her. We ate quickly because Daniel had to be ready to leave the *yishuv* at eight thirty. His new job as a salesman selling toys all over central Israel was about to begin. I threw some fruit and a packet of pretzels into a plastic bag. And I smiled at Daniel. Daniel, who had made it possible for me to come back here. Daniel, who was going to be working so hard to make it sure it would be good for us here.

I walked him to the car. "I'm going to let everyone know that I'm available to tutor kids in English," I said.

"Good," Daniel said. "It's good to be busy. And I'll be home late."

***

About a month later, when I realized that most of the kids in Migdal Yam were too young to need tutoring in English, I signed up as a lifeguard at the pool on the edge of the *yishuv*. It was on the spur of the moment. I'd gotten my lifeguard certificate back in high school, and I was glad to be doing something with the long, empty days. But something, some instinct I couldn't place, stopped me from telling Daniel about it. I davened that he'd be okay with it.

"Where you going?" Daniel asked. He pointed to the bag in my hand.

It was early morning. The sun hadn't begun to launch silver lances of light, and the air was still cool. I'd walked Daniel to his car to say goodbye.

"Lifeguard duty," I said.

Daniel unlocked the car door and settled into the driver's seat. "Here?"

I nodded. I was excited to be starting my first job. So why did I feel a tightening in my chest? As if someone were squeezing all the air out of my lungs?

Daniel put his head back on the headrest. "It's not so modest..."

"The pool is open only for women..."

"Walking around in a bathing suit all day..."

I swallowed. I couldn't spend every morning at home. "I'll wear a shirt."

Daniel nodded. "Hashem wants people to be modest," he said.

I knew that he didn't want me to go. But he wasn't actually telling me not to go...so I could go. Right?

"Don't you want Hashem to love you?"

Of course I wanted Hashem to love me. I swallowed again. "I'll wear a shirt," I said again. I wasn't sure why I had to do that, but I was sure that I wanted Hashem to love me.

Daniel started the car. I wanted him to wish me luck. To tell me I was a great swimmer. To tell me to enjoy the sun, the water, the new friends I'd be making. But he didn't. Instead, his question hung in the air. It was a question that was to mold the direction of our lives. What would I do to make sure that Hashem loved me?

***

Two months later, we had moved into our new house. Our lift had arrived. Our leather couches were in the living room and the tuna in the kitchen cabinets. I had an enormous oven. My enormous washing machine and dryer stood side by side. I was waiting to be able to throw in load after load of baby clothes. When Yemima came over to visit, she'd laugh and tell me that my furniture was bigger than my house. She was right; we were in a house, but it was Israeli-sized. One evening, I was asleep on the couch when Daniel finally came in. His footsteps shuffled along the newly polished tiles. The wicker armchair creaked when he dumped his briefcase into it. The second armchair creaked as he sank into it. Daniel didn't like the leather couches and never used them. He wanted to live like all the other Israelis. And that meant cheap, creaky furniture. I shifted and opened my eyes.

"You're so late," I said.

Daniel was drumming his fingers on his jeans.

A new habit. I hated the rapid beat. It made me nervous. But I didn't tell him to stop. I had other things on my mind. I'd reviewed what I wanted to say hundreds of times.

"Why don't you come home earlier...so we can...talk," I said. "You're so not...nice to me." There, I'd said it. I'd said what I wanted to say since we moved here. *Nice* was a safe word. It didn't really mean that much. I closed my eyes quickly. I was surprised. Shocked, really, that I'd said it. Maybe if I kept my eyes closed, Daniel wouldn't answer. Not that I had to worry too much... *nice* was a safe word. So he couldn't get mad.

"Not nice?" Daniel's voice was smooth. He never raised his voice.

I opened my eyes. No. He wasn't nice. I wanted him to share his day with me. To tell me where he'd been, who he'd seen. I wanted him to share his life.

Daniel curled the corner of his lip up. "If you were nice to me, I'd be nice to you," he said.

He was still drumming.

"I am nice," I said, still tapping into the courage that I'd found to say something was wrong.

"No, you're not."

I shut my eyes again. I swung my legs over the edge of the couch and sat up. I had to try. I had to tell Daniel what was wrong. I fished around, in that deep place in my chest that was filled with half thoughts, to find something that made sense. Breathless, almost, I tried again. "You don't talk so much," I said.

Daniel stopped drumming. I heard him standing up.

"If you were nice, I'd come home earlier," he said. He walked to the kitchen.

A single plate banged against the surface of the table. The table I'd picked out with Ima so many months ago. I missed her. I missed my family. And now Daniel was mad at me. I should have kept quiet.

The next day, Daniel came home with a box full of little plants. He dropped the box on the kitchen table. "You can plant these," he said.

He didn't tell me where he'd bought them and didn't ask me which ones I liked best.

I picked up the pot with the red callie and put it next to the yellow. I put the purple African daisy alongside. It was a burst of color. Strong color. Bold colors that I loved. I looked up. "They're gorgeous."

Daniel shrugged. "We can plant them in front of the porch," he said.

In the garden, I tipped the plants out of the plastic containers, while Daniel dug holes in the sandy soil. I dropped the plants into the holes and patted down the soil around the stems.

"You have to daven that they'll grow well," Daniel said.

I hadn't been fair to Daniel, I decided. He was trying to be nice. We were both trying, and that was what marriage was about. It was all about getting used to each other.

Three months after we'd moved to Israel, I'd gotten used to our relationship. It wasn't all bad. There were the good parts. So I stopped complaining and arguing. I stopped pushing Daniel to be what I wanted. I learned to accept him. This was a normal marriage with its ups and downs. And if I wanted it to be a good marriage, I had to think about how I could be nice to Daniel. I started thinking about what he would want me to do instead of thinking about what I wanted him to do.

1993

One-month-old Yael had been screaming all day.

By the time Daniel came home, I wanted my mother. I watched Daniel sit down. I wanted to throw Yael into his arms. But something kept Yael glued to my chest. I shifted from leg to leg, willing the words to bubble out, willing them to stay in. And then, without realizing it, I heard my voice. "Why do I always have to take care of her? You have to do your share." I laid Yael across my arm and jiggled her the way Reut, who had four kids, had shown me. And then my knees began to wobble. I stumbled to the couch.

Daniel took Yael from me and rocked her in his arms till she was quiet. "You have to kiss her, Racheli," he said. "Sing to her. Cuddle her. Talk to her." Daniel stroked Yael's head and handed her back.

I wanted to be a good mother. I had to try harder.

Daniel bent down toward his shoes and untied the laces slowly. "You don't have to take care of her all the time," he said. "Another few months and you can send her to a babysitter." He pulled off one shoe.

Daniel leaned forward, his elbows on his knees. "We don't have to have a big family. We can have one kid and go on ski trips every year."

Was that really what I wanted? Yael had finally fallen asleep. I felt my heartbeat slowing.

"Is that what you want? One kid and ski trips?"

Yael twitched on my arm. *Yes*, I wanted to shout...but I didn't. Because I wanted a house filled with kids. Like the other women on the *yishuv*. Like good Jewish women throughout history. I wanted my yard to look like a page in the catalogue of Toys "R" Us. Filled with a climbing frame, a swing set, and a slide. And lots of cute kids. I wanted a big family of kids who would be good Jews. I davened for that. Every day.

I shook my head.

Daniel moved toward the bookcase. He ran his fingers over the books...I'd never realized we had so many...and pulled one out. He turned back to smile at me.

It was in that smile, full of warmth, that I found the strength to keep going.

1994

A year later, Shimmy was born. Yossi and Dov, who were both living in Israel, came early the day of the bris. I was already at the hall in the shul, setting up the tables for the lunchtime seudah. "The napkins need to be folded this way," I told Yossi, folding the blue and white napkins into the shape of a fan. I fanned Yael, who was holding onto my skirt.

"No one looks at napkins," Yossi said. "And besides, you shouldn't be folding them. Go home and get into bed."

I remembered Yossi taking me for rides on Champion. I could almost smell the musky scent of his freshly groomed coat. I was exhausted.

"Where's Daniel?" Dov asked.

"He's learning. He'll be here to help set up soon." I hoped that this once, Daniel would leave his books and come help.

The door to the hall swung open. "You didn't put the drinks into the fridge." It was Daniel. The straps of his tefillin swung across his chest when he pushed his bangs back. "People like cold drinks."

Yossi looked up. "You put them in the fridge. Racheli's going home."

Daniel didn't move. Yael was pulling at my skirt. I bent to pick her up. What was I supposed to do? Who was I supposed to stand by? Yossi didn't want me to tire myself out. But he didn't realize that I was fine. Really fine. And Daniel…he'd been learning all morning. Of course he didn't have the head to put drinks in the fridge. He was probably thinking of the speech that he'd prepared. "I can do it," I said, "before I go home."

But Yossi was already heading for the kitchen. Daniel sat down at the head table and opened a *sefer*.

"He's got his head in a book again?" Gila said in my ear.

"Gila! So glad you could come!" I said, giving her a kiss.

"Wouldn't miss it. Now that I'm back in Israel, I'm going to be the best aunt ever! I can't believe you have two kids now, Racheli!"

I looked toward the window.

"Don't worry," Gila said, "I parked my motorbike around the corner where Daniel can't see."

"Thanks, Gila," I said. "Daniel's just in a better mood if he doesn't see it."

"I do it for you, Racheli, but he really shouldn't have an opinion about my motorbike," Gila said, and she stole a look at Daniel as she started folding napkins.

***

It was a hot, still night. The last light in the neighboring houses had flicked off hours ago, it seemed. Even the crickets had settled down to sleep. But Shimmy was cutting a tooth, and that meant that I was cutting a path through the grass in the front yard. I shuffled slowly, one foot inching in front of the other, Shimmy hugged close to my chest. I was dizzy with exhaustion, and if I moved any faster, I would stumble. I leaned against the swing set, and then Shimmy yelped. I started my circuit again.

And then I heard Daniel's car in the driveway. He was back from traveling around to stores. I knew that I was supposed to hope that he'd done well, ask him about new clients…but I couldn't find the energy.

"You there, Racheli?"

I grunted. A funny sound. As if all of the life had been drained out of me and all that was left was one last whoosh of dull air.

Daniel took Shimmy.

A triangle of light spilled out from the living room into the yard. Enough for me to see the jut of Daniel's chin. His eyes were shadowed.

"We're not going to Yossi's house anymore," he said. He took Shimmy.

I tried to breathe in. To push the warm air past the lump in my throat. Yossi and Esther had been living in Petach Tikvah since they got married. We'd spent a Shabbat with them about two months ago, and Yossi wanted to know when we were going again.

"Yossi isn't religious enough," Daniel said.

I breathed in harder. Past the lump.

"He has a TV. And he isn't religious enough."

Shimmy whimpered, and Daniel cuddled him close. Then he handed him back. He was so heavy. Too heavy for me to carry. I wanted to tell Daniel that Yossi didn't switch on the TV when we were there. That we had to visit them because they had invited us. But the words remained stuck behind the lump in my throat. I didn't have the energy to argue. And who said that Daniel wasn't right? Abba had always done what was right for the family. Daniel too would do only what was right for our family.

***

When Yael was almost two years old and Shimmy was nine months old, I signed up for a six-month course to learn how to be an aerobics instructor. I didn't tell Daniel until my parents had paid for the course. And then I waited for the right time. It came one Friday afternoon. Everything at home was ready for Shabbat, and we were at the beach. We sat just beyond the reach of the waves, where the sand was packed hard and smooth. Daniel was watching the kids. I hugged my knees and looked out to sea. We were lucky. So lucky that we could do this…take time off to be a family together.

I watched Daniel helping Yael to pat wet sand into the red bucket. He tipped it upside down, and the beginning of a sandcastle was born. "So I thought…I thought that I'd go into aerobics." The words popped out, almost by themselves.

Daniel smoothed the sides of the sandcastle.

He looked up. "Are you sure you want to jump and dance in front of everyone?" he asked. Daniel's hands were moving faster against the sides of the little sandcastle. Smoothing, smoothing. "Why do you always have to be the center of things? Why can't you just stay at home with the kids?"

I dug my fingers into the hard sand beside me. What was Daniel talking about? I was at home with the kids. All day. While Daniel was out. I needed to breathe. To see people. Why couldn't I explain it to Daniel? How come it sounded so wrong now? Sea water was welling up in the hollows that I had dug with my fingers. The sand was crying tears.

I turned back to look at the sea. I focused on the still, quiet line where the sky bent down to touch the water. I had to bend further. I had to change myself so that Daniel would be happy with me. But I wanted to be an aerobics teacher. To dance, leap, jump, spin.

Daniel left the sandcastle and came to sit next to me. "I didn't say that you shouldn't study aerobics – study whatever you like – I just thought that you enjoyed staying at home and taking care of the kids."

He reached forward for a tiny shell, half-hidden in the sand. "You do a great job. I don't want to take away the kids' special time with you."

I smiled. A shaky smile, but a smile. Good words from Daniel meant everything to me.

A week later, I began to travel into Beer Sheva once a week. Two bus rides. Two kids. I didn't ask Daniel to watch the children, because I knew this wasn't something he wanted me to do. I'm not sure how I had the courage to go week after week. It was physically draining, and I knew that Daniel would have preferred for me to stay at home. Thinking back, I suppose it shows how desperate I was to try to hold on to something that expressed my essence.

I opened my first aerobics class as soon as I finished the course. Eight women came to exercise in my living room.

One evening, class ran late. Daniel came in as I was seeing Reut to the door.

In the kitchen behind me, I heard Daniel banging the lid of the pot onto the counter. The clatter of cutlery against a plate. I hoped he'd enjoy the fish in tomato sauce. Yemima's recipe. I joined him in the kitchen.

Daniel looked up from his plate. "You need to work on yourself to become a better person," he said.

I wasn't sure what he meant. I was a good mother. I stayed at home with the kids. I took them to the park. I cooked. I cleaned.

"You have great inner qualities that just need to be discovered. If you were less busy with outside things, then you'd be able to hear your inner soul talking to you," Daniel said.

I kept quiet. I'd learned that silence worked.

"That way you'd come closer to Hashem…not only to people," he said. "You have to speak to Hashem."

I was ready to work on myself, but I wasn't sure what to change. And what about Daniel working on himself?

I picked up an empty packet of Bamba from under the table. I'd told Yaeli to throw it into the garbage. I folded the packet in half and then into quarters. "So what should I work on?" I asked.

Daniel looked up from his plate, but he didn't answer.

"What kind of work?" I asked again.

"You know what you need to do," Daniel said. "Talk less and listen more to what's going on around you. That way all the noise in your head will slowly disappear. You'll be able to fill your time with meaning. You'll be happier; we'll all be happier; a family growing in the path of Hashem."

It sounded so good. Of course I wanted to keep Daniel and the whole family happy. They were everything to me. If they were happy, I'd be happy. We'd be happy. I closed my gym class. Yemima and the other women didn't come anymore.

***

Gila came for a visit. She had bought a child-size helmet for Yael and wanted to take her for a ride. I knew Daniel didn't like the bike, but he was at work. He wouldn't have to know about it. With Yael's tiny arms hugging her waist, Gila drove up and down the road outside our house close to a hundred times. The little kids who congregated in my yard every afternoon were there to ooh and aah. I'm not sure if they made all the noise or if it was their mothers. Either way, Yaeli enjoyed being the center of the show.

In the evening, Gila noticed that our wedding picture was no longer in its place of honor above the couch. "What's with your wedding picture?" she asked me.

"The picture?" My eyes flew to where it used to be, over the sofa. "We took it down ages ago," I said.

"Why on earth…?" Gila asked me.

I shrugged and pulled a piece of lint out of Yaeli's hair…picked up Shimmy…put him down. "It wasn't that…that modest," I said.

Gila's jaw dropped, and she stood there for a minute opening and closing her mouth like she wanted to say something. But I looked away, and she didn't say a word.

1995

"I don't want to be a salesman anymore," Daniel said from the table where he was learning from a new book he had brought home the night before.

Shimmy was on my lap, and Yael was sitting beside me. We were sticking orange and yellow stickers onto the trees we had painted the day before.

"This isn't what Hashem wants from me."

I helped Yael peel off another sticker from one of the strips I had cut.

"Is this what I'm going to do with my life?" Daniel asked. "Convince some store owner to buy soccer balls in the summer and stuffed toys in the winter? For the next forty years?"

"You're good at it," I said, although I didn't know if he was or not. He never told me much about how his day had gone.

Shimmy was squirming. If Daniel wasn't going to sell toys, how were we going to live?

"I need to serve Hashem in a better way," Daniel said.

A better way? Daniel was doing just fine. Davening in shul three times a day, learning whenever he could. What more was he supposed to do?

Daniel stood up. He put his fists on the table and leaned forward. His knuckles turned white. And then he said, "I'm going to learn in yeshiva."

Yeshiva. I put the stickers down. "How are we going to survive?" I asked. "Can you do it? Really just give up working?"

"Don't you want me to learn Torah?"

I picked a stray sticker off the table. How I was I supposed to tell him I wasn't sure that this was a good move? "But we have bills to pay…" I said.

"Life is about more than bills. Don't you want me to learn?"

Of course I did. I was doing everything I could to make sure that Daniel could learn as much as he wanted to. It was good for us. In this world and in the next. Daniel had told me so many times.

"What will we do for money?" I asked.

Daniel pushed his hand through his hair. "Ask your parents to help out in the meantime. I've already asked my mother. With help, we'll manage."

I didn't want to ask my parents. They had helped us with the house. They were already giving us a monthly stipend. I didn't want to ask for more. But I also didn't want to argue with Daniel.

I didn't call my parents. And I didn't tell Daniel that I hadn't. When I thought about calling, I davened that it would somehow work out.

Daniel began spending his days in a *kollel* on Moshav Azariyah, a ten-minute drive away. Life carried on more or less like when he had been working. So much so that I didn't realize what was happening, until I went to the grocery store in Migdal Yam a month later.

Yoram, the owner, was at the till, chewing a toothpick.

"No rush…but when you have a chance, put some money in your account," he said, pushing my stuff down the counter to make room for the next customer.

I told Daniel that we had to pay the bill later that night when he came home.

His eyes darkened.

I looked away.

"Racheli, do you know how happy I am learning? People need to make sacrifices to stay in learning," he said. "You don't know what it means to make sacrifices. You want me to stay in learning, don't you?"

I didn't know if I wanted that. Maybe I didn't. Maybe I just wanted to be able to pay our bills.

"Didn't you speak to your parents?" Daniel asked.

I didn't answer. We'd never fought. We wouldn't fight now.

In the end, I asked my parents if they would help us for the next short while. None of us realized how long the short while would last.

About two months later, Daniel decided that he needed a change. His stipend had been minimal, but with the additional help from our parents, we'd been managing. Now he was leaving the *kollel* in Moshav Azariyah for a smaller *kollel* in Netivot, a town nearby. Daniel told me about the move one evening when we were taking the kids for a walk around the parameter of Migdal Yam.

"There's no stipend in Netivot," he said, tossing the ball ahead again.

I pushed Shimmy's carriage over a bump in the path. No stipend? How were we going to manage? I opened my mouth and quickly closed it. Last time I'd tried to tell Daniel that we needed to be practical, we had nearly fought.

"I start tomorrow."

A flock of birds circled above. Heading home for the night. No stipend. I'd probably have to ask my parents for more money. I cleared my throat. "Isn't all learning the same…no matter where you are?" I said.

"This is a better place for me," Daniel said.

Daniel's stipend hadn't been much, but it had helped. We had to have that extra cash. "Maybe…maybe you should ask the guys who travel with you to pay something for gas," I said.

Daniel frowned.

"I'm going alone. No one else is leaving the *kollel* in Azariyah."

I wondered why only Daniel was leaving Azariyah, but I didn't ask him. Besides, I was proud of him. Glad that he'd found a better place to learn. He was always growing… I wished I could grow like him.

***

Daniel had been in the *kollel* in Netivot for about two months when he spoke to me about my baseball cap. "I think you should cover your hair with something else, not a cap," he said. We were walking along the beach. Yael and Shimmy were playing with the waves, wetting their feet and splashing each other.

"I like my cap," I said.

Daniel turned to face the sea. "Who else wears a baseball cap?" he asked.

No other woman in Migdal Yam wore a baseball cap. And that didn't bother me. My cap was part of me. It was me. Baseball caps were fine in my family. My sisters-in-law wore them some of the time. "My father thinks a cap is fine. So do my brothers," I said.

Daniel was quiet. He ground his heel into the sand, lifted his foot, and began to grind another hole next to the first. "A scarf, or whatever the other women wear… It's more modest, Racheli."

I looked at Daniel. Sure, longer sleeves were better than short sleeves. I could see that. But covered was covered. It wasn't as if my hair wasn't covered. My cap covered it just fine. Why wasn't a baseball cap okay? I knew what I wanted to say, but I didn't say a word. I just ground my heel into the sand. Exactly like Daniel was doing. "Daniel…"

Daniel was walking toward the children.

What was I going to wear instead of a cap? I didn't own a single scarf. "Why? Why do I need to change?" I shouted into the wind. The sea breeze whipped my words away. Daniel hadn't heard me. "Daniel…" I shouted louder. "It can't be that hard. I'll try."

Daniel was standing between the children, holding their hands. He turned around, waved, and winked.

I looked at the row of footprints he'd left behind. A large wave bubbled past him, all the way up my toes. It receded, leaving the sand smooth and shiny without a trace of footprints. Yemima wore scarves. I liked the way she twisted them around her head. I could ask her. If Daniel was asking, it meant it was important to him. It wasn't so hard, surely. I was going to make Daniel happy. Make Hashem happy.

Later that night, I lay in bed wide awake. Daniel was right. Scarves were more modest. True, Abba didn't think so. And neither did Yossi or Dov. It didn't matter too much. I had to do what Daniel wanted. What he wanted, I wanted.

1996

It was drizzling. I'd have to use the dryer, but I didn't want to, because it drove the electricity bill so high. I bent down and tugged at the wet clothes. My belly pushed against my lungs, and I struggled for breath. This time it was going to be a winter baby. I threw the clothes into the dryer and moved to the living room window. Rain was a blessing. A day of rain was as great as the day that the Torah was given, a day full of salvation. Suddenly I saw

Daniel driving up. He should have been on his way to *kollel* in Netivot. Had he forgotten something? Was he sick?

The door flung open. A gust of cold, air heavy with the scent of damp soil rushed in.

"I'm going to Ashdod," Daniel said.

Ashdod? What was in Ashdod?

"There's a rabbi there…Rav Benayun. I'm going to learn with him."

"But you learn in Netivot…"

Daniel scowled.

Something inside me tightened. "Aren't you happy in Netivot?"

"The rabbi in the *kollel* is always busy…too busy. I need to have a connection with someone. Not be just another face in a full room."

I looked outside. It was pouring now. So hard that the drops fell like bullets.

"I need someone to guide me," Daniel said. He pulled out a kitchen chair and began drumming on the table.

The tabletop was covered with cornflake crumbs and spilled sugar. It was easier to wipe up the spill than to focus on what Daniel was saying.

"This rabbi can read palms."

"Like a fortune teller," I said.

"Fortune tellers are shams," Daniel snapped. "No one believes them. If they get something right, it's only by chance. This is real, Racheli. It's based on the Torah."

"It's good to have a mentor," I said. Yemima was my mentor…sort of. So was Reut. Tikvah, the nurse on the moshav, was also my mentor…although she was much older than me. Yes, a mentor was a good idea. This rabbi in Ashdod…he would give Daniel a more direct connection to the Torah. And if he could read palms, well, that was probably good too. Daniel knew what was good. I pressed my forefinger into a sugar crystal that I'd missed. "Sounds okay…" I was wondering about a stipend. But I didn't ask. If we spoke about money, we might fight. I didn't want to fight.

Daniel stood up and came close. "This rabbi, Racheli, he can read minds too," he said. "But he denies it. One of the guys asked him, just like that, and Rav Benayun shook his head."

"A mind reader? There are mind readers today?"

Daniel nodded. "He's humble too. It's important to be humble."

I knew the Baal Shem Tov was a mind reader. I glanced out the window. But were there really people who could read minds today? The rain had stopped. The rabbi in Ashdod was probably very holy .

Daniel stood up. "I need to leave now," he said. "I don't want to be late."

Later, as I listened to the whirr of the dryer, I realized that I would have to ask my parents for more money. But this time I would ask for enough to cover the expenses of a growing family. I couldn't live worrying about the expense every time I had to use the dryer.

***

"Avner…my father is my light. It's a beautiful name, Racheli. Just the kind of idealistic name that I'd expect you to choose." Gila hugged me. I looked at her jingling wrist full of bracelets, and she met my eyes before flashing a look at Daniel. He was shuckeling back and forth, his long *peyot* swaying, as he concentrated intently on the *berachot* for the bris.

"That's quite a beard he's grown, Racheli," Gila whispered. I loved Daniel's beard. It wasn't only his hair that was growing. He was serving Hashem with all his might. When we went to the *seudah* after the bris in the hall at the edge of the *yishuv*, Daniel stayed back in shul to learn. His Torah learning was holding up the world.

Gila stayed after Yossi and Dov left with their families. Ima couldn't fly out from New York, and Gila said she figured she'd better step into her shoes for the day. So she spent the day at Migdal Yam, helping me and baby Avner settle into home. Gila told me I should have spent a couple of days in a mother and baby home…but I preferred to be at home with the kids and Daniel.

When the rain stopped, Gila wanted to take the kids for a ride on her motorbike. Breathe in some fresh air before supper and bedtime, she said. She'd already buttoned them into their coats when Daniel came home.

"Gila," I said, "a bike ride isn't a good idea because the roads are slippery."

Gila looked at me without saying anything, but she didn't take the kids out on her bike.

In the evening, Gila bathed Yael and Shimmy and put them to bed. Just as she sank into the couch next to me and the baby for a schmooze, Daniel asked me to make him a cup of tea.

"Heellooo," Gila started to say, but I stopped her before Daniel heard. I got up and fixed him a cup of tea. And brought it to him with a smile. Gila gave me a sour look.

She didn't know how important it was to always serve your husband with a smile. I dropped onto the couch and took Avner.

Gila kicked off her shoes and curled her legs under her. "What happened to your cat, Racheli?" she asked.

I didn't answer. Instead, I stared into Avner's face. Gila wouldn't have understood how important it was not to have *tamei* animals in the house.

Gila turned quiet. And then she said she wanted to make it home before the rain began falling again.

Her fingers were already curled around the handlebars of her bike when she blurted out, "Daniel should fix his own tea."

"It's fine, Gila," I told her. I stood very tall and straight so she could see how proud I was of the home I was building. "I like to make Daniel a cup of tea." Gila couldn't understand about having a husband. She couldn't really know about serving Hashem.

"Yeah...but not today. Not after you just had a baby..."

I stepped back. "Well...thanks for the help with the kids," I said.

Gila looked at me for a long moment, and then she said, "Something tells me that you need more than help with the kids."

"What help?" I asked. Gila looked so worried.

"Nothing. Forget it," she said.

I stood there in the driveway for a moment longer, watching the storm clouds blowing in from the sea.

1997

One day, a few months later, when the winter afternoons were getting a little longer and a little warmer, I took the children to the park. The wind was blowing, and the park was almost empty. Great. Yael and Shimmy could have the swings for as a long as they liked. In New York, this wind wouldn't have been called a wind. It was more like a chilly breeze. With the delicious hint of salt. The kids clambered on by themselves, and I stood between the swings, Avner balanced on my hip, pushing them back and forth. My skirt flapped around my legs. I'd taken to wearing loose, baggy clothing. It hid the extra weight that I was still carrying even though Avner was six months old. And anyway, Daniel didn't mind the way I dressed. I sang loudly…songs that they had learned in *gan*, songs that I remembered from my own childhood, songs that I made up right then. The wind was getting stronger. It blew a stray candy wrapper across the park and against my shin. The wrapper stuck. I laughed. Not because it was funny…but because…because everything was so good in my life. I was busy with our growing family, Daniel was learning, we had a gorgeous house in Israel. We were blessed.

Avner had fallen asleep, so I moved away to tuck him into his stroller. Yael carried on singing. A gust of wind blew the end of my scarf across my face. It was getting cold. Almost like fall in New York. I thought of Ima, Faygie, Ayelet, and their kids. Growing up so far away. Suddenly, I missed them. If I were in New York, I could have taken the kids to visit Ima in the afternoon. Instead of sitting in an empty park.

Suddenly, I heard a voice behind me. "Racheli?"

I turned around. My eyes were watering from the wind. Tikvah Guttman… with a coat. I should have brought coats.

"Mammaleh…out now?" She shook her head. "Too cold," she said.

"New York is colder," I said.

Tikvah waved to the children. She looked around the park and then she sat down next to me.

As the nurse on Migdal Yam, Tikvah never had time to sit and talk. When she wasn't at work in Soroka Hospital in Beer Sheva, she was usually busy tending to grazed knees and splinters.

"You work too hard," she said. She patted my hand. Her palm was rough, but her touch was warm. "Daniel…he has to go to the store sometimes, buy bread and milk in the mornings, stand in line on Friday for the grape juice and challah…"

"I bake challah."

Tikvah rubbed my hand harder. "He has to take the kids to the park on Shabbat in the afternoon. Let you rest in bed with this little *tzaddik*."

I didn't like people telling me what to do. Or Daniel. "He's learning."

"It's not good to learn so much and let your wife do all the work."

And I certainly didn't like anyone to tell me that Daniel was doing something wrong. Gila had tried. A wife was supposed to support her husband.

Stand by his side. I wanted to stand up. Leave Tikvah alone on the bench… but her eyes were too warm.

"You work hard too," I said.

Tikvah sighed. She waved to the children again.

Besides, I wasn't tired. I had plenty of energy to do everything. I didn't feel worn out and weak.

That evening, Daniel came home late. Much too late to tickle the kids or even give them a kiss. They'd been in bed for two hours. Maybe three. I was baking granola. The granola in Israel didn't taste like the granola I was used to, and Dina, who'd made aliyah from Los Angeles, had given me her never-fail recipe. Bring to boil a cup of oil and a cup of honey.

Daniel headed straight for the couch. He was carrying a heavy box that had once held bottles of Osem ketchup.

"Late today," I said. I was out of honey. Oh, well. Brown sugar was also a sweetener.

"Look what I have," he said.

"Where were you?" I headed to the couch.

"Look."

I wanted to know where he had been, but I looked. The box was full of books and CDs. Some of the disks had slipped off the top of the pile. Half-concealed, they glittered between the books and the sides of the box.

"*Likutei Moharan*," Daniel said. "I'm studying all of Rebbe Nachman's writings."

"Why?" It was a stupid question. I probably would never have asked it… but I'd met Tikvah that afternoon, and she'd told me that Daniel shouldn't have been learning so much. And he'd come home so late.

"Why?" Daniel pushed the box off his lap and closed the flaps of cardboard over the books. Hiding them all. "Because it's Torah."

"Did Rav Benayun tell you about these books?"

Daniel shrugged. "He probably reads them. I don't know. I don't see him that much anymore. Everyone reads them. And when I'm done with these, I'll read the others. On wisdom, halachah, kind words, raising children."

More books. More learning. I wanted to finish mixing my granola. I measured oats, coconut, sesame and sunflower seeds into a bowl. So if Daniel didn't see Rav Benayun anymore, where was he spending his days?

I poured the granola into trays and pushed it into the oven. I was suddenly tired. I'd been awake since six in the morning. I sat at the kitchen table, wishing that Dina had never given me the recipe for granola. I wanted Daniel to ask me about my day. To tell me he couldn't wait to taste my granola.

He poked at a stray sunflower seed on the counter. "It's a mitzvah to always be happy," he said. He went to the couch, pulled a book out of his box, and turned a few pages. "It's probably the most important mitzvah in the whole Torah…to be happy."

A few days later, I woke up later than usual. I could hear Yael and Shimmy laughing in the living room. I sprung up faster than a jack-in-the-box. Daniel was standing by the front door, about to leave for shul, Yael was clinging to one of his legs, Shimmy to the other. And Daniel was tickling them with the tzitzit of his tallit. He glanced up and caught me watching them.

"It's my happiness cloak," he said. "We have to be really, really happy when we do a mitzvah, and praying is a big mitzvah."

***

Daniel had always been a big reader, and now he began to read even more. There was usually a copy of *Likutei Moharan* in his hands, or lying face down on his lap. There were volumes and volumes of this book, he had told me. He'd probably never finish reading it. Something inside me was…resentful. Suddenly, I wasn't quite so proud about how much he was reading, learning. True, we'd rarely had deep, meaningful conversations, and it had never bothered me before. After all, I'd known all along, from the nights we'd spent staring silently into the flames of a bonfire, from the afternoons we'd spent playing cards, that the man I was marrying wasn't someone who would spend hours sharing his thoughts. But now, with Daniel tied to *Likutei Moharan* day and night, I felt a flicker of resentment. And I was curious to know what he was reading about, why it mattered so much. I knew that I had to catch him in the right mood before I could ask. The right mood didn't happen until a few weeks later.

Ayelet had come to Jerusalem that year, just before Pesach. I hadn't seen her since we had made aliyah four years earlier, and I was excited for her to meet the children. Daniel wasn't part of any *kollel* at this point and spent most of his day learning alone. I wasn't sure where, and I'd learned that he didn't like to be asked. But since he made his own times, he offered to drive us all to Jerusalem. He'd learn in a shul while we spent the day with Ayelet and her kids. Of course, I'd have preferred for Daniel to come with me, but I knew that he wouldn't agree to see Ayelet. Ayelet and her family weren't religious enough. Like Yossi and Dov weren't religious enough. I was lucky he'd agreed to let me and the children see her.

The kids, dressed in matching red and blue striped shirts, were happy to start off by gazing quietly out the windows as we drove along. I could feel my soul expanding like the flat, green fields that stretched out on either side of the highway. I wanted to reach out, put my arms around this beautiful land, like I wrapped them around an enormous gym ball, hug the land close to my chest. This was where we belonged. The children began to tire of the long drive, so Daniel started to sing. One after the other, all the songs we knew.

I stared out the window contentedly. A Bedouin boy was herding his sheep in the distance. I glanced at Daniel. Now was my chance to ask him about what he was reading. He should share something. Anything.

"You read so much these days," I said. "Tell me more about what you're reading."

Daniel kept his eyes on the road. "It's just…things. Religious things."

"So tell me. Talk to me about it."

Daniel's fingers tightened around the steering wheel. His profile hardened. "You need to read," he said. "You don't read. If you read, then we'd have something to talk about."

My chest tightened. My heart shrank, shriveled within me. I had to read before we could talk. And so I read a lot over Pesach, while the kids were busy in our yard with their friends. Climbing, swinging, sliding on the climbing frame from Toys "R" Us that Daniel had assembled. I also listened to the CDs on parenting that Daniel had brought home.

I related to everything I read about. To everything I heard on the CDs. I was in the midst of raising my kids, precious Jewish souls, and I wanted to do it right. When Yemima told me about a parenting course in Jerusalem and offered to watch the kids until I got back, I signed up. Daniel didn't say yes and he didn't say no. He just kept quiet…which was what he did most of the time anyway. It was easier this time. I wasn't schlepping to a course with two kids in tow like I had done when I'd gone to the aerobics course. By the time the course was over, six months later, I knew that I wanted to share with other women the tools that I had learned. I began offering afternoon classes. Women came with their children, and the kids would play around while I gave over the things that I had learned. I didn't ask Daniel anymore about what he was reading. I didn't ask where he was learning or what he did all day. It was better that way.

One night, after I'd given a parenting class that had gone well, I riffled through my file of notes until I found a plastic folder filled with cards printed with slogans. I found the one that I wanted and stuck it on my fridge with a magnet: "I have a Godly intrinsic worth that isn't dependent on what people think of me. Others do not establish my worth."

1998

Smack in the middle of winter, I gave birth to a beautiful baby boy. After three days in the hospital, I was back home. The children had been living with neighbors to make it easier for Daniel, even though he was usually at home, and they had missed us. Coming home was chaotic, but I was happy to be back with the family.

To cut down on the cost of the bris, I decided to cook the food myself. I'd taken care of the meat balls (I still disliked chicken balls) and kid-friendly schnitzel when Yemima and Reut figured out what I was up to. Luckily for me, they took over, and my neighbors cooked the rest of the food. Sadly, my parents weren't able to come over from New York. Gila was visiting them, so she was also absent. Yossi and Dov came with their families, and although I was happy to see them, I busied myself with my older kids, the baby, and the other guests. I didn't want either of my brothers to start asking me about what Daniel was doing (I wasn't sure myself) and how I was managing. But Yossi was smarter than me.

I was nursing baby Yaakov in a side room off the main hall when someone knocked.

I didn't answer. I was feeling shaky from all the exertion. And I wanted to be alone.

"Racheli?"

The door opened a crack, and then Yossi came in.

As he walked toward me, I remembered the dog Yoram from the grocery store had brought to Migdal Yam after his brother died and no one else wanted the enormous animal. I missed having animals around me since Daniel had put Kitty in the car and let her off somewhere in Jerusalem. As soon as I'd seen the dog outside the grocery store I'd wanted to stroke it, but when I had stepped toward it, it growled. Now I felt like that dog. I felt my hackles rising.

"Mazal tov, Racheli." Yossi remained standing behind me.

"Thanks."

"I…Noa and I, the children…we miss you," he said.

My arms tightened around Yaakov. I had my own family now. A husband and children. I didn't need any more. Right? I looked at Yaakov's face. I didn't need any more.

"We'd like to see you…not just when you have a baby."

I felt it. A strange choking in my throat. A burning inside my nose. I was going to cry. I missed Yossi. I missed my family. But what was I supposed to do? Daniel didn't want us to go there. I squeezed my eyes shut. And he was right. I also didn't want my children around a TV screen. I kept quiet, because I knew I couldn't squeeze any words past the rock in my throat.

Yossi shuffled his feet. "So I thought that maybe we could take the kids out…Yael and Shimmy…to the Science Museum. That way, they won't be in our house, and the cousins can get to know each other a little."

He wouldn't…couldn't…suggest that to Daniel. "You…can't…," I said.

"Why not?"

"Because…because…" I didn't know why not.

"Why can't I take them to the Science Museum?"

I didn't know why. Daniel wouldn't want it. He would never, ever, let Yossi take Yael and Shimmy there. Or anywhere else. Yossi and Dov weren't religious enough.

I tried to turn in the plastic chair that I was sitting on. I felt the legs of the chair curve with my weight. I wanted to see Yossi. I missed him. I never thought about him – I didn't let myself. But now that he was here, in the room with me, I realized how much I missed him. His beard was still red, but it had faded. It was more the color of honey.

"Daniel isn't right, Racheli."

Right? Of course Daniel was right. He was always right. Anger sprouted inside me, smothering any tender feelings. "You don't understand," I said.

"*You* don't understand, Racheli."

I struggled to stand up. My legs were shaky. My arms were trembling. I couldn't let Yaakov fall. How could a newborn weigh so much?

"Sit down, Racheli. I'm leaving."

Yossi's voice was gruff.

***

Of course I defended Daniel when Yossi tried to tell me that he was doing something wrong. I defended him because I believed in him. He was doing what was right for our family. He was a good husband and father. I loved him. The children loved him. People didn't understand. They peered into your life from the outside and decided that this was good and this was bad. And even though the mud they slung slid off, it left a mark.

I suppose that was why, when Daniel came home late a few days later, after I had fed, bathed, and put the four kids to sleep by myself, something erupted. He wasn't in *kollel*. He should be helping out.

I stayed in bed. I didn't go to greet him, to warm up his supper, like I usually did.

I heard him coming into the room.

"Why are you always home so late?" The words slurred out my mouth by themselves. And as I heard them, my fingers curled around the edge of my blanket.

Daniel didn't answer. He walked to the window and pulled down the blind. The glow from the security light in our garden disappeared. "Why are you always arguing? Why are you always fighting with me?" he said softly. He never yelled. He didn't need to.

I curled my fingers more tightly around my blanket. In the dark, I could see Yossi's face. An echo of disapproval rang in my ears. And that made me say something more.

"I'm not arguing…I want you to come home to be with us." I took a deep breath. "I think that…I think that you're arguing."

Daniel turned from the window.

My stomach heaved. It was squeezing its way into my throat.

Daniel began walking out of the room. He stopped at the door. "I'm not arguing either," he said.

***

That summer, during the Three Weeks, a well-known rabbi from Jerusalem came to Migdal Yam to give us a lecture. We often had these kinds of events, and I usually couldn't go because there was no one to babysit the children. But this time, Yemima insisted that I had to go. And to make it easier for me, she sent along her eldest daughter to babysit.

Couples drifted into the hall together. I wished Daniel had come, but he never came to these events. The men sat on one side of the hall and the women on the other. At the end of the lecture, there was a question and answer session. Someone asked a question and before the rabbi answered, another question was shouted out. People whispered amongst themselves. This was the kind of give and take that I had been used to in high school. The kind of relaxed banter where I'd always had something to say. And then it popped out. A witty remark. The same kind of remark that used to make all the kids laugh until their bellies ached. It happened again…everyone in the hall laughed. The lecturer smiled. And he waited for the hall to quieten before he could continue.

At the end of the lecture, I walked out of the hall with Yemima and her husband. Daniel was at the door. I hadn't realized that this time, this once, he'd come to the lecture.

"Everyone's telling me how funny you are," he said. "They say you should study to be a medical clown. What do I need to hear that for?"

I lagged behind Daniel. So I'd be a clown…big deal. What was wrong with laughing?

"Do you think it's kosher to make everyone look at you like that? Do you think that it makes Hashem happy?"

I didn't know. I didn't know if Hashem was happy or not with what I did. But I knew that I should have kept my mouth shut.

Daniel sensed my regret. His voice softened a tiny fraction. "You don't need to go to lectures," he said. "All the goodness that you need is in the house."

We'd reached our house, but we didn't go in.

"Don't you want Hashem to love you?" Daniel asked. "If you don't behave right, He won't be happy with you."

"Hashem loves me the way I am," I said.

"How can Hashem love everyone the way they are? He loves people who are good."

Daniel walked away. I managed to thank the babysitter and send her off.

The children were in bed. The house was quiet. So quiet I could hear the storm in my heart. I sat at the kitchen table and put my head on my arms. Daniel was angry with me. I hated it when he was angry. I didn't have my parents or my siblings close by. I didn't have a job or a hobby. I had Daniel and the kids. They were my life. I had to be a good wife and a good mother. I had to make it work. Daniel was frustrated. He'd never hurt me purposely. He hardly ever went to learn with Rav Benayun anymore. Of course he was frustrated. Everyone needed to belong somewhere. And he couldn't find his place. My heart ached. Daniel had tried so hard to find a place where he belonged, but he was still searching. When would it end? Tears soaked my sleeves.

Penina was one of those people who always kept her doors unlocked and expected others to do the same. She knocked and walked right in. "What's wrong?" She pushed some tissues into my hand.

"Nothing."

"You don't cry for nothing. Where do you keep your oil?"

I blew my nose.

Penina opened the cabinets. "It's Daniel, isn't it?" The doors slammed shut. "You're out of oil." She turned the faucet on.

She was going to wash my dishes. "No, it's not," I said automatically. "It's not Daniel." I needed more tissues. "And don't do my dishes."

Penina sniffed. "Marriage is always hard," she said.

Right. Marriage was hard. It wasn't Daniel.

"But some marriages are harder. You need to talk to someone. Where's the *chalavi* sponge?" she said.

I pulled the dairy sponge out from under the pot I'd used to cook pasta for supper. Talk to someone. I didn't need to talk to someone. I had Daniel to talk to. It was me. I had to try harder. I turned on the faucet at the meat sink. We stood next to each other washing my dishes. The warm water, the soapy bubbles, the friendship…they all came together to wash away the pain. Soon Daniel would find another *kollel*, another *rav*. He would find where he belonged, and he'd be happy.

***

Our lives could have continued like that. A sprinkle of discomfort. A little itch that could be ignored. Plenty of people live lives that aren't ideal, but they keep plodding forward anyway. Sometimes content, sometimes upset. Life can flow forward smoothly even when everything isn't perfect, right?

But what happens when something major happens to disrupt the flow of life? When a challenge, a test, a *nisayon*, comes into your life? When something happens that magnifies the faults? In some families, the test brings out the good. The individuals rise to the challenge. They may have singed wings, but they emerge whole. They rise higher and higher, become brighter and brighter. They are like a soaring phoenix that everyone can learn from, wants to emulate.

But what happens when someone doesn't stand up to the challenge? When she makes bad choice after bad choice? When she builds a funeral pyre with her own hands? When she brings destruction into her home?

If you're honest enough, you can't blame those bad choices on your childhood or your marriage. Because you made those choices. You decided. So if you can't paint the backdrop of your life in solid black, then you have to take responsibility for all those bad choices. You have to acknowledge that the personal holocaust your family lived through was a holocaust that you built with your own hands.

And once you do that, how can there ever, *ever* be any hope for you?

PART THREE

Things fall apart; the center cannot hold;
Mere anarchy is loosed upon the world,
The blood-dimmed tide is loosed, and everywhere
The ceremony of innocence is drowned…
– William Butler Yeats, "The Second Coming"

CHAPTER SEVEN

Things Fall Apart

The Muslim Quarter, 1999

Daniel didn't find another *kollel*, and he didn't find another rabbi. Instead, at the beginning of the winter, when I was in my ninth month, expecting my fifth child, he discovered another direction in life. I don't know whom he spoke to, but I quickly learned that this new direction meant that we had to join the sixty Jewish families who were already living in the Muslim Quarter in the Old City. There was a long waiting list of people like us, idealists, who wanted to move into one of the tiny apartments that had been purchased by an organization that worked to ensure a Jewish presence in the Muslim Quarter. But somehow, despite the list, we got in fast.

My family couldn't believe it when I told them what we had decided to do. But I had answers. I told them everything that Daniel had told me. I was used to parroting someone else's opinion. I had done it with chicken balls – when I'd told my classmates that chicken balls were way, way better than meat balls because that was what Yossi had said. I had done it at Hila's house when I repeated all the reasons my father had given us for why you had to live in Israel. And I did it now. "Jews have always lived in the Muslim Quarter. We're going to restore the glory to what belongs to us," I said. I heard the fear in Ima's voice coming over the phone line, but I plunged forward. "You taught me to do this. You taught me that there have to be Jews living all over Israel. You took me on marches to celebrate new *yishuvim* being built. I don't see the difference." I didn't tell Ima the other reasons for moving that Daniel had given me. I didn't know why, couldn't put into words the feelings I had, but I knew that they wouldn't like these other reasons. Daniel had told me that we would be near the holiest place on earth and we could be more religious, closer to Hashem.

It was harder with Yossi. We had conversations that left me feeling dizzy and wondering who was right. Yossi tore my heart in two. Because Yossi had always been right. But now I was married, and I had to follow my husband. Yossi didn't know what was right for my family. Daniel did. When he told me that we were crazy, fanatics even, Daniel told me that I could no longer talk to him. I was sad, but not angry. Because above all, I was relieved. Relieved that the fight was over.

***

The children were all asleep late afternoon when we finally drove into Lion's Gate.

The road was narrow, with high stone walls on either side. It was only a twenty-minute walk to the Jewish Quarter, but it was all dirt and garbage. Arabs hurried along the sides of the road. A woman in a shapeless brown gown stooped a little to stare into my window. I stared back and narrowed my eyes. I wasn't going to live here in fear. This was home now.

As soon as we parked, two guards, rifles thumping against their thighs, strode toward the car. "Hurry," one of them said.

I grabbed the bag at my feet.

"Quick," the guard with an enormous white *kippah* urged. "It's late already."

"Well, too bad," I told the guard. "It'll take time to move us in. We have little kids, and I'm expecting."

The guard shrugged. He stepped back and looked around, checking that everything was still quiet.

We shook the kids awake and unbuckled them. Was he surprised by my assertiveness? I didn't know. But I was surprised myself. I guess I realized, in that instant, how hostile this area really was and that I'd have to stand up for my family.

One glance and I realized that we hadn't just moved from Migdal Yam to the Muslim Quarter. We had moved two hundred years back in time. Instead of a house, we had a two-bedroom apartment that was a mishmash of nooks and crannies all added on at different periods. A house of Lego built by a madman. Gone was our garden with a view of the desert. Now we had fifty meters of dirty, cracked tiles. Despite this, I oohed and aahed over the the arched windows at the front of the five-hundred-square-foot apartment.

That evening, when the children were finally sleeping on their mattresses, I sat on a wooden stool that rocked and leaned against the wall behind me. I missed my couch. There was no room for it in this tiny place, and most of our furniture had been put in storage. I tried to imagine the Jewish family that had lived here hundreds of years ago.

Daniel stood opposite me. He looked different from what I was used to seeing. His shoulders weren't stiff. He was relaxed. Almost as if he were on vacation.

He rolled his shoulders, as if he couldn't quite believe that he'd rid himself of a weight. "We can be more religious here," he said. "It'll be good for us. For the children."

I laid my head against the wall behind me. Someone outside was shouting. Migdal Yam had been home for seven years. We'd had a beautiful home with a yard. Yael had started first grade. Loud words, all in Arabic, rolled in through the mesh on the windows.

"We'll be happy here," Daniel said. "We have each other. We're like Rabbi Akiva and Rachel. You're my Racheli who sacrificed so much for me to learn Torah." He smiled at me. Little lines spread out from the corners of his eyes. Happiness lines.

I smiled back. I wanted us to be happy. And I knew that if Daniel was happy, I would be happy too. It wasn't that much different from Ima moving to Israel so that Abba could farm cotton.

***

Life has to have a routine, wherever you live. Migdal Yam, the Muslim Quarter…it doesn't really matter where you are, the same things have to get done. Kids to *gan* and school, meals, baths, bed. I hurried to create some kind of normal structure for my family before I would give birth. Daniel spent a few days talking to different people and visiting different *kollelim* until he settled into Kollel Keter Malchut, somewhere in the Jewish Quarter. Many of the men whose families lived in the Muslim Quarter, like we did, learned here. Daniel began spending most of his days and sometimes part of his nights there. I wasn't sure what they did there all the time, but Daniel told me there was a lot of praying for different things. Something about special prayers that could only be said at midnight.

Whenever we left the house, we had to be accompanied by an armed security guard. My day started with a mad rush to get Yael to the school bus that was waiting in the parking lot in the Jewish Quarter. The guard, who was always stationed on our rooftop, would come down to walk us to the Jewish Quarter. After that, I was left alone to get the four kids up all the steps that lead to the parking lot. Usually, we made it, thanks to my BOB stroller. The stroller seated one child, but because it was such a strong carriage, I could fit three kids on it and, occasionally, four. But sometimes, we missed the bus and then I had to decide if I was going to drive Yael to school after I'd taken Shimmy and Avner to *cheder* or let her stay at home.

The afternoons, I spent keeping the children happy and busy, which wasn't easy. They were used to a large house and a garden, and now they were living in a matchbox. For the first few days, I took them to the Kotel to say Tehillim. Even though Yael was only starting first grade, she already knew how to read in English and Hebrew. We sat right up against the Wall. I let the children touch the cool stones, and then we began to say the Tehillim that they knew by heart. By the third day, the children were more interested in pulling out the notes stuck in the crevices than in saying Tehillim. At first, I was disappointed. We were at the holiest place on earth, and they didn't want to use the opportunity. But then I remembered something that I used to teach in my parenting class. It was all about age. Saying Tehillim every afternoon wasn't appropriate for their age.

And they needed to play. They were kids. So I decided that I'd pack up lunch and take the children to a different park in the city every afternoon. Sometimes I'd leave in the morning to take them all to school and come back only in the evening. Yes, it was exhausting, but we were all stifled by our tiny apartment, and I was ready to do anything to avoid going back to the house.

I suppose that I should have spoken to them about the move. Yael, certainly, was old enough to tell me about her feelings. Tell me how she was managing in her new school. But I never did have these kinds of conversations. I wasn't used to them, and besides, I was always running. Trying to keep everything together singlehandedly, while Daniel learned. Keeping our mouse hole in order was impossible. I hadn't unpacked properly because there was no space for what we had brought with us. In my ninth month, I didn't have the energy to do it anyway. Where the mess of clothes and toys ended, the dirt began. It was the complete opposite of the home I had kept in Migdal Yam. Grocery shopping was awful because getting the groceries from the van into the house was a logistic nightmare. I was always trying to make sure there was cooked food available. And trying to keep the kids happy.

Making new friends isn't easy, but I missed my friends from Migdal Yam badly, and I needed some company, so I tried. About two minutes' walk from us lived a group of six families. Tzila's family was one of them. And her husband also learned in Keter Malchut. We hit it off from our first week in the Muslim Quarter when she came around with an apple pie. Tzila was a little older than me, and her family had been living in the Muslim Quarter for ten years. The inside of her house was so neat and clean that I never invited her to come to our home. Tzila had lace curtains on the windows, woven rugs on the stone floors, and potted geraniums in old kettles and pickle tins.

Accompanied by the guard, I'd hurry over to Tzila's house. My three-wheeled BOB stroller could bump across the uneven paving and over the garbage pretty fast. Two kids inside, one holding onto each side, I thumped my way behind the guard, hurrying to keep up.

"Why do you live here?" I asked her one afternoon when despite, or because of the rain, I'd rushed over. My sneakers were drenched. I'd taken off the kids' shoes, and I didn't know how I was going to ever dry them.

"It's idealism," she said. "It's uplifting, magical, and addictive. You can't leave here. This is the place where our forefathers walked, the closest place to the Beit Hamikdash. Don't you feel the spiritual connection?"

I didn't. Idealism and a longing for a spiritual connection had brought my parents to Israel to be cotton farmers. Idealism had brought Daniel and me to Migdal Yam. It had brought us here to the Muslim Quarter. But now, faced with reality, my idealism was running out the door. Could people really raise normal kids here?

Most nights, when Daniel would finally get home, I cried. He would sit opposite me at the gouged table and look into my eyes. "It'll get better," he said.

I wanted to believe him. It was so hard, and yet, despite all the difficulty, I loved Daniel, and I believed that what he was doing was right. And so I davened that, somehow, it would get better.

***

Three weeks after we had moved in, on Shabbat morning, baby Ahuva was ready to make her way into the world. Daniel was already in shul. I sent Shimmy and Yael to get the guards and run to the shul that Daniel was in.

Daniel drove our car from the Jewish Quarter were we usually parked to the Muslim Quarter. The children had instructions to go to Tzila's house until Daniel got back.

Our new life in the Muslim Quarter had drained me of every ounce of strength. And yet Ahuva's birth was the easiest of all my births. Finally, I was settled into my bed in the maternity ward. I lay back. Felt air whoosh out of the pillow that was covered with protective plastic. Daniel's eyes were red after being awake all night, but they were soft. Like melted chocolate.

"I'll leave the van here and take the bus home," Daniel said. "That way you can get home easily."

Daniel wanted me to drive myself home. I had imagined us walking into the house together. Showing the new baby to all the kids. Letting them hold her hands, count her tiny fingers. But Daniel was already standing up.

He pulled open the curtain around my bed. I was used to managing alone. I was young, strong. Hashem had blessed me with plenty of energy. But Daniel… I looked at his back. How was he going to manage the house and the children alone? "I left two boxes in the freezer," I said. "Schnitzel."

He turned around. "You'll be okay, right?"

I nodded. Daniel was busy learning. He couldn't just come and go when he wanted. And besides, I was used to doing everything myself. This was no different.

***

Sunday morning, Gila came to visit me. I was surprised, because she hadn't been in contact much since Avner's bris, two years earlier. And she'd been in New York for Yaakov's bris, so she'd missed that. It wasn't as if I had the time to call her. I was barely managing to keep my head above water.

"How're you managing in the Old City?" Gila asked after she'd taken the baby out of my arms.

"Okay," I said.

Gila laid the baby on her lap and stared at her little face. "She looks like you, Racheli," she said.

I nodded. I thought of all the Sundays that Gila and I had spent hiking around New York. All the times she'd visited us on Migdal Yam. And part of me missed her. Missed her visits and the tinkling bracelets. I felt my eyes burning.

"So...what do you want me to do for you? Get you a fresh salad bursting with vitamins? Or a calorie-laden Danish? Or both?" She kissed the baby.

I shook my head. "I'm fine here," I said. "Maybe..." I wasn't sure it was a good idea to ask Gila to the visit the kids in the Old City. But Daniel was looking after them alone. It wasn't like Migdal Yam, where we had a slew of friends. It was probably hard for him. And the kids. "Want to take some supper to the kids and see if Daniel needs help?"

Gila tossed back her hair. "I asked what *you* need, Racheli," she said. "Daniel's a big boy."

I should have kept quiet. I tried to smile, but my lips were frozen.

Gila snuggled the baby onto her shoulder. "She smells like...it's that yummy baby smell."

I could tell that was Gila's way of saying sorry. Maybe...maybe she didn't feel welcome anymore when she came to visit. It would have been easier if she didn't have the motorbike. She always wanted to give the kids rides on the bike, and Daniel didn't like it.

"I wish Ima were here," I said suddenly. The words popped out. And suddenly I realized how much I missed Ima. And Faygie. And Ayelet and my brothers. The burning behind my eyes grew stronger.

"Hey, Racheli," Gila came closer to my bed and kissed my cheek. "It's cool. I'll take them pizza and bathe the kids if that's what you want." She handed back the baby and got ready to leave. She stood at the door.

Like she wanted to say something else. I felt my stomach tensing up. But Gila just smiled a sad kind of smile and waved goodbye.

***

Coming back home with baby Ahuva was...not easy. There were no neighbors knocking on the door to bring me a meal, no one offering to watch the kids, no one to talk to. One afternoon, when it was raining so hard that I couldn't muster the energy to rush to Tzila's house, I did an arts and crafts project with the children. Ima had sent it before we left Migdal Yam. It was kinda cozy, sitting around the table coloring the stiff plastic outlines of a daddy, a mommy, four children, a dog, and a cat. I decided that I had to do it more often. Instead of trying to clean up the mess. The mess that never ended.

After we'd colored the outlines, we cut them out, and I put them on a baking tray and slipped it into the oven. Five minutes later, I pulled the tray out. The plastic had shrunk and thickened. The little figures were smaller versions of themselves. I stared at them as they cooled. And suddenly a sick feeling filled me. Trickled through my tired arms and legs until every part of me felt like it was dying. I was a plastic cutout. Cut away from everything familiar, from family and friends. I was shriveled and shrunken.

***

"Mothers read to their kids at bedtime," Daniel said. We were walking along one of the alleys in the Old City and had stopped outside a bookstore. He had come back late the night before. Rav Yigal had kept him and another few men back for a special class in Kabbalah. He'd woken up late, and with all the kids out, I was free to put Ahuva into the stroller and walk him to Keter Malchut. Daniel pointed to a stand of thin, colorful books.

"I do read to the kids," I said. Just the other night I'd read for the hundredth time the story about the dog who didn't want to have a bath. Daniel's brow furrowed. He picked up one of the books. "You need to read them Jewish stories. Stories about rabbis and *tzaddikim*. It's important."

Daniel always told us long, long stories at the Shabbat table. The stories were about the Baal Shem Tov and what he had done. The kids were young and couldn't sit still at the table for the hours and hours that Daniel wanted them to be there. I wasn't sure I wanted to tell them those kind of stories. I liked the story about the dog. It was cute. And it rhymed. I picked up another book. About Rabbi Akiva. Maybe Daniel was right. A pity to read junk when I could be telling them about rabbis and *tzaddikim*. Teaching them how to be better people.

That night I started with the first story. About Rabbi Chanina ben Dosa's wife, who was so poor that she didn't have any food. But she didn't complain. When her nosy neighbor came to poke around, the coals in her oven turned into challahs.

"It can't happen today," Shimmy said. He gnawed the cuff of his pajamas with his teeth.

"Why not?" I said. "Hashem can do anything." The children had to learn that Hashem was in charge of the world. Daniel was right: these stories could teach them so much.

The stories became a nightly ritual. Pajamas, teeth brushed, one last drink of water and then…one story, two, sometimes three. Stories of *tzaddikim*.

***

One night when Daniel came home, the children were sleeping. Even Ahuva. She was a good baby. She didn't cry endlessly. It was as if she knew that I couldn't – absolutely couldn't – cope with any more pressure. The first thing I noticed was that he wasn't wearing the clothes he'd been wearing when he left the house in the morning.

"What happened to your clothes?" I said.

Daniel shrugged. He stepped across the clothes on the floor to get to the door of the kids' room and looked in. Then he turned around to face me.

"It's better to dress this way," he said. "Important people wear black pants and white shirts."

I looked at him. From head to toe. "Where are your sneakers? They cost us a lot of money."

"Don't you want me to dress like the other guys in the yeshiva?" Daniel said.

"They all dress like that?" I hadn't realized that the yeshiva was that kind of place. Then again, I hadn't asked. And, anyway, Daniel wasn't very good at sharing his days with me.

Daniel pushed aside a pile of books and sat on the couch. "All of them. And their wives wear tights. Socks. The kids too."

"Who told you how their wives dress?" Daniel was drumming on his knee. He'd done that, long ago, when he'd been an unhappy salesman. Now the habit was back. I hated the sound.

Daniel didn't answer.

I wasn't going to dress like them. Women I didn't even know. I dressed fine. I covered my hair with a scarf, not a baseball cap. Wore sleeves that covered my elbows. That was enough.

"It's good to be more religious. Now that we're living in this holy place, we have to dress properly," Daniel said.

"We can be more religious without wearing more clothes," I said. I picked up some of the kids' clothes. Were these clean? Dirty? I didn't want more clothes to take care of. "Who told you I have to wear tights?"

"Rav Tzefanyah."

"Who's that?"

"He's a rabbi. He learns in a shul near Keter Malchut."

I threw the clothes toward the washing machine. Another rabbi. Daniel had a rabbi. Rav Yigal. Why did he need another rabbi? I looked at Daniel.

I sat on the couch. Pulled out some Lego bricks that had slipped down the side of the couch. Daniel didn't like questions. There should be a box to keep them in. In Migdal Yam, each toy had had its own box. I missed my old house. "You have a *kollel*," I said. "Why don't you talk to the rabbi in the *kollel*?"

Daniel frowned. "Yael?"

I turned around. Yael had woken up. She stood in the doorway of the kids' room, twisting a strand of hair around and around her finger.

"Come for a kiss and then go back to bed," Daniel said. He looked at me. "You don't understand anything. You can't just sit and learn in a yeshiva. You have to have a rabbi who knows you, who can guide you," he said.

I didn't want Daniel to have a rabbi who told him I had to wear tights. I didn't want Yael to wear tights. No one I knew wore tights. Abba had never made us wear tights.

Yael stepped over the piles of clothes and climbed onto my lap. She was clutching something in her hand. It was one of the plastic cutouts we had made together. It was the mother.

I took the cutout and rubbed it between my fingers. Shrunken and shriveled. My parents were in America. Daniel didn't want me talking too much to my family here. I'd left my friends behind in Migdal Yam. I didn't have anyone to talk to.

***

I suppose that visiting someone who lives in the Muslim Quarter is a novelty. It was that novelty and probably the memory of old friendship that brought Perrie and Reuven to my doorstep. With a security guard. Left alone, Perrie and Reuven had to step into the mess they could see beyond the slightly open door.

They'd gotten married at around the same time as Daniel and I. They were having a second honeymoon while Perrie's mom babysat their three kids back home. Back home meant New York.

By pushing away some of the toys behind the door, I was able to open the door wide enough for them to come in. I had just managed to put the five kids through bath time and we had started on supper. Bread dipped in yogurts.

Reuven pushed back some of the junk on the couch so that Perrie could sit down.

"Remember when we went to the Brooklyn Botanic Gardens to see the cherry blossoms?" Perrie said, pretending that she was used to the mess in front of her, behind her, around her.

Her voice was pretty and pink. Like her Prada jacket.

She tugged at the gold tab of the zipper on her jacket. Her mauve nails clicked against it.

Four hungry kids, cramped around the table, stared. I gave out more bread.

If Daniel had been home, he would have told her that it wasn't modest to draw attention to your hands by painting your nails.

I was so exhausted that I didn't even realize how absurd the whole thing was. Maybe three-year-old Avner, who was always astute, realized that something was out of place. Maybe he was just hungry and wanted to finish eating. Or maybe plastic spoons shouldn't be so flexible. Avner left the table, his half-eaten yogurt in hand, and leaned against the stone arch that separated the kitchen and the living room. He dug his spoon into his yogurt, but before it reached his mouth, the spoon bent, bounced, and a spoonful of yogurt flicked across the room – splat! – onto Perrie's jacket.

Perrie jolted. She stared at the splatter. The yogurt dribbled down in two uneven lines.

Ahuva cried, and I picked her up. I should have felt a flush of heat. Said something to Avner. But nothing came out of my mouth. I just signaled to Yael to go and fetch a tissue.

Yael ran to the bathroom and came back with two squares of toilet paper. Right…we were out of tissues. She was about to dab at the mark, but Perrie had recovered enough to take over the damage control.

Reuven opened his mouth and closed it.

Perrie wiped the mark, folded the sodden toilet paper into a square and dabbed again. Then she puffed at a stray strand of her sheitel. It floated off her face.

She should be wearing a scarf.

She smiled.

Smiled. She could still smile.

"They keep you busy." Perrie stood up. "Mine do too."

Ahuva had stopped crying, but I laid her against my shoulder anyway. "I need to call the guard," I said.

Reuven turned back to the window. He poked at the mesh where the kids had stuffed some stray papers. "You were right, Racheli," he said. "Audis are the best."

Ten minutes later, the kids were in bed. No teeth brushed. I curled up on Yaakov's mattress. It was his turn to fall asleep next to Ima. Perrie's taste had always been great. She could wear a pink Prada jacket, and it could look pretty. Not that pretty meant right. No, it wasn't right to wear flashy colors like that. I closed my eyes. I wished that she had stayed longer. Old friends were like well-worn slippers. A snug fit that made your heart warm and fuzzy.

CHAPTER EIGHT

The Stage Is Set

2000

The watery chill of winter had begun to evaporate. In the park, the tree that grew beside the bench I always sat on was beginning to grow new shoots. I touched the hard, shiny green tips gently. Asparagus. The tips, with their tiny leaves folded over the top, reminded me of the asparagus that Ima used to sometimes serve. Long ago. So long ago that I sometimes wondered if I had ever lived in Forest Hills.

"Read me a story." Avner pulled a book out from under the stroller and sat next to me.

The other kids were busy on the climbing frame. Yael was walking around with Ahuva balanced on her hip. She had grown, and her skirt was too short, but her tights covered her legs well.

Shira arrived and maneuvered her stroller into the space between the bench and the tree. She unstrapped two-year-old Hodaya. Shira sat down and smiled.

Avner opened the book and put it on my lap. Soon we were caught up in the story. The Arizal and his students were learning Torah at the *kever* of Hosea ben Beeri. Suddenly the Arizal's face clouded. He had seen that a plague of locusts was approaching Tzefat. All because the city had ignored the plight of a poor water carrier whose bucket had broken. With no way to provide for his family, the water carrier cried and complained to Hashem. The Arizal instructed one of his students to collect money and take it to the water carrier and to tell him that the town would never again ignore his plight.

Avner knew the story by heart. He knew that even though the locusts had approached Tzefat, they had veered off at the last moment. And yet he asked, as he always did, "They all had food, right, Ima?"

I nodded. The Arizal had saved them all from starving.

Avner jumped up, and the book slipped off my lap. He grabbed a packet of pretzels out of the bag hanging on the handle of the stroller and ran off to share them.

Shira had taken out her tapestry. She'd finished the trees, I saw. Now she was starting on the walls of the house. She threaded her needle with gray thread.

Suddenly she looked up. "You always read to them in the park," she said. "It's nice."

I stared at the picture on the cover. A black cloud was hovering over the city. Millions of tiny dots, each one a machine of destruction. And below the cloud, a circle of men in turbans were bent over a book. The cloud fascinated me. I stood up to check on the children. Sometimes I felt that the black cloud – not really a black cloud, just a…a dark…heavy something – was looming over our house. Daniel was different…not at ease like when we'd first arrived. But it was a dumb feeling. Because everything was fine in our life. Maybe hard sometimes, but that was okay. It would get better.

"Do you think it's true?" I asked Shira.

"What?"

"The story. Could the Arizal really see the locusts coming?"

Shira stuck her needle into her tapestry and looked up. "He didn't actually see them," she said. "If he had seen them, really seen them, it would have been too late to do anything about it," she said. "I think that he sensed them. Sensed them and somehow linked it to the water carrier." Shira straightened a stitch with the tip of her needle.

She was right. *Tzaddikim* could sense things. See things that we couldn't see. Yaakov was at the top of the climbing frame. I walked to the slide and bent down to watch him whizz out.

The sky was darkening. Enormous clouds nudged each other in a mad rush to cover the sun. It was going to rain again.

***

The children stood behind their chairs. Shimmy on Daniel's right, Yael on the left, and the rest of us further down. From the other end of the table, I looked at Daniel. His hat was pulled slightly forward, his shoulders stiff in his jacket. I had gotten used to how he looked, and I even liked it. Dignified.

Important. A soldier of Hashem. He picked up a *bentsher*, but he didn't start saying Kiddush. He picked up the Kiddush cup, tilted his head to the ceiling, and closed his eyes. His lips began to move. Behind him the candles, seven bright flames, flickered.

Yaakov was the first to move. Two steps and he was sitting astride the arm of the couch. I ignored him. Daniel's eyes were still closed. I wondered what he was thinking. Wished I was part of it.

He began to murmur. He picked up the new siddur that he had bought that morning and opened it. He ran his finger up and down the table of contents. When he finally found the page he wanted, Avner was pushing Yaakov off the couch. Yaakov fell backwards. He rolled onto his belly and swatted Avner's legs.

Daniel yelled. "I need to have *kavanot*. Think the right thoughts. How can I do it with such a racket going on?"

The boys slinked back to the table and stood behind their chairs. I stared at them. "Abba needs to concentrate. You can help him by being quiet." Shimmy stood straighter. He was old enough to understand.

Daniel began murmuring once more. Twenty minutes later, by the time he got to the familiar words of Kiddush, my feet were throbbing. The ingrown toenail that I didn't have time to take care of was burning like fire. I slipped off my shoes.

"Why can't they stand still?" Daniel grumbled.

I didn't answer. Daniel wasn't asking me to share what I'd given over in my parenting classes. So long ago. I herded the children to the basin to wash their hands.

Daniel looked at my feet. "Where're your shoes? Kiddush is a holy time. How can you stand there without shoes?"

I pushed a chair nearer to the sink so that Yaakov could reach the faucet. My shoes. I should tell Daniel about my toe. But now wasn't the right time. I mustn't think about ingrown toenails at this holy time.

It was late when the meal was over. Even Yael had fallen asleep at the table. Probably toward the end of the long, complicated story about the Baal Shem Tov and a beautiful bird on a ladder. I'd been busy serving the food, putting the little ones to bed. Finally, I could stretch out on the couch. The table, scattered with crusts of challah, would wait until the next day. I thought of the mouse I'd seen a few days ago. I'd forgotten to check the trap that I had set up. I hoped we hadn't caught it. And then hoped we had.

I opened my eyes when Daniel handed me a bag. Something hard. A book. Someone shouted in Arabic outside. Banged on our door. The guard on the roof yelled out. And I heard the sound of bare feet slapping against stone.

Daniel was back at the head of the table.

I pulled the book out of the bag. A siddur. I had a siddur. My fingers slid over the cream binding. I opened the cover and heard the spine crack.

"Edot Hamizrach," Daniel said. "Rav Tzefanyah says that we must daven according to this *nusach*."

"Why?"

Daniel stood up. "Because this is the proper and more correct form of the prayers. All the *tzaddikim* davened this *nusach*." He pulled his hat off and tossed it onto the table, onto the challah crumbs.

I curled up into a ball. I couldn't get up. Didn't have the energy to get into bed. A man was supposed to choose a rabbi to guide him. It was a halachah. Maybe. Daniel had told me once that he wasn't sure if it was a minhag or a halachah. But it didn't matter either way, I realized. He had chosen a rabbi. That was his job to do. Just as mine was cooking, taking care of the kids. He had chosen a rabbi, and we were following him. I didn't need to ask questions. Daniel knew what the best thing was for us. Besides, Rav Tzefanyah was probably a holy man.

***

I didn't like my new siddur. Didn't like the feel of the cover, the differences in the prayers. I knew it was important to get used to the new *nusach*, and so I didn't complain to Daniel…even though it was so hard for me. But one day, after I'd been trying to daven while two children fought over the new dolls' stroller I had bought for them, a complaint slipped out. "I can't daven well because it feels so strange," I said. "The words don't flow anymore."

Daniel stared at me. "This is the *derech* of Hashem," he said. "Do you want to come close to Hashem?"

Of course I did.

"This is the way, but if you don't want to, I can't make you do it." That was Daniel. He never forced me to do anything.

I began to wake up very early in the morning a few times a week, before dawn, to go and daven at the Kotel. Daniel was still sleeping, so the children were never alone. Sometimes I had to wait fifteen minutes until a guard came. When that happened, I had very little time left to daven before I had to get back home to wake the children. The plaza was always flooded with warm, yellow light. The quiet was so thick that you could rub it between your fingers. I had my regular spot, on the far right, close to the little room where some of the regulars davened. In this spot, I got to know my new siddur better. I tried to think about what Daniel had told me about how we were supposed to be happy when we were doing a mitzvah. Tried to feel happy that I was davening. Even if the words weren't all familiar. After a couple of months, the pages for Shacharit were smudged, a little wrinkled where my tears had fallen. The siddur began to look like it belonged to me.

Those mornings, when I was standing close to the Kotel, I would crane my neck up and watch the sky turn pink above the top of the Wall. Was this the time when the Kohanim used to bring the *korban tamid*? Some days I'd feel almost a pain in my chest, the longing for the Beit Hamikdash was so strong. On those days, when I walked home, I suppose that the soles of my shoes hit the stones like they always did, but I felt like I was floating.

***

"You actually did it. Gave up your huge house and garden for this!" Dina flopped onto the couch and looked around her. "It's a hole in a time warp. Just a couple of rooms plastered together at who knows how many different times in the past."

Dina was the first friend from Migdal Yam who'd come to visit, so I let her comment pass and just said, "It's in the Old City." As if that explained everything. Dina had come for Shabbat because her husband Avi had traveled to Denver to be with his sick father. She'd told me that he'd had to leave his construction company with the manager. And she needed a break. Besides, I owned her one for the granola recipe that she'd given me when we were still on Migdal Yam.

Dina pulled her baby onto her lap. She'd left the older kids with neighbors in Migdal Yam. She stared at Daniel, who was sitting at the table, a book open in front of him. He'd barely looked up when we came in. Dina was taking in

Daniel's big beard, the black and white clothing. She was going to say something, I knew it. "Have some apple pie," I suggested. "It'll be a while before we eat." The apple pie that was mom's secret recipe, and I knew Dina loved it.

During Kiddush, which took at least half an hour, I avoided looking at Dina. She'd never had much patience, and I didn't feel like hearing her opinion. I guess growing up in Los Angeles, in the heart of movie heaven, made you pretty loud. Louder than me, even. After the soup, Daniel told us a story from the Baal Shem Tov. The kids fell asleep at the table and on the couch. Dina was struggling to keep her eyes open. But I enjoyed listening to Daniel. He was usually out learning, and Shabbat was the only time we could spend hours together.

In the afternoon, we went for a walk. After the usual rush through the Muslim Quarter, we got to the Jewish Quarter. Daniel and the kids started up the stairs, but I stopped and waited for Dina to catch her breath. Finally she was ready to start pulling her stroller up.

"What is this?" she puffed.

I watched her pulling hard, trying to dislodge the brake on her stroller from the edge of the step. "The steps?" I asked.

She jerked her thumb at Daniel, somewhere above us. "He should be helping you."

"Daniel? He doesn't carry on Shabbat."

"Doesn't carry? Are you crazy? What's with these stringencies? And stop smiling so sweetly."

We went back years, Dina and I, so she probably felt she had some kind of right to give her opinion.

"Black and white and Kiddush till the morning and he floats ahead while you schlep."

"Black and white isn't a stringency. It's…" I handed out candies to the kids, who'd come back to us. "It's…nice."

"You're not real," Dina snapped. "And the steps!"

"It's…nice."

"It's not nice. It's hard!" Dina stared at me.

"I'm happy to do it for him."

"You mean lugging a stroller with two kids up a million steps is a privilege."

I kept quiet. I'd learned that you can avoid a lot of arguments by keeping quiet.

Dina yanked her stroller up another step and then stopped. Suddenly she grinned. "This kind of stuff, black and white and Kiddush when it's almost midnight, it's not for me. I don't know how you manage to listen to Daniel's long stories and look so interested...but I guess it's kinda neat. Maybe I'll try to focus more on what Avi's telling me instead of letting the kids distract me. It's good for a marriage."

I laughed. Even Dina had to admit that Daniel and I were on the right track.

***

Kever Shimshon is on the top of a hill in the pine forest around Moshav Eshtaol, near Beit Shemesh. We had set out for a picnic on the last day of Chol Hamoed Pesach. We didn't stop at the entrance to the park. We drove further, along narrow roads, winding little tracks that twisted and turned endlessly. Shimmy spotted the clearing first. A private spot with two tables, a slide, and a seesaw. We spent a couple of hours over a late lunch. The children played and gathered pinecones that I promised we would spray with silver spray paint. Daniel was busy reading a booklet that Rav Tzefanyah had given to the circle that learned with him.

"What's it about?" I asked Daniel.

"Holy things," Daniel said. He closed the book. "Things that Rav Tzefanyah explains to us. He teaches our circle things that other people don't know." He picked up a pine needle and began snapping it into pieces.

Something inside me swelled. Daniel was part of a select circle. A circle of people studying stuff that not everyone could understand. Suddenly I thought of Perrie and Reuven. It was a different life back in New York. And it was so far away. I was proud of Daniel for learning Torah. Proud of us and what we were doing. I pushed together a pile of pine needles with my feet and reached down for a handful.

"Someone who understands the things in this book has *ruach hakodesh*," Daniel says.

My head jerked up fast. Did Daniel have *ruach hakodesh*?

Daniel linked his fingers behind his head and stretched.

"Do you?"

"What?"

"Have *ruach hakodesh*?"

He smiled. "*Ruach hakodesh* is for holy people. Rabbis," he said.

When the children came running back, we set off along the track leading to the *kever* of Shimshon. Ten minutes later, we were standing at the bottom of a small hill. The children ran up.

Daniel and I walked up the hill slowly. There were white stones over the *kever*, a long rectangle at the top of the hill. A Chassid was at the foot of the *kever*, swaying over a *shtender*. All around me the hills, covered with pine trees, stretched out. On the right, the buildings of Beit Shemesh, rows of homes and patches of industrial zones, curved and curled around the lower hills. I felt my soul widening, expanding. A cool breeze blew up.

I spotted our children, a small, tight circle of bodies, wandering in the tall grass on the slopes below the *kever*. Daniel and I walked onto the roof of what had once been a house. I peered through thick cracks in the ground into the cave below. I rubbed my foot across the remains of a mosaic. Daniel sat on the wall, his legs partially hiding two hollows in the thick stones where a woman had once crushed spices or maybe wheat.

Daniel stared out to the hills. "If you have *ruach hakodesh*, you can read people's minds," he said.

I knew that *tzaddikim* could read minds. I'd read so many stories about *tzaddikim*.

"Rav Tzefanyah reads minds." Daniel looked at me. One eyebrow twitched.

So there were people even today who could read minds. I hadn't known that. I thought that mind reading was something that didn't happen anymore. Like prophecy. I looked across the hills, all the way to the end, where the last hill met the sky. Had Rav Tzefanyah read Daniel's mind? The words tumbled out. "What did he tell you?"

Daniel didn't answer.

I hadn't really expected an answer. I wouldn't want anyone to read my mind. What if I was thinking things that I wouldn't want anyone to know? Maybe Rav Tzefanyah had read things that Daniel didn't want to share. I moved a little closer to Daniel. It could have been…embarrassing.

Daniel stood up. "I'm going to daven at the *kever*," he said.

Only when I was all alone did I dare let my thoughts wander in a different direction. What if Rav Tzefanyah couldn't really read minds? What if he'd told Daniel things that weren't true?

I looked across to the *kever*. Daniel was standing, hands clasped behind him, his face tilted up, his eyes probably closed. Perfectly still. Suddenly Shimmy appeared. He stood next to Daniel. Clasped his hands behind him. Other mothers would have wanted to take a photo. But I didn't need to. I knew that this moment of father and son davening together was something I'd never forget.

***

Not long after Pesach, I stopped visiting Tzila, my friend in the Muslim Quarter, as frequently as I used to. I told her that the weather was warmer, and the kids needed the afternoons in the park. It was true, but there were other reasons too. Daniel was no longer part of Kollel Keter Malchut, where most of the men like him learned. Tzila knew that Daniel was spending his time with Rav Tzefanyah. Her husband had told her stuff about him, and she'd hinted that she wasn't sure that Rav Tzefanyah and his circle was… She'd stood up to pluck the dead leaves off her geraniums at this point. Pushed apart the stems to reach the crinkled brown leaves. And then she'd said that there were other places where Daniel would grow better. Well, Daniel wasn't a geranium. Daniel had moved beyond Keter Malchut. He needed something more. And I didn't want a friend who thought she could tell us what to do. So what if she was older than me? So what if she had lived in the Muslim Quarter for much longer than me? That didn't give her the right to criticize.

So I cut down on my visits. But there was another reason. The main reason. We had been in the Muslim Quarter for seven months. And I couldn't live there any longer. I wasn't a proactive person. I wasn't the type to think about changing something, and certainly not the type to make decisions, but the miserable physical conditions of life in the Muslim Quarter were too much even for me. The tiny apartment, the constant struggle with the logistics of it all…I couldn't carry on. And I had told Daniel that I wanted to move out. So there was no point trying to become good friends with someone I'd soon be saying goodbye to. I knew that we couldn't move back to Migdal Yam. Daniel wanted a more religious lifestyle than the *yishuv* could offer us. And besides, he was spending more and more time with Rav Tzefanyah. He had finally found a rabbi, a mentor who would bring out all of his strengths, and we had to stay close by. So I suggested that we move into the Jewish Quarter. That meant more money. Daniel told me to ask my parents. This time, I didn't hesitate like before when I had to ask them for money. I was far, far too miserable. My parents were delighted that we'd come to our senses and agreed to help us out. Like they always did.

A few weeks later, I was looking for an apartment in the Jewish Quarter.

As soon as we had signed a contract, we began moving our things into our new home. Our new apartment was large , airy, full of light…and best of all, I didn't need a guard to get in and out. None of us was sad to say goodbye to the Muslim Quarter.

***

Not long after we moved in, Daniel came home early. He usually wasn't home during the day. He walked out to the porch immediately. I followed him. He was leaning on the green wrought-iron fence that surrounded the porch.

He didn't turn around. But I knew that he'd heard my footsteps. And I knew something was on his mind. Maybe it was the rush in his steps, the stiffness of his shoulders.

Daniel picked at the flaking paint.

I'd already bought two tins to repaint the bars.

He turned his face toward me. "Rav Tzefanyah walked from the mountain tops at Chevron all the way to the Dead Sea and back in just one hour without any food or water," Daniel said.

His cheeks were flushed. I knew Daniel. I could sense his pent-up energy.

"Really, it should take a couple of days, maybe even weeks, to get there and back. He had *kefitzat haderech*. The long way was shorted by a miracle."

Kefitzat haderech. That was something that happened to holy people. Like Avraham when he was chasing the four kings who kidnapped Lot, or Eliezer, when he left Charan to find a wife for Yitzchak. "That sounds…unbelievable," I said. *Unbelievable* was a safe word. Because I couldn't believe Daniel. And I couldn't tell him that.

"It happened to the Baal Shem Tov too," Daniel said. "He had *kefitzat haderech* when he traveled to Vienna to save someone." He eased his fingernail under the peeling paint and pulled off an enormous flake of green paint.

Daniel stared at me. "He was accompanied by lions."

My breath caught in my throat. "Lions?" Rav Tzefanyah had tamed lions? Maybe it had been a dream…some dreams could be almost real.

Daniel's mouth was a thin line. His lips white. "Can you believe it, Racheli?"

I didn't answer him.

"He's a miracle worker…imagine…we've merited to know a *tzaddik*." Daniel turned away and leaned over the fence. In the street below, a young boy sped by on his bike, a cup stuck in the spokes of the wheel making a tremendous racket. Daniel looked up suddenly.

I stared at him. "It sounds just like the *tzaddikim* stories that I read to the children all the time," I said.

"Does it sound strange?" he asked.

I shook my head.

"If it sounds strange, it's because you're not used to hearing these things. If I could talk to you about them…and I can't…I mustn't…then you'd understand that there's a whole world you know nothing about," Daniel said. His eyes were filled with a bright light. He turned away.

People didn't just meet a real *tzaddik* every day, and here Daniel was privileged to know one personally. I wanted to be part of Daniel's world. We were married. We loved each other. Of course there were things I didn't understand. He was always reading, learning all day, how was I supposed to know the things he knew?

Daniel began to walk away. Slowly now. The urgency was gone.

I spoke to Daniel's back. "He walked with lions?"

Daniel turned. "Do you realize what that means?"

I stared at my husband. His eyes were shiny now.

"Do you know who my *rav* is?"

I didn't. I wouldn't have been able to recognize him if I had walked past him on the street. But I already knew that he had *ruach hakodesh*. And now Daniel was telling me other…strange…wondrous things.

"He's a holy man, Racheli."

I wanted to ask Daniel a million things. Who had seen the *rav* walking so far? Or had the *rav* just told them that he'd done it? I pushed those thoughts away very quickly. If Daniel said so, then of course it was true. I looked at the geraniums I had bought the day before. I needed to plant them in the boxes that would hang from the fence. Daniel had stopped walking away. He was waiting for me. Something inside me was ripping in two. "Is he like the Baal Shem Tov?" I asked him.

***

At the start of the summer, Abba came to Israel to check up on the farm on Ayin Yaffa. He came to visit us in the new apartment. He slept over for a night, so he had a chance to see Daniel when he got back after night *kollel.*

As soon as Daniel came in, Abba unzipped his carry-on and pulled out a new, tan-colored leather briefcase. "Trieste. Top of the range," he said, running his hand over the soft leather. "Inside is a list of contacts waiting to hear from you."

Daniel didn't answer.

I knew it was hard for him to keep quiet. I put a slice of baked salmon on a plate, added the cabbage salad I'd prepared especially for Abba, and prayed… prayed that Daniel would find the strength not to answer Abba.

"You've been learning for what…five years?" Abba said. "It's time to go back to work. A man can work and also make set times for learning. It's not right to just learn and have others support you. You're a strong, young man… I'm sure you could find a great job."

Daniel ate in silence.

"A man has a responsibility to provide for his family," Abba muttered. He banged the briefcase onto the table and then began walking out of the room. "Talk to him, Racheli," he said.

I moved to the sink. Turned on the hot water. Watched it splash against the flecks of salmon stuck on the plates. I was angry. Angry with Abba for putting me in this position. Angry with Daniel.

Daniel's fork clattered against his plate. "He doesn't understand. He doesn't value learning for the sake of learning," he said. "Some people have dollar signs for pupils."

Daniel wasn't angry. Unbelievable. It was as if…as if Abba's words meant nothing to him. He was…he was like the *tzaddik* in the story that I'd read to the children…the *tzaddik* who got yelled at for collecting tzedakah…he'd just walked away. I felt some of the tension drifting off me. He was good, Daniel, so good. "Maybe you should take him to meet Rav Tzefanyah," I said. "Let him meet a really holy person."

Daniel stared at me. He rubbed the back of his neck. "You need to be able to appreciate greatness when you see it."

I didn't know if that meant that he was going to take Abba to the *kollel* or not. But the next morning when I woke up, Daniel's bed was already empty.

***

I didn't have anyone to talk to. Ima, Abba, and my older sisters weren't in Israel. Daniel didn't like me to talk to my brothers or to Gila, because they weren't religious enough. Ditto for my friends from Migdal Yam. We had drifted away from the community that we had moved to the Old City to join. Sure, I made friends with the other mothers at the park, but there was no one to open my heart to. Somehow, I was still upbeat and cheery. It was just part of me. Instead of feeling angry and resentful, I put all of my energy into my family. I poured my heart into Daniel and the children. I did everything in the house so that Daniel was free to go to *kollel.* I took the children to parks all over Jerusalem, baked with them at home, did arts and crafts. But however busy I kept myself, I was lonely without a circle of friends. Daniel became my only friend.

One night, Dina called me to say she was out on a date with Avi and that they were at the Kotel.

"We thought we'd come visit you in your new house. It's a million steps up from the Kotel, but hey, Avi carries…during the week and on Shabbat too." Dina's voice was light and happy.

I stopped folding the laundry and looked over at Daniel, who was learning with Shimmy and Avner. Daniel liked to stick to his routine, but I so much wanted to see a friend. "Come over," I said.

Dina settled on the couch as soon as they arrived.

I handed her a plate of chocolate chip cookies that I'd baked with Yael. "We made them together," I said. "Yael's my right hand. She's seven already."

"You still real big into doing all the household stuff with the kids?" Dina asked. "I'm the type who'll rush to get everything done when it's quiet."

I smiled. I didn't tell her that I had to work that way, because Daniel didn't do much in the way of household chores. And that was exactly the way I wanted it.

Dina looked around. All five kids were still awake. Even though it was already ten o'clock.

"The kids have so much Torah running through their minds that they can't get to sleep," I said. Funny, how I felt that I had to defend myself.

"Hey, Racheli, it's kinda cool," Dina said. "You sound like those Yiddishe mammes of the past. Full of simple, pure, satisfying pride." Dina handed her baby to Avi.

Avi was on the couch next to Dina. He should have been talking to Daniel. They'd been good friends in Migdal Yam. Daniel should be making more of an effort to be friendly.

"Avi, take a good look," Dina said. "See how important it is to learn with your sons? Do that in our house, and I'll sound like Racheli…but just make sure it's at a normal time, not in the middle of the night. That way Shooey'll have Torah running through his head all the time."

Half an hour later, Daniel closed his book, and the kids scattered. "I'm going to shul," he said.

I felt bad for Avi, but I didn't say anything to Daniel. I picked up the empty plate.

Dina followed me to the kitchen. "What's next, Racheli?" she said.

I was quiet.

"I'm talking about the long coat. We're long-distance sisters. I gave you my granola recipe. And I never, ever give that out. What's with the coat?"

I watched a stream of water splash onto the plate. "It's all about *hashkafah*," I said. "Daniel knows what's best for us."

Dina and Avi left quickly. It was already late, and she said something about the babysitter waiting at home. I leaned against the door after I saw them out. For some reason, the visit had exhausted me. Avi's voice drifted through the door.

"Something is veering off target," he said.

***

It was Shavuot night. Daniel had taken Shimmy and Avner to learn in a shul near the house. I wondered why Daniel hadn't taken them to Rav Tzefanyah to learn, but I hadn't asked. He'd been tense, jumpy, for the last couple of days, and I didn't want to irritate him with my questions. He was always out learning till too late at night, driving himself too hard. He needed to rest a little.

When Daniel woke me up, I felt like my head was glued to my pillow. I was in the beginning of my sixth pregnancy, and I was exhausted all the time. I groped for the clock on my bedside table. It was just past midnight, and I'd been asleep for only an hour. Daniel wanted me to say the entire Sefer Tehillim with him. I had all of the next day to say Tehillim. But he so rarely asked me to do something with him that I got out of bed and shuffled to the living room. Maybe this all had something to do with the package that Daniel had brought in, late that afternoon. He'd stuffed it into the back of the closet in our bedroom, and I'd resisted the urge to take a peek. If it was a gift, I wanted it to remain a surprise.

The sounds of excited laughter drifted in through the open window. A circle of boys hurrying to a *shiur*. But inside the house, it was still and quiet. I sank into the couch, grateful that we'd finally brought our furniture from storage in Migdal Yam to Jerusalem. I curled my legs under me and opened my Tehillim. I liked it when we did things together. Daniel's eyes were closed, but his lips were moving. He knew all of Tehillim by heart. I wanted to sit next to him at the table, but the couch was too comfortable.

I'd been saying Tehillim for two minutes when Daniel made a funny, choking sound. Like he was gagging. "You okay?" His cheeks were two red blotches, above the line of his beard.

Daniel wasn't looking at me. He was staring at something behind me. "You know about *gilgulim*, reincarnations, right?"

What did I know? Sure, I'd heard some stories. I'd read something the other week, in one of the *parashah* sheets Daniel sometimes brought home. "Ruth was a *gilgul* of one of Lot's daughters," I said. There must have been more. But at least I knew about one. This time Daniel couldn't tell me that I never read.

"Yitzchak was a *gilgul* of Chavah," Daniel said. He closed his Tehillim and pushed it away.

Weren't men reincarnated as men and women as women?

Daniel rolled his shoulders, as if to shrug off the tension. "Reincarnation is all about fixing things up..."

Sure, I knew that. "You do something wrong, and you come back to fix it up. Like if you forget that you owe someone money, you might have to come back to repay it."

Daniel frowned. He didn't like to be interrupted. "Yeah, kinda like that. But sometimes, it's about bigger things. Sometimes it's about stuff that affects the whole world."

Like Ruth. David Hamelech was born from her. He was her grandson, or maybe her great-grandson. But this time I kept quiet.

"Batsheva." Daniel rubbed the knuckle of his thumb against his eyelids.

Was she a *gilgul*? I didn't know.

"Racheli, Rav Tzefanyah says that you're a *gilgul* of Batsheva."

Me? A *gilgul*? I laughed. A short bark. I wasn't a *gilgul* of anyone. I was Racheli.

"Don't laugh." Daniel's eyes were bright.

I didn't want Daniel to get angry. To lose the closeness between us. "I don't mean to laugh…it's just…weird… hard to believe." I looked at Daniel. And then something hit me in the chest. A wave of shock. His eyes were bright with…energy. Daniel really believed that I was a *gilgul*. Could I really be a *gilgul* of such a holy woman? I stared into my Sefer Tehillim. The letters were blurry. It couldn't be…maybe Rav Tzefanyah was wrong…mixed up. I couldn't be a *gilgul*. Not of Batsheva. I opened my mouth. Forced the words out. "I can't be," I said.

"Rav Tzefanyah says you are."

Rav Tzefanyah was wrong. He'd never seen me. How could he know who I was?

"He reads minds, Racheli. I told you that already." Daniel rubbed his entire hand over his eyes.

I stood up, and the Tehillim fell off my lap. This was crazy. "I don't feel like a *gilgul*. And I don't think we should talk about it."

Daniel was looking at me. Staring at me as if he could see something inside of me that I couldn't.

"I told you that Rav Tzefanyah walked all the way to the Dead Sea with lions. Lions are a sign of kingship."

I didn't want to think of Rav Tzefanyah and his lions. I wanted Daniel to tell me that he knew Rav Tzefanyah was wrong. That I was Racheli. Only Racheli.

"He says…the *rav* told me that he's a *gilgul* of David Hamelech."

I stared at Daniel. The *rav* couldn't be David Hamelech. People would know if David Hamelech were here.

Daniel stared at me. "That means…" he stopped. His face was shiny. He was breathless. As if he'd been on a hike in the middle of summer. "David Hamelech married Batsheva," he said.

Something smashed into me for a second time, under my ribs. Pushed all the air out of my chest. I sucked in. Tried to get air into my lungs. I was falling. Falling. Lights were flickering. A soft boom filled my ears. David Hamelech had married Batsheva. That meant…

"Racheli?"

I stumbled back. Felt the edge of the couch press against my calves. I fell backwards. "I'm married to you, Daniel," I said. "We're married to each other."

"I know," he said.

Daniel knew. He knew that this time the *rav* was wrong. Daniel's eyes were bright. Too bright. And, suddenly, the tears were falling. Running down his cheeks, sticking to the hairs of his beard. Wetting the front of his suit. Daniel didn't wipe them away. A terrible groan filled the air. "I love you," he said.

Daniel rarely told me that he loved me.

He stumbled toward the bedroom. I heard him rummaging in the back of the closet, but he couldn't find his package in the dark. When he finally came back to the living room, he was holding something white in his hands. The pile of fabric slipped out of his hands. He bent down and picked it up. He shook apart a white shirt, white pants, some kind of white hat, two strips of white cloth.

I stared. Fascinated. I wanted to look away, but I couldn't. I had never seen *tachrichim*. So how did I know what they were?

"I'm going to die soon," he said. His voice was a thin waver. "I have to die because I am Uriah Hachiti." Daniel shrugged off his jacket. "Uriah wasn't Batsheva's real *zivug*." He began pulling the shirt of the *tachrichim* over his shirt. His *kippah* slipped off his head. His arm stuck in the sleeve, and he shook it. "Racheli, you are Batsheva, and you will marry Rav Tzefanyah. You will marry David Hamelech."

***

About a week after Daniel told me that he was going to die, Abba came to Israel on a week-long business trip. He said something about deciding which direction he was going with the cotton business. About starting to use an agent to get the cotton to the market. He was planning to spend a night with each of the children to give out the gifts that Ima had sent.

"I'm coming to you first, sweetheart, because you're my favorite," he said when he called.

Daniel was sitting at the table, a book open in front of him. I pressed the phone against my leg. "It's Abba. He wants to come over," I whispered.

Daniel didn't look up. He just shook his head.

A wave of heat that began in my stomach crept toward my neck. This was Abba. Of course I wanted to see him. "Daniel!" My voice was urgent.

Daniel looked up.

He was pale. And I was sure he'd lost weight.

"You can do what you want, Racheli, but it isn't right for him to come here."

The heat slunk up steadily, and my head began to burn. Daniel was right. He only wanted what was good for us. For the family. Last time Abba was here, he'd pressured Daniel about getting a job. And we were going through so much now. We couldn't handle anything more. "I'm not feeling so well," I told Abba.

"Of course you're not feeling great. You're expecting, looking after five kids and Daniel. And it's hot."

I heard Abba sigh. My palms were clammy. I wiped them on my skirt. I glanced at Daniel. Abba couldn't come here, but I could still see him. Daniel hadn't told me not to. "I'll meet you at Yaffa Gate in the evening," I said in a rush.

"Yaffa Gate? Why should you come out if you're not feeling well?"

"Yaffa Gate. After I put the kids to bed."

"I want to see the kids. I'll take you all out to eat."

"No, I don't do those kinds of things anymore."

"Racheli, what's going on?"

Abba's voice was loud. And then I heard him sigh. "I know exactly what's going on. Daniel's still angry about me pushing him to get back to work."

"Abba, please." I glanced at Daniel, but he didn't look up.

In the evening, I met Abba at Yaffa Gate. As soon as I spotted him sitting on a low wall waiting for me, I felt lighter. Younger. A little girl again. But Abba was too tense to let me savor the moment.

"It's crazy, Racheli. We're perched on this wall like a couple of pigeons that don't have the brains to put together a nest when I should be treating you to a meal in a fancy restaurant."

I didn't answer.

"What's this with not eating in restaurants?"

"It's better this way."

Abba stared at me. I knew that there was more, much more, that he wanted to say, but I began telling him about the children and what they were doing. I could still be bright and cheerful. Make Abba smile and laugh. After an hour, I stood up. "I need to go now," I said.

Abba handed me a large bag. "Give the toys to the kids," he said. And then he smiled, "You look okay. Same Racheli as usual. Same smile."

***

There are some words that should never be spoken in a marriage. When you take a concept and give it shape with words, you are giving it substance. The suggestion that one of you could be married to someone else is sowing rot within your marriage. It's the fissure in a façade. The purity of the marital unit begins to crumble. At first, Daniel and I were horrified, but over time, as incredible as it seems, the preposterous idea that he was Uriah Hachiti, I was Batsheva, and Rav Tzefanyah was David Hamelech began to make sense. This idea came between us, hammering a hole in the bottom of our boat. It began to sink.

Over the next two months, every night, when Daniel came back from yeshiva, he would change into his *tachrichim*. Most nights we stayed up together for two or three hours saying Tehillim and pleading with Hashem not to take Daniel. I didn't want Daniel to die. He didn't want to die. I had never spent so much time together with Daniel, not even when we were first married. The more time we spent together, the closer we became. We were begging, pleading, with Hashem for our lives, so we should have been distraught. Oddly though, there was something intensely sweet about these hours in the middle of the night. Maybe because we were working together to keep our marriage intact. Maybe because we knew that our time together was limited. Maybe because we never spoke to anyone about what we were going through. Daniel warned me time and time again that I was not allowed to discuss with anyone what was happening to us. These were Kabbalistic concepts that no one would understand. There was no one I would have felt comfortable talking to anyway.

The day before Tisha b'Av, Daniel spent the day davening at the Kotel. He came home just before the fast began and refused to eat anything. He didn't go to shul to daven. Instead, he changed into his *tachrichim* and sat hunched over in a corner of the living room. Yael was seven years old, and Shimmy was six. They were old enough to understand that something was very wrong. Abba should have been in shul like everyone else. So I told him that Daniel didn't feel well. I told them that Abba wore special clothes on Tisha b'Av, like he wore his *kittel* on Yom Kippur. When the children were finally in bed, I sat opposite Daniel, waiting for him to talk.

His skin had paled to the point that it was hard to tell where he ended and the *tachrichim* began. His eyes were dark, vacant hollows.

Finally Daniel looked up from the *kinnot* that he was holding.

Dread is a strange feeling. You don't want something to happen, and at the same time, you do want it to happen so that it will be over. Dread paralyzes you so that you stop breathing.

Daniel looked at me without seeing me. "It's tonight, Racheli. Rav Tzefanyah said that tonight, I'm going to die."

Finally my breath came. Short gasps that hurt my lungs. It was going to happen. Daniel was going to die. Just like all the Jews had died in the desert. On the saddest day in Jewish history. Why wasn't I crying? I was going to be a widow.

We spent our last hours together davening. Daniel wouldn't talk. He recited *kinnot*. One after the other after the other. In a raspy voice that wasn't his.

I still wasn't crying. Did that mean I didn't really love Daniel? Did it mean that my soul knew that I wasn't really going to be a widow? Maybe my soul knew that I was going to remarry after Daniel died. But Daniel…I loved Daniel. Was I crying without tears?

I kept glancing at the clock. Staring back at Daniel. What did a person who was going to die look like? Could I call Hatzalah? Was I supposed to just let him die? There were so many questions I should have asked him. But I couldn't. He wasn't there, with me. His soul was already in a different place.

Time passed. Hour after hour. At one point, I was so tired that I closed my eyes. My head must have fallen forward, because I jerked awake. I stared at Daniel. He was still davening. He looked the same as he usually did. Pale, but alive. And then I heard the birds beginning to sing. I tried to stand up. My legs were stiff. I hobbled to the window. The sky was turning gray. The sun rose slower than ever before that morning. But it rose…and Daniel was still alive.

After that, some of the fear left us. We didn't speak about what had happened that night. We spoke around it. Spoke around it as if our prayers had created a delicate and fragile shell that could protect us as long as our words didn't try to define the miracle. Daniel continued to sleep in *tachrichim.* But by now, they had become pajamas. I threw them into the wash with the white load and hung them on the lines on our porch. I bought Daniel a second set, but he complained that the fabric was too rough against his skin, so I pushed them to the back of the closet and prayed we'd never use them.

Sometimes, when I was out in a park with the children, I wondered what would happen to us if Daniel died and I married Rav Tzefanyah. Rav Tzefanyah, I knew from Daniel, had never married. How would he manage with a household of children? Six children. Because there was another child on the way. Each child brought down its own *mazal,* I knew. Maybe this child would bring down the power to nullify Rav Tzefanyah's words for good.

***

In January 2001, a group of adults and children from Azariyah, where Daniel used to learn, were on a field trip in the south. As they drove along what was supposed to be a peaceful road, a mortar shell exploded twenty or thirty meters away. Shrapnel tore into the bus, killing five adults on the spot. Four children were badly wounded. We had friends on Azariyah.

It was Gila who called to tell us the news. Yael picked up the second line when she realized that Gila was on the line. She was distraught. "They don't have hands," she said. "How will they get dressed? How will they write?"

Gila told her that we had to daven for them. And then she told her that she would come pick her up and that they would spend the afternoon putting together a puzzle and eating ice cream. Yael was thrilled. I had to call her back to cancel, of course.

"What's up, Racheli?" Gila said. "Yael needs to take her mind off this horrible tragedy. Why can't I take her out?"

I was never the type to hide behind excuses. And so I told her straight out. "Your motorbike isn't modest. And Yael is too old to ride a bike."

"I'll pick her up in a cab," Gila said.

She just didn't understand. "You have a TV. A computer."

"I won't switch them on," Gila said.

I hesitated.

"I won't bring her to my apartment," Gila offered. "We'll go out. Somewhere in the Old City."

"I'll ask Daniel," I said, but I didn't call her back. Because I didn't need to ask Daniel.

After that I didn't hear from Gila anymore.

2001

I gave birth to a son in the middle of winter. I had hoped it would be a girl. It would have been easier if I'd have given birth to a girl. We wouldn't have had to deal with a bris. I wouldn't have had to meet Rav Tzefanyah.

The bris took place in the rooms of Rav Tzefanyah's *kollel.* It was a long walk, down a wet and slippery road, outside the actual walls of the Old City, but still close enough to be part of the Jewish Quarter. I had forgotten to put on my coat in the rush to get the children ready, and my sweater was damp from the drizzle. The room was filled with tables, chairs, and bookcases whose shelves had bent from the weight of the books they carried. A red piece of velvet over the only window flapped in the breeze. I sat in a corner, my baby in my arms, my children around me, as I waited for everything to begin.

Finally, a tight circle of men in long coats jostled forward. I saw Daniel and tried to smile. Next to him was a short man with large, flabby lips. I looked away quickly. Toward the open window. The curtain flapped back and forth. I blinked rapidly. If I blinked fast enough, would I be able to erase the image of Rav Tzefanyah? Rub it out before it became part of my memory…

Someone took the baby, and the men swept back, into the room where the bris was taking place. Soon my baby would be part of the Jewish people. He would be Meir, the one who would give light.

***

"I'm not suffering," I repeated as I stepped closer to Ima. She was standing at the stove. Stirring chopped celery into the soup. She hadn't been able to come for the bris, there had been a convention, something to do with Abba's business in New York that she had to attend. But she was here now, helping us to adjust to a new baby. It was the first time she had dropped everything, left New York for one reason only…to help me.

"You work too hard," Ima said again. "You never stop. It's not healthy for you."

I stuffed my hands into the deep pockets of my house robe. Maybe I should have made the effort to get dressed. I looked at Ima. "I love what I'm doing. I'm lucky to have a family, a husband and children to look after. This is just how life is. It's my job to take care of the house and the family."

I gave Ima a hug and inhaled the tangy-sweet smell of rose perfume mixed with a whiff of celery. Strange, but not unpleasant. I pulled back to switch the kettle on. I needed a cup of hot coffee.

Ima added water to the pot. "Daniel should help a little," she said. "Until the children grow up and can take over."

Daniel. It was always about Daniel. Ima. Abba. Yossi. Gila. Tzila. Everyone wanted Daniel to do this or not to do that. Why couldn't they see what he was doing? The crazy hours he spent learning, always learning. Building a spiritual fortress for the Jewish people. I was tired of people telling me all the time that it wasn't enough. Tired of the criticism. Tired of defending him all the time. And this time was one time too many. I swung around. My lungs full of air. My mouth full of the words I wanted to yell.

And then I stopped. Ima was standing very still. Her eyes closed. She quivered. A tremor. A little shake. As if all the emotions inside her were bubbling, boiling, building up to an explosion that she wouldn't let happen.

One step, two. And then my arms were around Ima, hugging her tight. So tight that I could feel her heart beating against mine. Gently, she freed one arm and then the other. She wrapped her arms around me and hugged me back.

I laughed. Or did I sob? "Who says Daniel needs to help? Let him learn." I choked the words out. "I'm happy with my family, my beautiful house."

I hugged Ima tight and somewhere, in the space between her arms where the smell of roses was the strongest, I let myself feel that sometimes, it really was hard. But if it was hard, I reasoned as I pulled back and fumbled in the pocket of my robe for a tissue, it was only because I wasn't being good enough. I had to change, improve myself so that it wouldn't be hard at all. If it hurt sometimes, it was my fault.

***

Toward the end of that year, Daniel met Rav Natas. Someone who knew Rav Natas had come to Rav Tzefanyah's *kollel* and whispered to Daniel that he knew a hidden *tzaddik*. Someone who was much greater than Rav Tzefanyah. Daniel, always the searcher, had gone to meet this *rav*. By the time Daniel told me about Rav Natas, he had already been to the new yeshiva three or four times. It was a hot night in summer. The kind of night where the air stands still. Where smells creep in from the street and hang like old cobwebs in the corners of the room.

"I've met a young *ilui*, a genius," Daniel said. "He has a few boys with him. In a yeshiva in Mekor Baruch." He was holding a notebook in his hands. "He's opening up new gates of knowledge for me."

Over the next few weeks, I learned that the *rav*, Rav Natas, lead a close-knit circle of young men who gathered in a basement in Mekor Baruch. Daniel began going to Mekor Baruch a few times a week. Rav Tzefanyah was angry and warned Daniel not to go there any longer. If Daniel refused to listen and insisted on going to Mekor Baruch, he would no longer be welcome in the *kollel*.

I listened to Daniel telling me about Rav Tzefanyah's threat. And I didn't know what to tell him.

"He can't tell me what to do," Daniel said. "I can learn anywhere I want." Daniel began dividing his time between Rav Tzefanyah and Rav Natas. And Rav Tzefanyah never mentioned his threat again.

***

Meir was an easy baby and developed into an easy toddler, which was wonderful because by the time he was almost a year old, I was once again expecting. With less energy than normal, I was spending more time in the house. Which was why I began teaching seven-year-old Shimmy to read English. I'd imagined that it would be easy. After all, Yael had picked up reading almost effortlessly. We began with letter recognition. I also decided to teach Shimmy how to write his name. Two days later, he had it right. I gave him five shekels and sent him with Yael to the store to buy himself a treat.

It took longer than I thought. By the time Shimmy and Yael came back, I had finished giving the other children supper. Shimmy came in waving a half-finished packet of chocolate buttons. I was spooning the last of the scrambled eggs into Ahuva's mouth when I saw the packaging. Shimmy had begged me to buy those chocolates earlier in the week. I'd checked the *hechsher*. We didn't use it. The chocolates had gone back on the shelf even though Shimmy had whined until we left the store. Now, sent to buy a treat with Yael, he'd finally gotten what he wanted.

I reached for the packet and pulled it out of his sticky fingers.

Daniel was very careful about what we ate. I had found him checking the labels on the groceries in the cabinets. "I told you we don't eat these," I said.

Shimmy shrugged.

"I'm going to tell Abba." I herded the younger children toward the bathroom. I don't remember if Shimmy and Yael helped themselves to bread that night. I do remember that I didn't make them scrambled eggs.

2002

One Shabbat night, a few months later, Daniel was particularly tense. To make things worse, I was also in a bad mood. Dov's eldest son, Yehudah, was celebrating his bar mitzvah, and we weren't taking part in the family Shabbat. Petach Tikva, where Dov lived, wasn't religious enough, Daniel had said. The family wasn't religious enough. Our children couldn't mix with their cousins. I knew all the reasons, hadn't expected to go, but it still hurt. Kiddush took so long to get through that every one of the six children was crying by the time Daniel was done. No one got grape juice. The crying intensified. Somehow we made it through the first course.

The kids slinked off their chairs, one by one, and for once Daniel didn't shout at them and tell them to come back. He stared at a purple spot on the tablecloth. Somehow beet juice had leaked under the plastic. He finally looked up. His fingers hovered over his lips, raked at his beard.

"Rav Tzefanyah spoke to me today. Alone. After everyone had left already. I was putting all the books back in their places." Daniel stopped.

He was talking too much. Daniel never spoke so much. What had happened? I poked at a crumb of challah. "And…?" He hadn't heard me. I was about to prompt him again.

"And nothing." Daniel stopped chewing his finger and sat straight. He looked around the table. "Why can't you keep the children at the table? What kind of a Shabbat table is this?" he said. "Bring the children back to the table."

The next day, Daniel and I went to the bar mitzvah party that was being held on a moshav near Petach Tikva. The children stayed at home with a babysitter. Daniel gave me fifteen minutes to say mazal tov to everyone. Since I was nearing the end of my pregnancy, I had bought a special top to wear, black with swirls of silver and gray. I'd chosen it in one of the back stores in Meah Shearim, and I loved the way the swirls shimmered as the fabric moved. I fluttered between Ima, Ayelet, Faygie, Gila, relatives I hadn't seen in years, shared hugs and kisses, bits of news…and then it was over. Daniel was standing in the doorway waving.

Gila saw Daniel too. "I'll take you home later," she said. "I'll borrow Dov's car. Stay with us."

I shook my head. "I have to get back to the children."

Gila flicked her wrist and her bracelets jingled. There were more of them than I remembered. I could hear the familiar tinkle above the noise in the hall. Then she turned away. Without another word.

She was angry with me. I hated it when people were angry with me. Why couldn't she understand? I had a houseful of children. I stared at my family, all of them chatting and laughing, the children chasing each other between the tables. I reached up to straighten the back of my headscarf, tuck in the stray hairs…if they were different…more religious…then I could have stayed. It was their fault, not mine.

I met Daniel outside. Instead of heading to the car, he walked along the path that lead to the gardens surrounding the hall. He stopped beside a trellis covered with jasmine. The night air was thick, heavy with the sweet fragrance.

"People used to marry young," Daniel said. "In Yemen, girls got married when they were twelve years old."

Jasmine. I'd buy some jasmine plants and put them in garden boxes. They'd climb along the fence of the porch. And the fragrance would waft into our living room.

"Sometimes fathers would promise their baby daughters to someone else's son. And then, when they got older, they'd marry them."

Music. There was music drifting out of the hall. A slow song. So they were eating, the dancing hadn't started. I looked at Daniel. I didn't want to hear about weddings. I wanted to go back into the hall. To my family.

"Rav Tzefanyah..." Daniel stopped talking. "He wants to get married..." Daniel plucked off a long, slender jasmine blossom.

Rav Tzefanyah was getting married! I felt my heart leap into my throat. How long had Daniel known this for? "He's getting married?" Really? I was... free. Daniel and I were free. The waiting, the nightmare...it was over. Really over. I laughed. And then I stopped. "Daniel?"

He was swallowing so hard and so fast that in the dim light, I could see his Adam's apple bobbing up and down. "What's the matter? Aren't you happy? Don't you want to stay married to me?"

"He wants...he wants to marry Yael," Daniel said.

I stared at Daniel. I saw Yael lying on her stomach on the floor Shabbat afternoon, reading a book. Her legs up, bent at the knees, waving back and forth like thin reeds.

"He said that since she's your daughter, it's like marrying you, but it will be...better, he said, better, this way." Daniel pushed his hat back so far that I was sure it would fall off his head.

I opened my mouth. But my mouth was dry. So dry that my tongue couldn't move.

My legs wobbled. "She's a kid."

"He knows that. He knows everything." Daniel began gnawing at a fingernail. "What...there are ways to do these things..."

Do these things? What did Daniel mean? Yael was in third grade. The tremor in my knees was traveling up my legs. I put a hand against the trellis to steady myself. I felt it shake. He wasn't thinking of letting the *rav* marry Yael. He couldn't be thinking that.

"It's a *zechut*, Racheli..."

I remembered those flabby lips. I stared at Daniel. His eyes were…unfocused. There was something there I didn't recognize.

Daniel put his hand over his eyes. He massaged his eyelids. "I don't know…" He lowered his hand.

And then, I realized what Daniel was feeling. I realized because it was something I had trained myself not to feel. How many times had Daniel told me things, things that went against all I'd ever known? Things that didn't feel right? How many times? And when I'd heard these things, when they shook, rocked, and eventually toppled what I'd always known, I'd been…confused. Amongst the rubble of my thoughts, there had often been confusion. No one can live with confusion. I couldn't…so I had taught myself not to feel it. That was why I knew, with certainty, that Daniel was confused. Daniel didn't know what to do. And that frightened me the most. What would I do if Daniel didn't know how to guide us? Where would I turn? He had to figure it out. Had to know what to do.

We walked back to the car. As we passed the hall, I heard the voice of Mordechai Ben David. *Rachem, rachem b'chasdecha al amcha tzureinu. Show mercy, show kindness on your people…* I wanted to run through the open doors, ask Abba what to do. Ask Yossi or Dov. It was a crazy thought that didn't even flash coherently in my mind. It was only a feeling, an urge. I'd never ask them…because…because we didn't talk to them much anymore…and they would never understand us.

***

The following Sunday, when he came back from yeshiva, Daniel told me that Rav Tzefanyah wanted to meet Yael. To explain to her what her future role would be. To prepare her. We were to take Yael to the yeshiva on Tuesday afternoon. Tuesday was the best day, Daniel told me. On Tuesday Hashem had done two things: divided the seas from the dry land and also made vegetation and trees sprout. It was a double blessing.

Ahuva cried out in her sleep. I should go and check on her. But I couldn't. Couldn't peep into the bedroom that she shared with Yael. Couldn't look at Yael. My Yael. Tomorrow I would have to prepare her. Tell her that it was a merit for her. Tell her that this was a glorious destiny. Warn her that she couldn't speak to anyone about it. Because no one, no one, would understand. How would I tell her? Could I write a letter? Could I ask Daniel to tell her?

I heard Daniel getting ready for bed. But I didn't get off the couch. Maybe we should pray all night. Prayer had saved Daniel. It had saved me. Prayer could change a person's destiny. Daniel was calling me. But what if this…this marriage…was her destiny? What if it was really part of Hashem's plan for the Jewish people? Daniel couldn't find his *tachrichim*. Where had I put them? I didn't know. I got up. Rummaged in the back of the closet for the extra pair. Pulled it out. The pair he had always refused to wear.

Daniel rubbed the cotton fabric between his fingers. "Too rough," he said. "I can't sleep in these."

Where had I put the *tachrichim* when I made the beds in the morning? I couldn't think. Couldn't focus. If we had *neviim*, prophets, they would be able to tell us things. Tell us everything. But today, because of our sins, we were leaderless, sheep without a shepherd. With no one to advise us, to guide us.

And then, with the clarity that comes from desperation, I realized what we had to do.

"I don't want to take her," I told Daniel. "I don't want her to go to him."

"She has to. He told us to take her."

"Ask Rav Natas," I told Daniel. "Go to him and ask him what to do."

Daniel threw the rough *tachrichim* back into the closet. He banged closed the door. And then he nodded.

I waited for Daniel to say something. He couldn't be agreeing with me. Or could he? But he didn't say a word.

The first time I made a decision for the family was when we moved out of the Muslim Quarter. This was the second time. I should have felt a sense of elation. After all, maybe I had found a way of saving Yael from a marriage that I couldn't believe was right for her. But I didn't feel euphoric. Instead, I felt a sense of dread.

CHAPTER NINE

Natas Enters Our Lives

Mekor Baruch, 2002

We drove to Mekor Baruch just before two o'clock in the morning. I'd told Yael that we would be out in the middle of the night and that she was responsible for the children if they woke up, but I was anxious and hoped that the meeting wouldn't take long. The streets were quiet. Bathed in warm, yellow light. There was one white lamplight on the street. Daniel parked beside it. As I got out of the car, I craned my neck to see the top of the lamppost. A cloud of tiny moths fluttered around in never-ending circles, pulled by the bright light. I knew they would go around and around until they died.

Daniel hurried into the building and down the steps. Lower and lower into the building until we were on the basement floor. He knocked on a wooden door and waited. The olive wood mezuzah on the doorpost was the largest I had ever seen. A teen opened the door.

Rav Natas sat at the head of a long, heavy table. He was young. Younger than Daniel. His beard was sparse, pointed. The table was covered with books. Later Daniel told me that these were books on Kabbalah. The Rav was looking at a gold necklace with a stone pendant that was next to the books on the table. When Daniel came in, he lifted his head, but his eyes remained lowered.

He waved his hand, and we sat down. The teen who had opened the door stood at the Rav's side. Another teen stood at the other side.

Rav Natas nodded, and Daniel began the whole story. How he had met Rav Tzefanyah, who had walked from the mountains of Chevron to the Dead Sea in an hour accompanied by lions. How Rav Tzefanyah, who was a reincarnation of David Hamelech, had seen that Daniel was Uriah Hachiti and I was Batsheva, destined to marry him. And now, Daniel explained, Rav Tzefanyah had had a second revelation and knew that it was better for him to marry our daughter Yael.

"She's eight," I said.

Daniel frowned at me.

The Rav didn't speak. He rubbed his finger along the gold chain on the table. Polished the pendant, a brown stone with flecks of gold, between his finger and thumb.

My watch had slipped over my wrist, and I couldn't see the time.

The second attendant rubbed his eyelids with the tip of his finger. The skin around his eyes was whitish. He looked, I decided, like a panda.

Finally, Rav Natas turned to Daniel. "How does Rav Tzefanyah know these things?" he asked.

"I don't know."

"You don't know?" The Rav looked up. His eyes were green, flecked with the same gold specks that shone in the stone of the pendant.

Daniel reached up to touch his beard and then lowered his hand.

"Could he be wrong?" the Rav asked. As if he was weighing up the possibility himself.

Daniel hadn't told Rav Natas everything. He hadn't told him that he'd slept in *tachrichim* for eight months and that even though Rav Tzefanyah had told him that he would die, he hadn't died. I nudged him, but he ignored me.

"You are ready to give your daughter to a man who doesn't tell you how he knows things?" Rav Natas picked up the gold chain. He waited for it to stop swinging. Then he reached for a book. Flipped through the pages. Read something.

The attendant with blotchy skin walked to the bookcase that ran along the length of the room and picked out a notebook from one of the file boxes filled with similar notebooks. A brown notebook, like the one the children used in school. He pulled a pen out of his top pocket.

The Rav picked up the pendulum again. It began to swing back and forth. The Rav spoke. Short sentences, so low that I could catch only a word or two even though the room was silent. *Marriage, child, lies, gilgul, rasha.*

The attendant wrote down everything the Rav said.

Finally the Rav looked up, at Daniel. "Your daughter is forbidden from marrying him," he said. Then he stood up and left the room.

The attendant closed the notebook. He kissed it. "Rav Natas talks to angels," he said.

Tzaddikim could do things that we couldn't do. I knew that. I knew that Rav Tzefanyah could read minds. Now I knew that Rav Natas could speak to angels.

I don't know what Daniel told Rav Tzefanyah. How he explained why he didn't bring Yael the following day to the yeshiva. Perhaps he told him that it was too hard for me to give up my destiny. I didn't ask him. We didn't speak much about the meeting with Rav Natas. Didn't talk about how he had questioned Rav Tzefanyah's reliability. I was ecstatic that we were free…free of the fear of death…free of the fear of pushing Yael into a marriage that was all wrong. I didn't need anything more.

The days after Daniel and I came back from our first meeting with Rav Natas weren't easy days for Daniel. He was drumming with his fingertips, rolling his shoulders, rubbing his neck. Trying to get rid of tension. And disappointment. I realized that Daniel had been shaken, and I wasn't about to rub salt in his wounds. It had seemed to Daniel when he joined Rav Tzefanyah's yeshiva that he had finally found a mentor. And now he was no longer sure.

Over the next few weeks, Daniel began spending less of his time with Rav Tzefanyah and more with Rav Natas. Rav Natas had a small yeshiva, Daniel told me. Usually he had about five boys learning with him. They would come and go. But Eran and Yigal, the two attendants who had been with Rav Natas the night we had gone to the yeshiva, were always present. By the end of summer, when the sky was a dome of blue steel that kept in the heat, when the trees and the shrubs held up their dry branches and begged for rain, Rav Natas had become our spiritual guide. He remained our sole guide for the next six years.

***

During the weeks after that first meeting with Rav Natas, Daniel and I were giddy with relief. Rav Natas had saved us from Rav Tzefanyah and his strange ideas. We were still married to each other and would remain married to each other. Yael was safe in our family. When Aharon was born, a month after we first met Rav Natas, it was only right for us to choose Rav Natas to be sandek. But he refused. He insisted that the honor be given to my father. Daniel was torn. On the one hand, he wanted to do as Rav Natas told him. On the other, he didn't want my father to be sandek.

On the morning of the bris, which was held in our home, we still hadn't decided who was going to be given the honor. Even though both my brothers had come with their families, Daniel wouldn't consider asking them to be sandek. When Rav Natas arrived accompanied by the six or seven boys who learned in his yeshiva, my parents still hadn't arrived. The entrance to the Old City had been cordoned off because of a bomb threat. By the time my parents arrived, half an hour later, Rav Natas had agreed to be the sandek. He brought with him his own siddur that he kept staring into for the entire bris. The baby was called Aharon, to symbolize the peace that Daniel and I felt Rav Natas had brought into our family. My parents, always generous, had told me to call in a caterer, and so for the first time ever, I didn't have to cook a single thing for the meal. Rav Natas, however, didn't stay for the meal. As soon as the bris was over, he left, accompanied by his entourage.

***

About six months after Daniel began learning under Rav Natas, the circle of followers began to visit the graves, shrines, and tombs of *tzaddikim*. The trips would last all day long. We never knew when the Rav would decide that it was the right time to visit a *tzaddik*, or which *tzaddik* merited our visit. So Daniel was traveling all over the country at any time. Rabbi Eliezer ben Rabbi Yossi Haglili, Rabbi Yehuda ben Teima, Rabbi Nechunya ben Hakane, Rabbi Pinchas ben Yair, Rabbi Shimon ben Chalafta...the list of *tzaddikim* was endless. If the circle wasn't at the *kever* of a *tzaddik*, it was at the mikveh. For hours upon hours.

When Daniel had been part of the yeshiva in Azariyah, or with Rav Benayun in Ashdod, or in Keter Malchut, or even with Rav Tzefanyah, he had always had some sort of schedule. I knew what time he'd leave the house, when to expect him home. But with Rav Natas, routine became a forgotten word. I knew that Rav Natas was married, and I often wondered how his wife managed. They had one son, Yehoshua, so I assumed that his wife and I were both trying to cope with the same challenges. But we hadn't met, so I hadn't had the chance to speak to her. Besides, I was slowly beginning to understand that Rav Natas was working on *tikkunim*, deep rectifications that we knew little about. And if that was so, then the inconveniences of waiting for Daniel, helping him to prepare for a trip on the spur of the moment, the uncertainty of never knowing when he'd come home, these were little things in the grand scheme.

"What do you do there?" I asked Daniel one morning, when he finally came back after being away all night.

"We learn, talk a little"

"What else?"

"Eat."

Daniel had never shared much. "Who's there?"

"The circle. The usual guys."

"Do you like it?"

"It's okay," Daniel said.

I was naturally full of energy, enthusiasm. I wanted Daniel to experience vitality. Especially as I was putting so much effort into trying to make it happen for him. I also wasn't sure if Daniel wasn't sharing because he never talked much or if it was because the things that the circle was doing were secret. Or not understandable. Either way, I never really knew where Daniel had been, what he'd done, or whom he'd done it with. But since he seemed settled in himself, I busied myself with the house and the children.

***

"I found this dress for Ahuva." I pulled a pale blue dress with ruffles out of the bag. It was a week before Rosh Hashanah, and I'd been shopping for new clothing for all of the children.

Daniel closed his book. He looked up. But he didn't smile.

"She'll wear it for Sukkot," I said. Daniel didn't want us to wear new clothing on Rosh Hashanah. It was a day of judgment. On a day of judgment, he'd told me so many times, you don't stand in front of the Judge wearing new clothing. It was much better to wear white. Like the Kabbalists.

He nodded. He was thinking of something else, I realized. I kept quiet. I wanted to tell him that I'd found a dress for myself. Same color, different style. It would be cute...mother and daughter. But Yael...well, it had been harder to find something that we could agree on.

And then Daniel told me. "I'm going to Uman with the Rav."

Uman. What was Uman? Uman was where Breslover Chassidim went for Rosh Hashanah. How could Daniel go there? Leave me alone with six children?

"Three days, Racheli. It's not so long. Don't you want me to go with the Rav?"

I laid the dress facedown on the table. Folded the sleeves against the back. Folded up the skirt. "But I'll be alone."

"You won't be alone. You have the children. Don't you want me to go with the Rav?"

Of course I did. I didn't know much about Uman. I knew that thousands of Jews went there. It was a holy place, and I wanted Daniel to have the experience. I slipped the dress into the bag. "I washed your *kittel* yesterday." I told him.

The trip to the airport was a tremendous ceremony. I'd cooked and packed enough schnitzel, potato kugel, and cakes for the whole circle. The soup was frozen in two boxes that I had wrapped well with plastic wrap so that not a drop would spill out. The airport was full of people, packages, and bustle. Noise buzzed in a cloud so thick I could almost see it. And then they were gone. I drove home in the van, the Rav's wife and son in the back. I davened that it would be good for Daniel. For Rav Natas. The circle. But I felt strangely flat.

2003

By the time we hit winter, Rav Natas was regularly celebrating days of *hillula* for *tzaddikim*. Growing up in the States, we'd never heard much about days of *hillula*. It was a new concept for me. One I tried to get used to. Since it also meant that Daniel was away from the family even more, I had to work hard not to feel upset. Especially when he went to dangerous places. Like the night the circle went to the *kever* of Yosef Hatzaddik. Which is in Shechem. And since Shechem is a hornet's nest of terrorists, it meant going in a convoy on an armored bus. Tickets had to be booked in advance, which was why I knew about this trip before it happened.

"When a *tzaddik* dies, he leaves behind a light in this world," Daniel said. "Yosef Hatzaddik's light is there at the *kever*, and we can tap into it. Miracles happen to people who go there. Don't you want me to go there?"

Of course, I wanted him to go there. To tap into the light, the energy. It sounded…mystical. Spiritual. Something I wanted to be part of.

Daniel was tired when he eventually got back home. He had been awake all night. Shechem was a two-hour ride from Jerusalem, and the convoy had only arrived there at two in the morning. When they got back to Jerusalem, the Rav had taken the circle to the natural spring mikveh in the Lifta valley below the entrance to the city.

He poured maple syrup over the pancakes I had made and told me a little of what had happened. He told me that the bus had been packed with all kinds of people. Some religious and some not so religious. He told me about the holiness. How intense it had been. And I wished that I had been there. At the *kever* of Yosef Hatzaddik with the children.

"There are lots of things that we can't see," he said. "We can't see atoms and molecules, but they're there. It's like that with the Rav. He sees things that we can't see."

"What did he see?"

But Daniel didn't answer. He rolled his pancake up, and the maple syrup oozed out of the ends.

"What did he tell you?"

Daniel looked up. "Not everything that happens needs to be spoken about," he said. "The ways of a *tzaddik* are hidden."

I believed in *tzaddikim*. We had a hundred books about *tzaddikim*. Stories that I would read to the children every night. I didn't understand how *tzaddikim* did what they did. But no one could. I thought of the story of Rabbi Akiva Eiger. Who could understand how Rabbi Eiger could have known the reason why the son of Ettel in Lomza wasn't learning Torah as well as his brothers? Just the suggestion that their son had perhaps once eaten something not kosher had made the parents determined to track down if it could really have happened. And they had found out that it had really happened. And that was the reason he hadn't been able to learn as well as his brothers.

Yes, *tzaddikim* could see things that we couldn't see. I looked at Daniel, calmly reaching for another pancake. Could it be that we knew a *tzaddik*, a miracle worker? I so much wanted to be a part of it all. "Do you think that Rav Natas…that he could be a *tzaddik*?" I was breathless. We'd had such a bad experience with Rav Tzefanyah. Could it really be that Rav Natas was a miracle worker?

Daniel closed his eyes. As if he was afraid that I'd read the answer there. "We don't need to talk about everything," he said.

***

Hillula followed *hillula*. Most of the time, the *hillula* was at the *kever* of a *tzaddik*; sometimes it was in the basement, which we now called the yeshiva. Gradually, I became more involved with the circle. At first, my involvement centered on catering for the day of *hillula*. That included shopping for the groceries, preparing the food, and then delivering it to wherever the *hillula* was taking place. When the *hillula* was in the north of Israel, the drive would take me hours.

Sometimes, if I was lucky, the Rav would be present when I brought in the food. He would always thank me. Always without looking at me. And I'd feel a wave of gratitude and joy wash over me. So this was what it felt like to serve a someone who could work miracles.

When I was away, I would put Yael, who was now nine years old, in charge of the house and the children. Since I was so busy running errands for the circle, our home was often a mess. The clean, tidy apartment that I took so much pride in began to resemble the apartment we had left behind in the Muslim Quarter. But it didn't matter, because we were involved in something so big.

***

"Try this skirt on." I handed Yael a beige skirt with pink trim along the hem.

She glanced at it and continued looking through the skirts hanging on the rack. Like she'd done with every single item I'd picked out for her so far.

I'd seen a pink top in one of the stores we'd already been to that would be the perfect match. With long sleeves. Which store was it?

"I don't like it," Yael said.

I tugged at a black skirt. Too long. We'd been to every store in Geulah. Yael had been helping me so much over the last few months that I had decided to treat her to an afternoon of shopping in Geulah. Maybe an ice cream at the end. Shimmy and Avner were in *cheder*, and I'd called a babysitter to look after the other three children. "Take it, Yael." I pushed the beige skirt into her hands.

Yael pushed it back.

"It could look different when you try it on."

She pulled out a pale yellow skirt with flowers. "I don't like beige," she said. "No one wears beige anymore."

I didn't like the skirt she'd chosen. It was too bright. Too short. I held it up to the light coming through the store door. "It's see-through."

The saleslady hurried over. "It's not at all see-through," she said.

She was wearing a turquoise sequined top that was so tight she looked like a salami stuffed into its wrapper. Silver heels. What did she know about modesty?

"Yellow is the in color this season. So are flowers," the saleslady said.

Yael pulled the skirt out of my hands and held it against her. She moved to the mirror.

The saleslady stood behind Yael. "The color suits you. And we have a matching top. There's a discount on the second item…just for this week."

"Please, Ima?"

My feet were aching. I looked at my watch. We had to hurry. We had half an hour left till the babysitter had to leave. And I so much wanted Yael to have a new Shabbat outfit. "Try the beige skirt on," I said.

Yael threw the yellow skirt onto the rack. It slid off and landed in a crumpled heap.

"We'll try the store across the road," I said. It was our last hope. She was ruining the whole afternoon. We were supposed to be having a nice time together.

"All my friends go shopping on Yafo," she said. "No one comes to Geulah."

Yafo. Just the name of the street gave me a bad feeling. "We don't shop there. I don't want you to even think of going there," I said. Yafo Street was full of nonreligious people. She'd never find something for Shabbat there.

Yael was already crossing the street. Weaving her way between the slow-moving cars stuck on Malchei Yisrael.

I hurried after her. "Let's get something for weekday," I said.

"I don't need anything," she said without turning around.

***

The next time Abba was in Israel, Daniel let him come to the house. "I guess he forgave me for buying him a leather briefcase that cost three hundred dollars," Abba said, but I didn't answer him. I was just glad he was here; he was so excited to see the kids. Meir was a year old, and he was walking already. "Get up and go…it runs in our family," Abba said. "Which is exactly why you're able to move around like that. Migdal Yam. The Muslim Quarter. And now the real home in the Jewish Quarter. You have your hands full with six kids to look after," he said to me.

"I like taking care of them," I said, when I noticed he was looking around at the mess in the house.

"Of course you do, Racheli," he said, adding, "and you do the best you can. "This is how is it when you have little kids." Abba waved his arm around the room.

Just then Shimmy came running in yelling about how he'd almost made it to the van that was taking him to his swimming lesson and the driver had seen him and he'd yelled at him to wait and the driver had ignored him and closed the door.

"Slow down, sport, you're like a firework gone wrong," Abba said. "Where does he need to get to?" he asked me. "I'll take him. I was about to leave anyway."

"You don't need to take him," Daniel said.

He'd just walked in. "Daniel," Abba said in surprise, "you're home so early…" Abba looked at his watch.

Daniel looked at Shimmy. "You're already eight years old. You know how to tell the time. Get ready on time."

Shimmy hurled his bag against the wall. "It's not fair," he yelled.

"Kids need to learn how to take responsibility," Daniel said.

I was arranging the flowers Abba had brought in a vase. I didn't say a word.

"He's still young. Next time, he'll be ready fifteen minutes early so that he won't need to run for the van. Right, Shimmy?" Abba said.

"Sure, he'll be ready. Because he'll remember what happened this time," Daniel said.

Abba picked Shimmy up, wincing from his bad back, and carried him outside to the porch. I was glad he didn't argue with Daniel…because I knew that if he pushed Daniel too hard, I'd have to meet Abba at Yafo Gate again next visit.

***

About a year and a half after Rav Natas had become our Rav, Daniel started going away for Shabbat with the circle. It was one thing to be left alone with six small children during the week, but it was another to be left alone for Shabbat. Especially since I didn't have any family or friends to turn to for company. Daniel would leave on Thursday night, and I never knew when he was coming back. Something didn't feel right. I didn't have anyone that I could turn to and sound it out. Feelings that I couldn't identify swam around in my chest. I ignored them, until one Thursday night at the end of a long day when two of the children had been fighting a stomach virus. Another Shabbat table without Daniel loomed ahead of me. Endless fights over how many knaidlach were in each bowl.

"It's hard for me alone," I said, watching him throw a towel into his carry-on. "The kids are small…and I miss you."

Daniel looked at me over the open lid of the suitcase.

"I…I think you should be here more. You know…for the kids."

Daniel was looking at me as if he couldn't understand me. I never stood in the way of things that he wanted to do.

"Maybe we can go out someplace. Like we did when we lived in Migdal Yam. For a picnic. To the beach even. Be a family."

Daniel zipped the suitcase closed. "Don't you want me to become a *tzaddik*?"

Of course I did. But I didn't know it would be so hard. I kept quiet.

"Don't you want to be a *tzaddikah*?"

I did. And so the words and feelings that had stirred within me settled back into their murky depths.

"Then this is what I have to do," Daniel said. "You're a good wife. You're helping me to serve a man who does miracles, and this way, I'll also become holy."

I heard Yaakov retching. I ran out of our bedroom. He was trying to make it to the bathroom, but he couldn't. He bent over, his hands on his stomach, and threw up.

Afterwards, when I had changed Yaakov's pajamas and was tucking him back into bed, Daniel came to find me. "You know I need to go," he said.

I nodded. "I hope it goes well," I said. I didn't ask when he'd be coming back. I wanted to be a good wife.

"You're a *tzaddikah*," Daniel said.

I wished it felt better, in the pit of my belly, to be a *tzaddikah*.

***

"I'm...unsettled, Racheli."

Ima was holding two-year-old Ahuva on her lap and stroking her hair while I sponged the crusty sores on her little face. "I think it's getting better," I said without looking up. The horrible rash had started with patches of red, itchy skin. And these had turned into little yellow-brown sores.

"It's not the impetigo," Ima said.

I was glad Ima was here. She'd come to Israel on a surprise visit. Just because she missed us. I was enjoying her visit, and I didn't want her to ruin it.

"It's making me worried. This whole thing. Why won't Daniel let the children visit their cousins? Why can't they go together to the science museum, to the zoo, to make pottery?"

I looked up. "You know why," I said. I pulled up Ahuva's sleeve. Small patches of red skin had appeared on her arms too. I hoped that the antibacterial wash that Ima had found at the pharmacy would work.

"A Barbie doll? Daniel's afraid that the children will be affected by a Barbie doll? Racheli, you had four Barbie dolls. At least." Ima smiled.

I didn't smile back. "It's not just the Barbie dolls," I said. "It's everything. If they were more...like us...then it would be different."

"Use a clean piece of cotton wool for her arms," Ima said. "It's a bacterial infection, and you'll spread it if you don't use a clean piece each time you wipe."

I pulled off a new piece of cotton wool. Daniel was right. Ima didn't understand. She couldn't understand. Because she wasn't part of it. She didn't have the merit to be part of Rav Natas's circle.

"We need to take her to the doctor," Ima said. "Impetigo's infectious. Maybe there's a prescription cream that we can use. Something to stop the itching. Why won't Daniel let you take her to the doctor?"

The door banged shut. I looked up. Daniel was home, even though it was only the middle of the morning. Good. Let him deal with Ima. I was tired of it.

"She needs to go to the doctor," Ima said to Daniel. "I told you that yesterday."

Daniel threw his wet towel on the table. He'd been to the mikveh.

"It'll go away by itself if we soak it and say more Tehillim," he said. "Her cheeks look better already." He came to stand next to us. "Shlomo Hamelech wrote down remedies for all the illnesses in the world, but the book was burned because people were no longer praying. We need to pray when we're sick, and this will help to rectify the mistake that people made…the mistake that they're still making."

Ima was quiet. She never argued with Daniel.

"When you're ready to move to Israel, you'll come and live with us," Daniel said to Ima. "And then you'll start to understand these things."

It wasn't the first time that Daniel had told Ima that when she came to Israel, she could come and live with us. Daniel never made that offer to Abba. He liked Ima. Because Ima didn't argue with him.

Daniel rolled his shoulders. "A doctor is a *shaliach* from Hashem," he said. "There aren't many reliable *frum* doctors, and they're difficult to find. That's why we need to pray first. And you see that prayer works. The scabs on her face are improving."

2004

Daniel had been learning in the yeshiva of Rav Natas for almost two years when, finally, Rav Natas told him that the next day of *hillula* could take place in our home. Until now, the Rav had been a vague presence in my life. Someone whom Daniel was close to.

I was ecstatic. It didn't matter whose *hillula* it was. What mattered was that it was going to take place in our home. Daniel had followed many rabbis since our marriage twelve years earlier, but the rabbis had been his rabbis only. I had always been on the outside. With Rav Natas, it was different. I had cooked so many meals for the circle, invested so much love and care into it. Now I was being included to an even greater extent.

Baked salmon, roast brisket, almond ice cream. I was busy for two days with all the cooking. The circle arrived later than I had expected, because they had been at the mikveh to prepare for the *hillula*. When they finally arrived, the children were tired and hungry.

The Rav's clothing was perfect. A white shirt creased so perfectly that I thought he had pulled it out of the packaging that day. A long black frock like the one worn by the principal of Shimmy's yeshiva. His wife, Tiferet, was wearing Shabbat clothes. I should have worn Shabbat clothes too. But it was too late to change now.

I spent the next hour serving the food. After each course, the Rav thanked me, without ever looking at me. I was honored that he was in our house and eating my food. Along with the feeling of honor, I was frustrated. Whereas the Rav's four-year-old son Yehoshua was sitting quietly on his chair the entire time, my children were running up and down, creating havoc. Shimmy was already ten years old, Avner nine. They were old enough to realize, to some extent, the greatness of Rav Natas. They should have been able to at least sit still. Like Yehoshua.

After I had put the four younger children to bed, I sat at the table. I had expected the meal to last another hour. But we sat at the table for four more hours. The Rav said a few *divrei Torah*. We said some Tehillim. And then the Rav began to tell us stories about *tzaddikim*. Long stories that wound this way and that way and back again. Shorter stories about *tzaddikim* who read the minds of their followers, who blessed their followers with wealth and health. I had a vivid imagination and could see the villages that the *tzaddikim* visited. Feel the cold that blew up the sleeves of their coats. I was there with the characters…watching them serve their Rebbe.

At the end of the last story, I felt a tremor pass through me. I allowed myself a glimpse at the *tzaddik* who was sitting at our table. He was showing Daniel how to become a good person. When the Rav eventually *bentshed*, he used the same siddur that he had used at Aharon's bris. And it took over an hour.

The Rav's students, including Daniel, sat quietly, as if they were used to sitting. Eran and Yigal, the attendant I'd named Panda, stood behind the Rav's chair. The skin around Yigal's lips had turned white, I noticed. At some point, Yael, Shimmy, and Avner fell asleep on the couch. Finally, at around midnight, the Rav signaled to Yigal. Yigal took a notebook and pen out of a bag he'd hung on the back of the Rav's chair. The same kind of school notebook I'd seen when we'd gone to the basement two years ago. The Rav pulled out the pendant that he was wearing under his shirt. He waited for it to hang still. Eran flipped through the pages of an old book and placed it on the table next to the Rav. The Rav intoned words. He looked upwards, his eyes alight with sheets of fire. Was he talking to angels? The pendant swung this way and that. Yigal balanced the notebook in the palm of his left hand and wrote notes. Finally, the Rav tucked the pendant back into his shirt and signaled for everyone to stand up. The *hillula* was over. Yehoshua, his son, was still awake. I hadn't heard him speak a word all night.

I stood up, slowly because my legs were stiff from sitting for so long. Finally, I could get to bed. Relief fluttered inside me. Suddenly, I felt someone looking at me. I turned my head toward the Rav and watched him closing his eyes. The Rav left without thanking me.

The next morning, I began to clean up. The children were still sleeping. I heard Daniel getting up. I rolled up the plastic tablecloth. Soon he was standing in the kitchen doorway. He had accompanied the Rav back to the yeshiva after the *hillula*. By the time he got home, I'd been sleeping.

I felt a cold splash on my tights. Orange juice was leaking out of the rolled-up tablecloth. "Is it…is it always like that?" I asked him.

"Like what?" He held up his tzitzit to check the knots.

Like what? Somehow I'd expected a *hillula* to be…different. Maybe some singing. I didn't know. I'd never been to a *hillula* before. But last night had been a little…a little I didn't know what. "I don't know…" I stuffed the rolled-up tablecloth into a garbage bag.

"On the day of *hillula*, a *tzaddik*'s soul returns to the world. We can get spiritual energy that his soul brings. But if you don't feel it…" Daniel shrugged and threw his tzitzit over his head.

I didn't feel it. I felt tired.

"I told you that you wouldn't understand," Daniel said.

Something inside me tensed. I wanted to understand. So much. But…why hadn't I enjoyed the *hillula*? Why didn't I feel what the others in the circle felt? I began to fold the white tablecloth. Maybe…maybe I wasn't a good enough person. I heard Aharon stirring in his crib and hoped that he would sleep for longer. Daniel could ask the Rav what I had to work on. But if he did that, then the Rav would know that I wasn't really such a *tzaddikah*. I didn't want that.

Daniel came back a little earlier that night, when I was still serving the children supper. He caught my eye and tilted his head toward the porch. I scanned the kitchen table. The children were busy eating the rolls that we had baked together. They would be quiet for another few minutes. I followed Daniel outside.

"You don't need to do it again," he said.

The *hillula*. I knew he meant the *hillula*.

Daniel rubbed the front of his shoe against the leg of his pants. "It's too hard for you," he said.

"No, it's not."

Daniel checked his shoe. "You don't feel the right things. You don't understand."

"But I want to understand," I said. "I want to be part of everything."

Daniel stared at me.

I leaned against the rails. I felt my back crushing the tendrils of jasmine and ivy. Of course the Rav had known what I was thinking…he had read my mind…seen the relief. I should have tried to feel the energy coming from the *tzaddik*'s soul. Whose *hillula* had it been, anyway? Instead, I had ruined it for myself. Ruined it because I was too tired to sit for so long. I had been given a chance to serve a miracle worker…and I had ruined it.

***

A month later, Daniel told me that Rav Natas had told him that women should wear shawls. I'd never worn a shawl. Shawls were things that my bubby had worn. Maybe. I wasn't even sure of that. I didn't argue, even though the change seemed so big. I'd grown used to change since I'd married Daniel. Daniel knew that I wanted to be a good Jew. That I would do anything to make Hashem happy with me. I had changed from a baseball cap to a headscarf. I could change more and begin wearing a shawl. So I went out, bought some pretty, velvety fabric, and found a seamstress to make me two beautiful shawls. I wore the shawl when I prayed and when I left the house, even if the weather was summery.

I had been wearing my shawls for a week when Daniel told me that the Rav had agreed to come to our home again. I wasn't sure why… Perhaps Daniel had pleaded my case. I didn't ask why the Rav had changed his mind. I didn't want Daniel to remind me that I had almost ruined everything. And besides, Daniel rarely answered my questions about the Rav.

The Rav arrived and the same scenario repeated itself: a few *divrei Torah*, eating, Tehillim, sitting at the table for hours and hours. I did not complain. I made sure not to even think about complaining. It was hard to try to control my thoughts when the children were so tired, pulling at my skirt, asking for another cup of soda. But I didn't want – couldn't allow – the Rav to tap into my negative thoughts again. When it got so hard that I was sure I was ruining it for everyone, I got up and went to the bathroom until I'd cleared my thoughts.

Slowly, the Rav began to come more often. No one was ever sure when it would happen. I got used to keeping the house well stocked so that I could put together a lavish meal within hours. Usually, when I was doing all the cooking, Yael would watch the children. Sometimes they went to the park by themselves. Our lives became one long day…or was it night? With Rav Natas, there were no routines, no schedules. Sometimes, the circle would leave to visit the *kever* of a *tzaddik* at nine o'clock at night. On those nights, Daniel didn't come home.

Some evenings, the Rav would tell us that he would be holding a *hillula* at our home that night. Instead of putting the children through a normal supper and bedtime routine, I would begin a marathon of cooking. On those nights, the *hillula* would begin only at around eleven o'clock at night. Then we would sit around the table for six, seven, eight hours. When I finally fell into bed, I was so exhausted that it was impossible to get the children to school the following morning. Daniel didn't encourage them to go to school, because he said that there were so many bad influences in the schools. Part of me felt that school was important, but I would never go against what Daniel had said. Besides, Yael, Shimmy, and Avner were old enough to get themselves out. If they wanted to, they could organize themselves to go to school. And if not…they could stay at home. The younger children would sleep until lunchtime. Of course, in the evening, they weren't ready to go to bed. And that meant another late night.

One evening, I was cooking for a *hillula* that was supposed to begin in an hour's time. Daniel had called to tell me when I was in the park with the children, and we had rushed home to prepare. We had rushed so much that Shimmy had forgotten the bouncing ball that he had been given in *cheder* for answering correctly three of the questions that a visiting rabbi had asked the class. By the time he ran back to get it, someone had taken it.

He was watching me peel potatoes instead of changing into a white shirt. Some of the peels flew to the floor.

"Pick them up," I said.

He didn't move. "The *hillula* is boring. I'm not coming," Shimmy said.

Automatically, I reached for another potato. But my mind was whirring. He couldn't say that. Mustn't say that. A lesson from my parenting classes flashed into my mind. "You can change your shirt now, or you can change after you have picked up the potato peels," I said.

"I don't want to come. I don't like sitting for so long. It's boring."

My stomach tightened. Boring. It wasn't boring. How could he say that? The Rav was doing important things at the *hillula*. I nicked my nail with the peeler. I glanced at Avner. He was on the floor, trying to pick up the wet peels that had stuck to the floor. I glanced at the clock. The Rav would be arriving in thirty minutes. The food wasn't ready. My stomach was a knot now. I couldn't think these thoughts. It wasn't right. I closed my eyes. Squeezed them tightly shut. He was right, wasn't he? Shimmy was right. The *hillula* would be boring. Just like the others had been.

"It's important. A *hillula* is important," I said. "We're lucky that we have a *rav* like Rav Natas. We're so lucky that we can help him to do all these *tikkunim*. Not everyone is as lucky as we are."

Shimmy still didn't move. "If you don't go change now, I'm going to tell Abba," I said. An empty threat. I would never, ever tell Daniel what Shimmy had said. I'd be crazy to tell him that one of our kids was rebelling. And besides, we never spoke about anything connected to the circle. The circle was holy. And if there were things that we didn't understand, it was okay. Because we weren't supposed to understand the ways of a *tzaddik*.

***

I was always shopping and cooking for the circle. Sometimes the Rav would give Daniel an envelope of money to cover the shopping bills, but most times, I covered the bill myself by asking my parents for more money. What had once been so difficult for me to do had become almost routine. When I wasn't shopping and cooking, I was driving the Rav and some of the circle members to the *kever* of this *tzaddik* or that *tzaddik*. Whatever I was doing, I was thinking of Rav Natas, the miracle worker that we were serving. So much so that when I bought clothing for my boys, I also bought clothing for his son. And all the time, I was waiting for the next *hillula*. I had begun to enjoy them.

At every *hillula* I felt a feeling of awe. It wasn't the same awe that I got when I went to the Kotel early in the morning, so early that the plaza was almost deserted. It was different...but it was still a feeling of holiness. Of love, even. And then there was the feeling that I had to follow the rules, be obedient. Like the time a policeman had stopped me for speeding and I had too many children in the back of the van and I knew that I had to get to Kfar Chananyah to deliver the food for the *hillula* of Chananyah ben Akshia. Why hadn't I listened to the rules of safe driving? Of course I wanted to listen to the safety rules. Rules were good for me. I followed the unspoken rules at a *hillula*. They helped me to believe that the *hillula* was wonderful. Inspiring. Exactly where I wanted to be.

At a *hillula*, I learned to eat even if I wasn't hungry, because this was the way to uplift the soul of the *tzaddik*. I learned to focus on how I was sitting, on what I was thinking, so that Rav Natas wouldn't see that I was anxious, uncomfortable. Because if he read my mind and saw these negative emotions, then he would stop coming to our home. I knew that he wouldn't forgive me a second time. And I didn't want to be pushed out of our circle. I wanted to belong to where Daniel belonged. Sometimes one of the kids tried to ask me for something during a *hillula*, but I shushed them because I had to stay focused on thinking the right thoughts.

We didn't really belong to our families anymore, and we had long since stopped being part of a bigger community. When Rav Natas entered our lives, our world became infused with new meaning. Now Rav Natas and his circle were our friends and family. We never knew what was going to happen or when it was going to happen. By the summer of that year, our lives revolved fully around the circle. Had more boys and men joined the circle? Who was closest to the Rav? The questions buzzed around my head. Flies buzzing over putrid meat. But there was no doubt. None at all. More than two years of being in the Rav's closest circle had cancelled out all doubts. The Rav knew everything. I didn't need to understand anything more. I never put these thoughts into words. Here, in the circle, you never voiced what you were thinking. Daniel never told me what the Rav had told him. I knew there were things they spoke about. That much he had told me. But everything was a secret. Nothing was shared. And it didn't matter, because we had been chosen to be close to the holiest of the holy.

***

That year, we stopped eating milk products on Pesach. The Rav didn't eat them, and as part of his circle, we had to follow his customs. It was hard to get used to. I had always made plenty of cheesecakes on Pesach. I didn't like black coffee. The older children complained. But I understood that if this was what the Rav did, we also had to do it. And I expected them to understand too.

At around the same time, when Daniel was home for Shabbat, we began walking to the Rav's house for Seudah Shlishit. From the Old City to Mekor Baruch was a walk of about thirty minutes, and in the late afternoon, when the heat had subsided, it was a pleasant walk. We never took the children. Yael was in charge of them. Whenever I felt that it was too much for her, I would buy special treats for the children to share when they ate Seudah Shlishit alone. I never thought of staying at home with them. I treasured the walk with Daniel. We so rarely did things together. The walks there and back were quality time alone. And, besides, since Yael more or less managed, I wasn't willing to forgo time spent in the presence of the Rav.

There were usually five or six young students of the Rav gathered around the long table in his apartment. Tiferet, the Rav's wife, and I sat at the end of the table, opposite the Rav. Since Rav Natas didn't use electric lights on Shabbat, the room would gradually become dimmer and dimmer, until finally, the only light in the room came from a twenty-four hour candle in the corner next to the Shabbat candles. A tall bookcase, stacked neatly with many books, stood against one wall of the living room. The first time Daniel and I went, Rav Natas didn't speak much to anyone. I knew that Chassidic Rebbes used this auspicious time, the last minutes of Shabbat, to speak to their followers about deep things, ways to improve themselves, ways to bring about the final *geulah*. And I had expected the same here, but although Rav Natas said a few *divrei Torah*, nothing was too difficult for me to follow.

In all the times that we came to Rav Natas, I never saw him open a Gemara like I had seen Abba doing, running his finger down the small print in the center of the page, moving to the column along the sides. Instead, every now and again, Eran or Yigal would bring him an old book that was bound together with black duct tape. Daniel told me it was a book on Kabbalah. At other times, Rav Natas would read from his special siddur. It was the Siddur Hakavanot of the Rashash, Eran had told Shimmy one day. Although the Rav didn't speak much at these gatherings, didn't even interact much with us, I always felt that this was a reverent time, a time to gaze at our Rav. To soak up his wisdom. To fill that place in my chest that was no longer a hole. I was being a good soldier in Hashem's army because I was serving a *tzaddik*.

***

On Lag ba'Omer, Daniel went with the circle to Meron. The circle wasn't going to the *kever* of Rabbi Shimon bar Yochai, where hundreds of thousands of people were going to be. It was too crowded there for them. They would be going to a burial site of Rabbi Yossi ben Kisma. An underground cave midway down the mountainside under the *kever* of Rabbi Shimon. I cooked and packed food for the circle. Then I helped Daniel load everything in the van. But I didn't do any of this with a full heart. It wasn't fair. I wanted to go with Daniel. I wanted the family to be together. Like we always were on Lag ba'Omer. I wanted Daniel and I to take the children to the bonfires in the Old City, to watch him dance around them with the boys. I didn't want to do this alone.

In the late afternoon when Shimmy and Avner came back, dirty but happy from industriously building the biggest bonfire in the Old City, I'd made my decision. We were going to Meron. The children were thrilled. Shimmy and Avner forgot about their hard work. Someone else could light their fire. They were going to Meron.

At nine o'clock, we caught a specially chartered bus, and we arrived at Meron at midnight. The children had slept on the bus, so they weren't cranky. I was so excited to be doing something so adventurous. Even if I wasn't with the circle, I was close by. I was sure it was going to be fun. There were hundreds of thousands of people. And that was when I realized that it would be almost impossible to watch seven children by myself.

I found a tiny space where I could stand with the children without fear of getting crushed, and I called Daniel. "Guess where I am?" I shouted above the voices, the music, around me. "Meron," I said.

"What?" Daniel shouted. "Why did you come here?"

I felt all the energy draining out of me. Daniel was angry with me. I hated it when he was angry. Why had I come? For a single moment, I wondered how I was going to manage here with all the children. And then I decided that we were going to enjoy all the festivities. Later, I'd figure out how to get back home. I always managed. I was strong and capable. I'd manage this time too.

***

"We're going to the *kever* of Benayahu ben Yehoyada."

Daniel's voice. I turned over in bed and kept my eyes shut. I was expecting our eighth child. I was nauseated and had a terrible headache. The children were all in school. Aharon was sleeping in his crib, and I wasn't going to get out of bed until he woke up.

"The Rav said that we'll leave in an hour. You need to be ready."

Daniel's voice was closer now. At the foot of my bed. Or was he standing beside me? I opened my eyes. Daniel was smiling.

"You're coming too, Racheli. The Rav wants you to come too."

Me? I never went to the *kivrei tzaddikim*. Except to deliver the food. I wasn't welcome to stay. To take part in whatever the *tikkunim* and prayers. Daniel was looking at me. He stopped smiling. He could see I felt weak.

"Do you know who Benayahu ben Yehoyada was?"

I shook my head. A wave of pain pounded above my eyes. I closed them. This was the first time I was being told I could join them to go to the *kever* of a *tzaddik*. But my head hurt so much.

"David Hamelech's greatest warrior. He killed a lion. Killed an Egyptian with the sword that he pulled out of his hand. He helped Shlomo Hamelech capture the king of the demons, Ashmedai, so that he could find the *shamir*."

I wanted to go. Finally, I was being included. The Rav was a *tzaddik*. And I could be there, help to serve the Rav. I had to go. Get up. Get ready. Fetch the children from school. Another wave of pain. And with it came the nausea.

"Eran told me. He told me all these things about Benayahu ben Yehoyada." Daniel turned to leave the room. "I'll tell you more in the car on the way there."

"Where to?"

"To Biriyah. Near Tzefat."

Tzefat. I had to drive to Tzefat. A flutter of excitement. The children would be coming. A first time for them too. They were so young, and already we were involving them in holy work. I pushed myself up. Who would be in my van? Would I drive the Rav? Usually ladies who wore shawls didn't drive cars – it wasn't considered modest. But the Rav allowed me to drive, because driving was part of my way to serve him.

We arrived at the *kever* in the early afternoon. The Rav had driven up in the second car. I was upset that I hadn't had the merit to drive him up, but also relieved because I still wasn't feeling well. I should have been excited. This was my first time with the circle at the *kever* of a *tzaddik*. The men went through the blue doors that led into the room where the tomb was. Yehoshua followed his father. Tiferet, the Rav's wife and the only other woman in the circle, remained standing in a corner away from the men. But I couldn't stay in the room. My children were hungry because I hadn't had time to give them lunch. Behind the main building, I found a courtyard surrounded with trees. I set the food out on two wooden picnic tables. It was peaceful there. Cool. Shady. My headache had gone. I was even hungry.

"Benayahu ben Yehoyada was a big *tzaddik*," I told the children as I smeared ketchup into the pitas I had bought and stuffed them with cold cuts. "He helped Shlomo Hamelech find the *shamir*…so that he could cut the stones of the Beit Hamikdash without using any metal. The worm cut the stones into perfect squares."

The children weren't listening. Avner and Yaakov were fighting over which half of pita had more meat in it. Six-year-old Ahuva had sat Aharon on the end of the table and was busy feeding him a slice of turkey meat. Shimmy had wandered off somewhere. And Meir was complaining of a stomachache.

I wanted the children to be excited. To feel some of the spiritual energy that filled the forest around us. Shimmy was already eleven years old. He should be with Daniel, standing by the tomb. Saying Tehillim or whatever they were saying. It wasn't right that he'd wandered off. Why wasn't he excited about being here? The Rav would be angry with him. With us. The children wandered off toward the forest to look for wood to make a bonfire. Without Meir. He slouched against a tree trunk and refused to eat anything.

Half an hour later, the men emerged. Eran placed a chair at the head of the picnic table. We ate. Daniel noticed that Meir was slouched against the tree trunk, and he asked me what was wrong. When I told him, he told Eran. Eran whispered something into the Rav's ear. The Rav answered him. I knew that it was about Meir. "The children don't sit with us like they should," he said, looking at something behind me, something in the darkening sky.

Something inside me clenched. He was going to complain about the children. I knew they weren't like Yehoshua. I wanted them to sit like he did. To absorb the holiness of the Rav…but they were…what were they…young? They weren't bad. My heart was clenching upon itself, creasing up tighter and tighter until I couldn't breathe.

The Rav rubbed his fingers across the pendulum he wore. "You must buy celery and dip it into the water of a mikveh," he said. "Then Meir must eat the celery."

I didn't know where I was going to get celery. We weren't near any shops. But my heart started unfolding. He hadn't complained about the children.

The Rav began speaking. He told us about Benayahu ben Yehoyada. When the king of Persia was ill, Shlomo Hamelech knew that the milk of a lioness would cure him. Benayahu ben Yehoyada managed to tame a lioness sufficiently by feeding her goats until he was able to milk her. He told us other things. About how the Arizal had found his *kever* through *ruach hakodesh.* About how Benayahu had studied Kabbalah.

It began to get dark. Meir was falling asleep, so I told Yael to put him on the back seat of the van, where he could sleep. When Yaakov and Avner began to complain, I sent them into the forest to find more sticks so that we would be ready to make a fire if the Rav wanted.

We'd been sitting on the picnic benches for three hours when Yigal told me that the Rav wanted me to leave. It was too hard to do *tikkunim* with the children around. Before we left, I stopped to pray at the tomb. It was covered with a cloth of deep blue velvet that ended with a thick row of tassels. The trip here should have been fun. I should have been uplifted, but I was tired and nauseated. And now I had to drive back, alone in the dark. The next day, back in the Old City, I did buy celery. I dipped it into the waters of a mikveh. I managed to convince Meir to eat some by hiding tiny, chopped-up pieces in a spoonful of crunchy peanut butter. By that evening, Meir was feeling fine. And I knew that I'd seen a miracle.

***

One evening, three years after their last visit, Dina and Avi knocked on the door. Avi had let his workers off early because they were ahead of schedule in the housing project. After heading to the Kotel, they popped in at my house. On the worst possible night. We were in the middle of a *hillula*.

I sat Avi at the table with the men and motioned to Dina to join me in the kitchen. "What gives, Racheli?" Dina asked me. "You look like you're heading out for a party instead of like…a regular Tuesday night. And what's with the shawl?"

I sighed. I didn't have time for her questions. I needed to serve the food.

In between courses, Dina asked me, "Why is Daniel sitting beside the rabbi as if he were a guest in someone else's house?"

I tried to explain to her, "That's the Rav. He must sit at the head of the table." But Dina didn't understand any of it, of course.

"What's going on?" she asked me. "This isn't about black and white clothes or a long coat. Or not carrying on Shabbat and making your wife into a porter. Who is that bunch of losers hanging out in the living room listening to this rabbi? Who are the two guys standing behind his chair like some kind of bodyguards? And why are they saying Tehillim and then more Tehillim? This is really weird."

I just looked at her with pity. She really didn't understand a thing about the elevation of the *hillula*.

"What's up, Racheli?" Dina asked me again. "The whole truth and nothing but the truth," she said, trying to be playful. But this was no laughing matter.

"The Rav's here," I said.

"Rav?"

"Daniel has a new *rav*. A genius."

Her mouth fell open.

"We're honored by his visit."

"He's in Daniel's seat," she said.

"Daniel wants him to sit there."

"No way…you can't be serious."

I didn't get a chance to answer. There was shouting coming from the living room.

"Crazy…you hear…this is all crazy." It was Avi's voice. Loud, angry.

"The Rav says you must leave." That was Yigal.

Dina glanced at me. I split open a packet of wafers, carefully, along the serrated line. The food needed to be served.

Dina marched into the living room. I tried to stop her, but she was already through the door. Eran was nudging toward Avi. Avi stood his ground, a forearm raised, his biceps bulging.

"Avi," Dina yelled. "You move away now, you hear?"

Avi turned around.

The Rav stared at Dina. His eyes were dark slits. His lips were moving. I was afraid that he was cursing her.

"You tell your thugs to leave my husband alone," Dina yelled at him. Everyone turned to stare at her.

I found my voice. "Dina… Dina, you don't understand…"

Avi was pulling at Dina's arm. "Let's go," he said.

Dina called me the next day. I told her that she'd spoken disrespectfully to the Rav, but she didn't apologize. Not surprisingly, we didn't speak to each other again for a very long time after that.

***

After that first trip to the *kever* of Benayahu ben Yehoyada, the children and I almost always went with the circle to the different graves and tombs. We went about every two weeks. The children often missed school, but I didn't mind that much. The schools were full of children who were…different from our children. Daniel was happier that they were at home. No one ever called me to find out what was happening. And the children never spoke to their teachers about the trips, because they knew that whatever we did with the Rav wasn't something that we discussed with others.

Usually we went to places that weren't that well known. There were fewer people there. One day, we went to the *kever* of Rabbi Yehudah ben Teima on a mountaintop outside Moshav Dalton, near Tzefat. I was feeling much stronger by now, and I had packed a lavish picnic with meat loaf, chicken schnitzels, and mini meatballs.

The men stood by the *kever* intoning the teachings of Rabbi Yehudah ben Teima. *Be bold as a leopard, as light as an eagle, as quick as a deer, and as courageous as a lion to do the will of your Father in Heaven.* They davened from special booklets that the Rav had put together. I asked Hashem to help me to be a good wife, a good mother. A good soldier in His army. Finally, after about two hours, we sat down to eat. "We can always rely on your wife to bring the food," the Rav said to Daniel.

As we ate, the Rav told us more about the teachings of Rabbi Yehudah ben Teima. *The brazen one goes to Gehinnom, and the shame-faced goes to Gan Eden.* I could feel the energy in the air. The Rav was telling a story, but I couldn't hear clearly. A cool wind had blown up, and his words were being whipped away. Aharon was pulling at my skirt. He was tired, but I couldn't see Yael or Ahuva. I wanted to hear the Rav. I wanted to be part of the *tikkun*. I remained seated even though I couldn't hear clearly. Night fell. I was vaguely aware that the children had fallen asleep. Some in the car. Some on blankets under the trees.

May it be Your will, Hashem, our God, that You build Your city quickly in our days and give us a share in Your Torah. The Rav was talking again. He'd been quiet for so long. I repeated his words. Over and over, the circle repeated the words. And then the Rav was talking about darkness and evil. I didn't want to hear about bad things. I wanted to beg Hashem to rebuild Yerushalayim. Rebuild His city so that Jews could live in all of it. Even in the Muslim Quarter. It was four o'clock in the morning. And I was tired. So tired. But I couldn't get up. No one got up until the Rav told us to get up. I put my arms on the table and lay my head on top of them.

I woke up with the first rays of the sun. Everyone was sleeping. Suddenly Daniel was at my side. "The Rav said to take the children home," he said.

I looked at the head of the table. The Rav was there. He looked like he hadn't slept all night. "I want to stay. To be with the circle. Near the Rav," I said.

The Rav looked up. "She can stay," he said.

Daniel smiled at me.

Together with the children, I stayed on for another day and night. That night, the Rav began to talk about the evil in the world. Evil spirits that floated between heaven and earth. That lodged themselves in the bodies of living people. His words frightened me. All the more because I couldn't talk to Daniel about them. Couldn't talk to anyone about them. Because we were just one family and a handful of faithful followers who believed that we had a great secret to guard. There was no one to talk to and no one with whom to share our thoughts.

No one complained of being cold or tired. No one thought of taking a shower. We fell asleep, like on the first night, at the table. The next morning, Yigal drove away in my van and came back with pita, hummus, and tuna in brine because the tiny store on Dalton had run out of tuna in oil.

At the end of the third day, when the men left to go to the mikveh, I drove home with the children. Back at home, I tried to settle back into routine. Get the children into bed on time, wake them up for school. Reschedule a dentist appointment. The words of Rabbi Yehudah ben Teima had become a mantra in my head. *Be bold as a leopard, as light as an eagle, as quick as a deer, and as courageous as a lion to do the will of your Father in heaven.* I heard them intoned over and over. I encouraged the children to sing them. We made up a tune and danced in a circle, our arms linked. The Rav had spoken about the darkness and evil that he felt in the world, but I didn't want to think about darkness and evil. I wanted to think about how bold, light, quick, and courageous we had to be so that we could do Hashem's will. As we danced, I remembered the rabbi who had come to our *gan* so many years ago on Moshav Ayin Yaffa. I remembered what he said about being a soldier in the army of Hashem. And my heart swelled with joy. I was a soldier, and I was raising my own mini-army of soldiers. Ready to do mitzvot. To put more bricks in the walls of the Beit Hamikdash. Each one of the children was a tower of light in the world.

The circle didn't come back the next day. Or the next. I didn't even know when to expect Daniel back home. He eventually came home after four days. I had missed him so much, but I didn't tell him. Instead, I told him that I was happy he'd been able to go with the Rav.

Not long after this trip, a month before Chanukah, I gave birth to Hillel. I don't remember much about the birth. I do remember wondering if anyone had told the Rav that I was in labor. Was he praying for me?

***

We invited my family to the bris. Even Gila came. She'd missed Aharon's bris, because she'd been in the States, so I guess she thought that she'd make the effort to come this time. Even though she'd hardly been in touch with us over the last four years since we hadn't let her take Yael out for an ice cream after the terror attack near Azariyah.

She arrived early to help set up. That was Gila – always looking for a way to help out. But Yael and the children had a pretty good idea about how to set up for a *seudah*. They had done it often enough for a *hillula*. So Gila began folding napkins into a fancy swan shape.

"I've called you a few times," Gila said. "Did the kids give you my messages?"

I looked at the baby's tiny fingers. What was I supposed to tell her? That I knew she'd called, but Daniel didn't want me to talk to her too much? "It's busy here," I said.

Gila kept folding.

I watched her looking around the living room, and I saw it through her eyes. It was halfway decent. The caterer that Ima and Abba had called in had set up two long tables, and Yael had carried most of the mess to the bedrooms.

I leaned back against the couch. The same couch that we'd had in Migdal Yam. My house had been different then. Clean and tidy. Something I could be proud of. But now…I couldn't keep up with the housework like I used to. There was so much shopping and cooking to do for the *hillulas*. And besides, there were more children to take care of.

"You're not doing the bris in a shul?" Gila asked.

I closed my eyes. Gila and her questions. I wished she hadn't come early. Maybe it would have been better if she hadn't come at all. I couldn't explain it to her. Didn't want to. She wasn't part of the circle. She didn't have the merit.

"Doesn't Daniel belong to a shul?"

"Ima, I'm hungry." Ahuva stood in front of me with a roll in her hand.

"You can eat it if you wash your hands," I told her. And then I stood up, because the Rav and the circle had arrived. "It's the Rosh Yeshiva," I said to Gila. Finally the bris could begin, and she would stop asking so many questions.

This time Rav Natas had agreed to be the sandek without telling Daniel to ask Abba first. He kept his eyes tightly shut as he got ready to say the *berachot*. He was drawing up the right *kavanot*.

Yossi, who thought that the Rav had forgotten the words, went over to him with a siddur and pointed to the *berachah*. Ridiculous. It only showed me how much my family didn't understand.

I didn't enjoy the *seudah*. We sat with my family at one table. The Rav and the circle sat at the other table. It was so hard to make sure that the kids didn't talk to their cousins. Hard to see how my family didn't appreciate the Rav's greatness.

When I got up to get the mustard for Daniel, Gila cornered me behind the refrigerator door.

"What's up?" she asked. "You and Daniel…the kids…are you okay?"

I stared at Gila. "I'm fine," I said. Why couldn't she see it? Why did my family keep giving me the feeling the something was wrong? Why couldn't they just be happy for us, happy that we were part of something so big and so important?

2005

It had been three years since the first night that Daniel and I had gone to meet Rav Natas in his yeshiva. Only after three long years did the Rav agree to celebrate Purim in our home. I worked hard to get everything ready. I bought new drapes, cooked all the food, and set everything up. All the while knowing that I wasn't going to be part of the celebrations. Together with the children, I was going to the Rav's house in Mekor Baruch to spend Purim with Tiferet and their son. Bad enough that I wouldn't be part of it all. But I also didn't know when I would be able to come back home. It depended on when the Rav would call an end to the celebration.

Just before I left the house on Purim, I spoke to Daniel. "It's hard for me not to be part of it all," I said. "I want to see everyone together, hear the singing…"

Daniel had been sitting on the couch. He stood up. "Racheli, you *are* part of it all! We couldn't be here if it weren't for your good heart and good *middot*. Everything is perfect, and it's all thanks to you."

"I didn't mean that," I said. "I meant…"

Daniel stepped closer to me. "You need to be happy with the merit of preparing things for us. Be happy with the mitzvah," he said.

Shimmy ran in to tell me the van was loaded. I'd ruined things again. Why had I said anything? The children were excited to be going away. Why couldn't I share in their excitement? I guess I just really wanted to stay and see all the fun.

When I came back, three days later, the house was in more of a mess than it usually was. Daniel couldn't help me to clean up because he had gone to be with the Rav. The next year, and the year after that, I did the same thing. Prepared everything and left. But I never complained again.

2006

I pushed a hundred shekels into Shimmy's hand. "Cashews, sugared almonds, sunflower seeds...buy a lot of whatever you want," I told him. And then I was back at the stove. Lifting lids, stirring, tasting, adding salt. *Lichvod Shabbat kodesh. Lichvod Shabbat kodesh.* Please, Hashem, make the food tasty. Tastier than ever. Because finally, after four whole years, four years of refusing our invitations, of not wanting to impose, Rav Natas and his family were coming to our home for Shabbat. With all the members of our circle.

I scooped Hillel off the floor. He was learning how to crawl. He was at that crab stage when he had one leg bent under him and the other out in front so that he could scoot forward. Yummy delicious. "The *tzaddik* is coming," I sang and twirled. I put some measuring cups on the floor to keep him busy.

"Ahuva, the carrots..." Ahuva was eight years old. Plenty old enough to help out in the kitchen.

Ahuva put her book down. "Is he a big *tzaddik*?"

I handed her a peeler. "The biggest!" I said. "And we're lucky to know him. So lucky to be part of his circle."

"Where's everyone going to sleep?" Avner asked.

Sleep? I poured oil into a pot. Tzimmes. I hadn't made tzimmes in a long time. And Daniel loved the sweetness of carrots and prunes. Please, Hashem... let it be tasty. There wouldn't be much time for sleeping. We'd be sitting at the table for most of Shabbat. And the Rav would lead us in whatever we had to do. "The children will share one room. Yael's room," I said. The boys in the circle would take over the other rooms. Or they wouldn't. They could sleep on the couches just as well.

"It's a mitzvah to give up your bed for guests," Yael said.

She was folding napkins into fans and holding them in place at the table with a cup. She had it right. It was a mitzvah. Daniel and I were raising the children right. There were more important things in life to worry about than if you had a bed at night or not. Things like serving a *tzaddik*. I thought of all the different Chassidic rabbis that I'd read stories about. Rav Natas was a miracle worker like them. And we had the honor of serving him.

Shimmy came back an hour later with the cashews, sugared almonds, and an orange kitten that was barely moving. Where was Daniel? He didn't want animals in the house. And certainly not a cat. A cat was an impure animal.

"Can I keep him?"

"No." The kitten looked like Kitty, my kitten in Migdal Yam.

"I'll put her on the porch, in a box, under the jasmine."

The kitten opened her eyes. She was terrified. And too weak to move.

I looked around. "Don't tell anyone," I told Shimmy. "You need to find a syringe to drop milk into her mouth." I picked up the bags of nuts that Shimmy had dropped on the floor.

Shabbat was like an extended *hillula*. "See how careful Rav Natas is?" I was standing in the entrance to the laundry room, behind the row of men who had lined up to wash their hands. Yaakov was standing beside me. I tucked his shirt in. Again. His new pants were one size too big. I had misjudged when I'd bought them. "Look how he wipes the handles of the cup to make sure that there's no water left on them. That's how you wash for bread," I told Yaakov. It was important to point out these little things that weren't really so little. These were the things that made someone holy.

During the meals, six-year-old Yehoshua sat perfectly still by his father's side. When he got tired, his head flopped back, bent a little to the side, and he fell asleep. With his eyes half-open. As if he was ready to wake up at a moment's notice. My kids, in contrast, were…kids. It was hard to keep the younger ones at the table. And I knew that I shouldn't expect it. But the older children should have known better. Daniel was listening closely to what the Rav said, long stories about *tzaddikim* who performed miracles. When he wasn't listening to a story, he was reciting Tehillim. And I was busy serving the meal and trying to keep the older children at the table. At any one time, there were usually two or three of them missing. They would slip off their chairs quietly, and I'd find them in the corridor, where there was enough light to read, bent over an open book.

I was frustrated. Frustrated that Daniel and I couldn't discipline our children to behave like Yehoshua. Silent disappearing acts weren't a way to honor a *tzaddik*. And underneath the frustration, there was another feeling. A feeling that I wanted to push far, far away. But it slid around the room, curved around the corners, and finally wrapped itself like a rope around my neck. I was afraid. Afraid that the Rav would see their lack of respect. Become angry.

Blame me and Daniel. I hated it when anyone was angry with me. And I didn't want the Rav to complain about the children.

I glanced at Ahuva, curled up on the couch. She was seven years old. Twelve o'clock was way past her bedtime. Of course she'd fallen asleep. The meals were so long, and they were children. And then, my breath caught in my throat. I couldn't think like that. We all had to serve the Rav. The Rav would read my mind, see that I was making excuses for the children. I had to sit at the table and clear my thoughts. I had to calm myself. Make my thoughts pure and holy. So that the evil spirits that the Rav could see wouldn't come close. Wouldn't attach themselves to me. Please, Hashem…help me clear my mind.

That Shabbat slipped into Sunday and Monday, and still the Rav and his circle were at our home. I was exhausted from the constant cooking, the trips to the grocery to keep replenishing our stocks, the long hours of sitting at the table. But I was also exhilarated. We were part of a holy circle. Rav Natas was telling us stories about *tzaddikim*…people who could perform miracles. But those were all stories. Things that had happened years and years ago. We were lucky enough to have our own real miracle worker in our midst.

***

Three months passed before the Rav agreed to come to our home again for Shabbat. This time, immediately after he arrived, he took off his frock and changed into an elaborate dark blue robe with gold embroidery. On his head, in place of his usual *kippah* and hat, he wore a dark blue turban with gold trim. He sat at the head of the table, looking like a king. Tiferet came into the kitchen, where I was trying to at least clear the counters before Shabbat, and asked me if she could prepare a cup of tea for the Rav.

"Magnificent," I said, waving a dish towel in the direction of the Rav. It wasn't a word I normally used. But I'd seen it in an advertisement for exclusive jewelry in a magazine that Yael had brought home.

"I sewed it," Tiferet said, opening the right cabinet for a mug.

I felt a worm of jealousy burrow into me. She had sewed the Rav a robe. This was a magnificent robe that brought him honor. Made him into a king. I glanced at the Rav quickly. Over the food processor part that I was holding.

I didn't want him to sense me looking at him. It wouldn't be modest. The elaborate flowers, clinging to the stems that wound up either side of the robe, reached up to the heavens, carrying his holiness higher and higher.

"You're out of herbal tea," Tiferet said.

I wasn't. I had bought two boxes, because I knew that this was what the Rav liked to drink. I pulled them out. "You didn't do the embroidery," I said. Maybe she could sew, but she couldn't have done the embroidery.

"There are places where you can get it done," Tiferet said, dipping the tea bag into the hot water.

Which places? I wanted to know. Because I was going to tell Daniel that we had to present the Rav with a robe. And then I'd need to find a seamstress. Because I didn't know how to sew.

***

The next time I saw Rav Natas was at the *kever* of Abaye and Rava. He had driven up to Tzefat with the circle in the early morning. I followed later in the day with the children after I had finished cooking for everyone. I was driving fast to get there. I didn't want to miss out on anything. Once I reached Tzefat, I headed for Amuka. It was a familiar road. I'd driven it dozens of times. Just before I reached the army base, I turned into a road pointing to the gravesites of Abaye and Rava. I drove slowly up the steep slope and then parked in the clearing. Shimmy pointed out Mount Hermon in the distance. A patch of gray and green against the blue sky. I hurried the children along, our feet crunching against the stones on the sandy path. Finally, I saw it. A white cemented building with the usual blue dome. Steps, an arched corridor, more steps. The earthy smell of a cave. And then I saw the group. No one greeted us.

Rav Natas was reading from the Siddur Hakavanot. Putting together names of Hashem. Five members of the circle, as well as a stranger with *peyot* like small horns, stood around. Daniel was saying Tehillim. And then my eyes locked on the wooden staff that Rav Natas was holding. Strips of blue and yellow satin billowed from the end of the staff.

Yaakov ran to the low *kever* and began patting the stone. I handed Hillel to Yael. Eran. He was the one who talked more than anyone else. I looked for him. He was leaning against the wall of the cave, picking his teeth with the wooden toothpick that he always kept in his shirt pocket. "What's the Rav holding?"

"A staff." He propped the heel of his shoe against the wall. "Moshe Rabbeinu had a staff."

I knew that.

"Rav Natas carved the kabbalistic names of Hashem into the wood. So it has to stay covered. With special cloth."

Shimmy had joined us and he asked Eran, "Can he do miracles with it?"

"If you feel sick, he can touch you with it, and you'll feel better."

"Ask him to help Yigal with his white eyes and lips," Shimmy said.

Eran didn't answer. He continued picking his teeth.

I called the children to come to me. We began to say Tehillim together. I hoped that Rav Natas would end his prayers before the children got wild. Aharon, who had just turned four years old, didn't have much patience to stand still.

CHAPTER TEN

The Abuse Begins

2007

One morning toward the start of winter, Daniel woke me up early. I was exhausted. Avner had spent the previous afternoon clambering on top of a pile of building rubble that had been dumped at the edge of the parking lot. An old plank of wood full of nails had hit him, and one of the nails had embedded itself in his leg. I'd spent most of the night at the urgent care clinic attending to the wound. I pushed myself up on my elbow. Daniel was dressed. Ready to go out.

"I need you to help me plan a trip," he said.

I swung my feet over the edge of my bed. Where were my slippers? "Where are we going?" I asked. I was already used to getting ready to set out for a trip on short notice. The Rav could decide at any time that we had to leave. "I'll pack food?"

Daniel shook his head. "I'm going alone," he said.

"Alone? We always go together. All of us." Had I done something wrong? Had the Rav decided to shut me out of the circle?

"The Rav says that I must go alone. Without anyone else."

I found my slippers. I didn't ask Daniel why the Rav had told him to go alone. Of course the Rav had his reasons. We didn't need to know. And even if the Rav had given Daniel a reason, Daniel wouldn't have told me. We never discussed what the Rav did.

"Where are you going?"

"I need to go to seven *kivrei tzaddikim.*" Daniel pulled a piece of paper out of his pocket. "You always drive, Racheli. Tell me where I should go first."

I looked at the list. Yonatan ben Uziel, Rabbi Yossi Haglili, Rabbi Yossi ben Zimra, Hillel Hazaken, Shammai Hazaken, Rabbi Yochanan ben Zakkai, Rachel the wife of Rabbi Akiva. Tiberias. Daniel had to start in Tiberias with the gravesites of Rabbi Yochanan ben Zakkai and Rachel, then he'd go further north. I'd make him a travel guide.

Forty minutes later, Daniel was set to go. He looked at me. There was something strange in his eyes. Was it fear? What was Daniel afraid of?

***

Over the winter, Rav Natas and the circle began coming to our house regularly. Sometimes it was for a *hillula*, sometimes for Shabbat. Whenever they came, they lingered on. I was never sure if they were going to stay for a day, two, or even three. When they stayed, there was no day and no night to our lives. We would sit around the table until the Rav signaled that it was time to get up. Often that happened only at four o'clock in the morning. Then we would sleep. The men would get up to daven Shacharit close to lunchtime. Maybe they went to the mikveh before. I never knew what they were doing when they left the house. And Daniel never told me. It was all part of the secrecy.

At the beginning of the year, on the tenth of Shevat, we held a *hillula* for Rabbi Shalom Sharabi, the Rashash. The Rashash was a very big *tzaddik*, Daniel had told me. He had written the Siddur Hakavanot that the Rav always used, and so the Rav wanted this *hillula* to be the most elaborate one we had ever held. I had put a lot of effort into the meal, bought three kilos of fresh meat and cooked it in wine and fresh herbs. The table was laid with cream and gold disposables that Yael had bought especially. Yael was my right hand…she was the eldest, and I expected her to do everything I asked of her.

I stood in front of the mirror. Daniel and I had been married fifteen years. Under my eyes, I noticed tiny, gentle creases. Lines that had been penciled in by the artist of time.

The members of the circle arrived late, close to midnight, at our home. So late that all the children had fallen asleep. The Rav sat at the head of the table. The table looked beautiful. Yael had gone out to pick up the disposables. She was the eldest…it was her job to help out. Yigal took up his position to the right of the Rav.

Before Daniel sat down, I pulled him aside. "Where were you?" I asked him. "I thought you'd be here three hours ago."

Daniel shrugged and tried to move away.

Eran edged past us. "The Rashash was the father of all Kabbalists," he said. "It takes time to prepare for such a *hillula*."

Two-year-old Hillel heard the noise. He woke up, slipped off the couch. He ran to Daniel and hugged his legs.

Daniel shook off his pudgy arms and pushed him away. "Where are the kids? They should be here. Why can't you organize anything?"

I wanted to tell Daniel that we'd waited for them for hours, but I didn't. Because I could tell, by the stiffness in his shoulders, the way his lips had disappeared into his beard, that something was wrong. "What's the matter?" I asked.

He frowned. "Nothing."

He shuffled toward the end of the table, as if he had to convince his feet to follow each other forward, and sat down. Why wasn't he sitting next to the Rav, like he usually did? It wasn't right. He always sat next to the Rav. And then I noticed the stranger. With curly *peyot* that stood out above his ears like two horns. I had first seen him at the *kever* of Abaye and Rava. He was sitting next to the Rav, in Daniel's usual seat. I hurried after Daniel. But Yigal was there, in front of me.

"The Rav wants you to serve the soup now," he said.

I hadn't made soup. I never made soup for a *hillula*. Soup was for Shabbat. How was I going to get soup? I looked for Daniel. He had to tell me what to do. But Daniel was hunched over, one hand covering his eyes. And then… somehow…maybe it was an idea sent to me by the Rav himself…I realized what I had to do.

"Ask the Rav if I can serve soup after the meat," I said.

In the kitchen, I began spooning the meat onto oval platters, pouring thick sauce over the slices. But it was only when Yigal told me that the Rav gave his permission that I woke Shimmy to carry them through to the living room.

It happened after the Rav had finished eating the meat. He looked up. His gray eyes were the color of water. "There is evil in this world," he said. "The evil brings darkness. Darkness and filth. Impurity."

I didn't like to hear about the evil. I didn't like the children to hear about it.

The Rav called to the stranger, "Emanuel." Emanuel brought him his staff, tightly wrapped in blue and yellow satin. The Rav put it on the table and began to unwrap it. After he unwrapped each section, he ran his fingers over the carved letters. His lips moved, but I didn't hear a sound.

Emanuel folded the fabric neatly and piled it up in front of the Rav.

"We need to empty the world of demons," he whispered. He lifted the bare staff and pointed it at Daniel.

In the kitchen, I stopped chopping onions and carrots for the soup. The staff was covered with the names of Hashem. He couldn't point it at Daniel. It was...dangerous. It could make something – I didn't know what – happen. I heard the knife clatter onto the floor. Watched it skid under the refrigerator.

"Demons are here."

The staff was still pointed at Daniel. But it couldn't be...not Daniel. Daniel was good...faithful. Out of the corner of my eyes, I saw Shimmy, his hands over his ears.

"This evil person must purify himself. He must purge his body." The Rav's soft voice snaked around the room. Incantation after incantation. Suddenly he stopped and stared at Emanuel. His eyebrows drew together until they were one black slash. "Are you concerned? Worried?"

Emanuel stiffened. His eyes slid left...right.

As if he wasn't sure the Rav was talking to him.

"If you doubt me..." he leaned toward Emanuel, making it clear that he was, in fact, talking to him, "...you can leave. Now."

Emanuel shook his head. Once.

I looked at Daniel. Daniel had to say something. Deny it. I wanted to put my hands over my ears. Like Shimmy had done. Block out the words that couldn't be true.

Each chant was softer than the one before, until all I could hear was a gentle swish. Like waves breaking on the shore. The Rav's eyes blazed with white fire. He was looking at me. Tremors ran up and down my arms like armies of ants. He mustn't read my mind. I had to change my thoughts. Whatever the Rav said was true. Always true.

Daniel put both his hands over his face. His fingers opened and closed like the leaves of fan.

He had to apologize. I willed him to stand up. Speak. Beg.

But Daniel didn't move. He kept his hands over his eyes and his lips sealed.

I leaned against the door of the refrigerator. I saw Shimmy back out of the living room, into the corridor. The Rav couldn't be right. But he was right. I had to say something. To defend Daniel. But I was a child again. A child trying to explain something to Ima, to Ayelet, to Yossi. The words of denial stuck to my tongue like a stubborn hair. Anger began to bubble inside me.

Daniel was my husband. He was part of me. I had to defend him. I pushed myself away from the refrigerator.

"An evil, dark man..." The stick was still pointing at Daniel, but it was wavering. Changing direction.

And then the Rav was staring at me. The flecks of silver in his eyes flashed. He mustn't read my thoughts. If he read my thoughts, he would...he would turn on me. Like he had turned on Daniel. And I wanted to serve the *tzaddik* that Daniel had brought into our lives. Into our home. The Rav stared at me, and the fire of my anger began to lessen. Why couldn't Daniel serve the Rav better? Why was he making trouble for us? Why did I always have to defend him? I turned away.

The soup was bubbling. I would serve it soon. But first I needed to breathe. I pushed aside the drapes and walked out onto the porch. Put my hands on the cold railing. I had never painted it. I rubbed my hands over the bar and felt the old paint flaking off some more.

"He's a stupid man."

My hands tightened around the bar. It was the Rav's voice. But the Rav had never spoken to me except to thank me for the food I cooked. "A stupid man who understands nothing."

I heard a swish of fabric. I turned around slowly and saw a dark blue shadow melt into the light coming from the living room.

***

The morning after the *hillula* of the Rashash, Daniel didn't get up for his usual minyan. I was glad. I wanted to tell him that he had to apologize to the Rav. Tell the Rav that he had done wrong. That he wanted to change. That he didn't want to be evil. I opened my eyes and watched him bend over to look for his shoes under the bed.

"You need to speak to him," I said.

"Who?"

"The Rav. Tell him that..." I couldn't tell Daniel that he had done wrong... "...that there was a mistake."

Daniel straightened up. "Don't talk like that."

I shivered. Could the Rav hear me? Hear me even though he wasn't in the house? I made myself think...fast...the Rav was right. He was always right.

And then another thought made its way into my mind. What had happened before the circle came to the house last night? What had Daniel done?

Daniel turned to face me. His eyes were bloodshot. As if he'd been awake all night. "I don't want you to talk like that about the Rav. It's not okay."

I knew it wasn't okay. The Rav would hear me, because he could tap into the heavenly spheres. But…Daniel…I wanted to tell Daniel that he should work on himself. Urge him to change whatever it was that the Rav saw, but… but I never told Daniel what to do. "Where are you going? To the yeshiva?" I had to help him. I loved him.

Daniel stood up.

It felt strange. Thinking that Daniel had to work on himself. Daniel had always told me that I had a lot of inner work to do. And now it was up to him to change. He had to see that. "Where are you going?" My voice was louder now. "To the yeshiva?" He had to go to the yeshiva. Fix things up.

Daniel rubbed the back of his neck. "No, not to the yeshiva. That's not what I need to do today," he said. He walked to the door.

I stuffed my face deep into my pillow. So deep that I could feel my nose rubbing against the mattress. Daniel's pain was mine. I knew that it hurt to be told to change…because Daniel had told me and hurt me so many times.

We never spoke about it again. But something had changed.

The next day, Daniel did go to yeshiva. When he came home, he was even quieter than usual. Without eating, he went to lie down. I had sent Yael to the grocery to buy oatmeal and chocolate chips so that we could bake together later in the evening, but she hadn't come home yet. Where was she? She should have been back by now. The children were playing with a Playmobil set that my mother had sent them. I followed Daniel into the bedroom.

"Emanuel was thrown out," he said, without opening his eyes. "The Rav told him to leave."

Emanuel…the newest member of the circle…who carried the staff of Rav Natas. "Leave?"

"He didn't know how to listen," Daniel said. "He asked too many questions."

What hadn't Emanuel listened to? What had he questioned? Had the Rav read his mind? There were so many things I wanted to ask Daniel about. But I didn't ask him one question. Because…because I wasn't like Emanuel. I knew that there were things that I couldn't understand.

"He missed his chance," Daniel said.

Suddenly I was glad that Daniel hadn't answered the Rav at the *hillula* of the Rashash. Rav Natas could have thrown him out. Told him to leave the group. I closed the bedroom door. Sat on the floor with the children and set up the goat pen with the Playmobil pieces. I felt bad for Emanuel. He wouldn't be part of the Rav's circle. He didn't have the merit to serve the Rav.

Life and the routine that wasn't a routine carried on. We still went as a group to *kivrei tzaddikim*. Rav Natas and the circle still came to our home for a *hillula*, once every few weeks. At every *hillula*, I felt the same old anxieties: Would I sufficiently control my thoughts? Sit correctly? Would the children behave? And now, in addition to these worries, I added a new one: Would the Rav lash out at Daniel again? He usually did. Daniel never defended himself. And no one else did either.

***

The sky was the color of old, yellowed newspaper. A hot wind, heavy with dust and stale smells, tossed faded candy wrappers and plastic bags high into the air. They floated up and then plummeted down when the gust sucked the life out of them. It was an evening in April, the third day of a relentless *sharav*. Daniel and I were sitting on the porch, trying to feel the ocean breeze that the weather man had promised us.

"The Rav told me to take Shimmy out of his school and put him in his yeshiva," Daniel said.

I blinked. Under my eyelids, dust particles moved up and down, sandpapering my eyes.

"He starts tomorrow. He'll come with me in the morning."

Shimmy was twelve years old. Soon after Rosh Hashanah, we'd celebrate his bar mitzvah. It wasn't the right time to move him. He needed his friends. I looked at Daniel. Willed him to tell me that it was good. That this was the best thing for Shimmy. But he was silent. So I didn't tell him my worries. Besides, if the Rav had decided, that meant that this was the best thing for Shimmy. For us. "That's…nice," I said. "There's no one else his age in the Rav's yeshiva. It's a special merit." I wondered if Shimmy had friends. He'd stopped bringing his friends to the house years ago. "He needs a Gemara. What are they learning?"

"There are books in the yeshiva." Daniel rolled his shoulders, his head. "My neck hurts," he said.

Was it from tension? Like the headaches I had started to get? I watched a ladybug speeding across the floor, stopping at a crack in the tiles. None of the children brought school friends to the house anymore. The younger kids weren't attending any school, so they never made school friends. The older kids did have friends that they had grown up with, but since our crazy lifestyle excluded any semblance of routine, it was hard to know when we'd be around. When these friends came around to the house, we were often away on a trip to the north. Or if we were at home, we were either all sleeping the daylight hours away, or the men were at the mikveh. As a result, the friends that came around kept missing the kids. Sure, some of the neighbors still dropped in occasionally. Five-year-old Shani from upstairs adored playing with Hillel. Aside from our hectic lifestyle, being the youngest child in the family meant he loved the extra attention. And on long Shabbat afternoons, there was more chance of us being around, and then while their parents rested, neighborhood kids would come around.

"Did you tell Shimmy?" I asked Daniel.

He shook his head. "You tell him."

I stood up. Where was Shimmy? Had he gone to *cheder* this morning? Was he at home? I didn't know. I couldn't keep track of the older children. Once, I remembered, I had known the names of all of their friends. Like I knew every child's favorite color, his favorite board game. When had I stopped paying attention to these things? I couldn't remember. Now, there was always shopping to do, cooking to do. My head was starting to hurt. A drumming set up behind my left eye. The Rav was going to teach Shimmy. A personal tutor. A tremendous merit. I had to bake a cake. The air was suddenly lighter, cooler. The *sharav* was finally lifting.

The following day, I sent Shimmy off with a coffee cake that I had baked especially for his first day in the yeshiva. All day, I waited for him to come back, to tell me how it had been. When Daniel finally came back in the evening, he came back alone.

"Where's Shimmy?" I asked.

"He's boarding at the yeshiva. He's big enough to sleep out."

A surge of disappointment filled me. I wanted to see him. Hear how it had gone. But I didn't say that. I smiled. "Did he enjoy it? Did you learn with him?"

Daniel rubbed his palms against his pants. "Why are you asking so many questions? Questions all the time. If the Rav said that this is good for him, then this is what we must do."

I knew Daniel was upset. Maybe Shimmy had acted up in the yeshiva. Embarrassed Daniel in front of the Rav. His first day. He should have made an effort to behave well. Why didn't he realize what a great merit he had? "Do you want a drink?" I asked Daniel.

He shook his head.

How was Shimmy going to manage without any clothes? Should I send him food? Did Tiferet cook for the boys in the yeshiva? Suddenly I noticed that Daniel wasn't only upset with Shimmy. He looked…strange.

Daniel swallowed. "They're molding him there, Racheli," he said. "Disciplining him so that…so that the evil will be purged." Daniel traced the outline of his lips with his fingers. Put his hand over his mouth.

It was good to be molded. Molded into a *tzaddik*. Rav Natas would help Shimmy. So why did Daniel look so…strange? I didn't want to think about the evil. Shimmy was a child. Children weren't evil. Rav Natas, who knew everything, knew that too. Surely.

The next morning, Daniel didn't go to yeshiva. He went to the Kotel. I had prepared a bag of things for Shimmy, and it stood by the door. Daniel would take it there later… But Daniel didn't come back.

Just before lunchtime, I was crouched at the door of the washing machine, pushing in a colored load, when I heard the front door opening. The children were all out. I thought it was Daniel. Then I heard the dull thump of Rav Natas's staff against the floor.

He had never come without a warning. Daniel wasn't here… Would he answer me if I called him? I stood up quickly. So quickly that I felt the blood rush to my head. And then I saw them. Rav Natas and behind him, Eran, Shimmy, and Yigal. The blood thundered in my head. Refused to go down. Shimmy was hurt. His lip was swollen, the color of a ripe plum. What had happened?

Rav Natas sat at the table and signaled for the others to sit down. Rav Natas didn't look at me. He stared at Shimmy. "I am molding him," he said.

Shimmy turned to look at me. A quick glance.

His eyes were full of fear. So much like the eyes of the wounded kitten that he had brought home and kept in a shoebox on the porch. I moved toward him. To put my hand on his shoulder. But Rav Natas lifted his hand, and I couldn't move.

"One day you will thank me for disciplining him. Without this, he could even murder you."

I stared at Shimmy. Could he hurt me? Hurt the children?

The Rav took out his pendulum. It swung back and forth before it hung still. "Is Shimmy dangerous?" he asked.

The pendulum swung back and forth.

"Must we help him to purge the evil inside him?"

The pendulum kept swinging in the same way.

"The angels are telling me that he has the stain of sin," Natas said. He stared at the pendulum again.

Shimmy…I had to bathe his lip.

Rav Natas looked up. "In a former *gilgul*, Shimmy attacked Yigal. You can see the signs around his eyes, his lips…"

I stared at the white patches on Yigal's face.

Rav Natas was gazing at the pendulum. It was swinging from side to side now. He looked at Yigal and nodded.

Yigal's arm went back. He slapped Shimmy's face. And I didn't move. I watched them stand up…the Rav, Yigal, Shimmy…I watched them walk out of the house.

When Daniel came back, an hour later…or was it two…I was on the couch. Frozen. The children had come in, taken food, and gone out. Ahuva had taken Hillel.

Daniel looked at me. "The Rav came?" he said.

I couldn't nod. Couldn't speak.

Daniel looked at me. Looked at the bag standing by the door. "I'm not going to the yeshiva today. I can't watch it."

I stared at Daniel. He knew. He knew, and he was leaving Shimmy there. Did that mean that it was okay? Did this have to happen to get rid of the evil inside him? When Yael asked me where Shimmy was, I explained to her that it was a special merit for Shimmy to learn in the same yeshiva as Abba. Later, I heard her repeating my words to the kids. She added that Shimmy had his own room and that he didn't have to keep it tidy. He could do whatever he wanted.

***

Three weeks after he began learning in Rav Natas's yeshiva, on a Shabbat morning, Shimmy walked home. The door opened quietly, and he slipped into his usual seat. Daniel was in the middle of testing six-year-old Meir on his *parashah* sheet.

I pushed my chair back, heard it clatter against the floor. I hadn't seen Shimmy since the morning he had come to the house with Rav Natas. He had called a few times, but he hadn't said much. Except to ask me to send him money and food with Daniel.

Daniel put down the *parashah* sheet.

"I'm not going back," Shimmy said to no one. He reached for the bowl of cholent.

It was cold already. I could tell by the way the gravy had formed a crust on top of the potatoes. His lip had healed, I saw.

He tipped the bowl toward an extra plate that was on the table, reached for the fork of one of the other kids and began to shovel potatoes and beans into his mouth.

Daniel stared at the tablecloth. He began pushing challah crumbs together to form a pile. "You have to go back," he said. He called Hillel, pulled him onto his lap, and began to sing a song.

Shimmy ate. He got up, went to the freezer, and began rummaging through the boxes there. "He hits me," Shimmy yelled into the freezer. He pulled his head out and stared at me. His eyes weren't filled with fear like they had been that morning when he had come home. Anger smoldered there.

Daniel finished his song. "You walk him back, Racheli," he said.

I didn't get up.

Daniel picked up the *parashah* sheet and rolled it into a tube. "You don't have to walk him back," he said. "You can decide not to. But then the evil inside him will grow. If he stays here, the work that the Rav has done will have to begin again. You don't want that, do you?"

I looked at Shimmy. He had pulled out the box of peanut butter cookies that Yael had baked and sat at the kitchen table. He stuffed one into his mouth, chewed, and before he swallowed, he stuffed another one into his mouth.

"You don't have to walk him back, but you'll have to tell the Rav why you didn't do it," he said.

I stood up. My legs were shaky, Jell-O that hadn't set. I took a water bottle out of the fridge. Two plastic cups. And I walked Shimmy back. Shimmy stayed in Rav Natas's yeshiva. He would come home, sometimes during the week, sometimes for Shabbat. His eyes were no longer filled with anger. They were empty. Sometimes, when he caught me looking at him, I noticed a flash of raw pain, or was it resignation, but it was never more than a flash, so fast that I wasn't sure I'd even seen it. Shimmy tried a couple more times to tell us that he was being hurt, but we just kept telling him to keep on listening to the Rav, since he knew best what was needed. So he suffered quietly, knowing that no one was going to save him. He never again complained about what Rav Natas was doing to him.

***

The following week, after an early Seudah Shlishit, Daniel and I got ready to walk to Rav Natas's house. I gave Yael the bag of nosh that I had bought and told her to take the kids to the park. Daniel and I didn't talk as we walked there. We'd never talked much, but after Shimmy joined the Rav's yeshiva, we talked even less.

When we got there, the Rav was in the middle of saying something. I wanted to hear him. Tiferet had set up some drinks and cookies. I sat at the end of the table, not anywhere near the three boys from the circle. Where were the other three boys? Tiferet came to sit near me. I didn't ask her where the other boys were, because we never discussed what was happening in the circle. Perhaps they had been sent away. Sent away for not listening to the Rav. I focused my thoughts. The Rav was holy. A *tzaddik* whom we could serve. Poor boys...why wouldn't they want to serve a *tzaddik* in whatever way he told them to?

The Rav spoke about the darkness in Mitzrayim. The evil forces that had ruled there. How these forces had escaped Mitzrayim with the Jews. How we had to destroy them. Were these the forces that clung to Daniel and to Shimmy? I didn't know. I didn't speak to angels. I didn't know how to read the minds of people. I looked at Rav Natas, watched him read from the books that Yigal passed him, watched how he made a *berachah* using his Siddur Hakavanot. I was lucky to serve him. Lucky that he knew how to rid the world of evil.

The room grew darker and darker. Orange light from the street lamps filtered into the house. The Rav stood up and left the room. The boys, together with Daniel, began to sing a song. The words were too loud. I couldn't make out Daniel's voice. He was singing too softly. Irritation scratched inside me. Tiferet was cutting up a watermelon, carving it into paper-thin slices. I never managed to do that. I needed to breathe. I wandered into the kitchen. The door to the back yard was open. I walked out.

Rav Natas was there, in front of the laundry lines. His eyes half-closed, swaying to the singing that drifted out from the living room.

I turned to go back in.

"Racheli…"

I stopped.

The Rav stepped closer. He kept his eyes on the ground. "Rav Tzefanyah…" he said. "Rav Tzefanyah was right."

Rav Tzefanyah? I didn't want to hear about him. And certainly not from the Rav.

"Almost right. You are a *gilgul.*"

No! It couldn't be true. I was Racheli. Only Racheli. The Rav himself had told me that I didn't need to marry Rav Tzefanyah. I backed away. Stumbled against the step of the kitchen door.

"You are not destined for Daniel."

Not destined for Daniel. I was married to Daniel. It couldn't be. The Rav was looking at me. Shots of silver sped through his pale eyes.

"But evil men cannot hear the voices of angels. You are a *gilgul*, but Rav Tzefanyah made a mistake. I saved you…because you are destined for me."

The Rav picked up the hem of his robe. "This must remain our secret," he said. "You don't want the heavenly courts to become angry with you." He walked past me. "And when the time is right, when the angels tell me…I will give you the message. And you will decide, you and Daniel…you will decide if you are going to follow your destiny." The Rav turned around. The light from a streetlamp picked up the embroidery on his robe, making it glitter. He didn't turn to face me, but I heard his voice drift over his shoulder. "The small children…the evil must be purged from them too. You will know what you have to do."

Behind me, the circle, three boys plus Daniel, began a second song. Now I could pick out Daniel's voice. I stared at the laundry lines. A green floor rag fluttered from them. Could it be? Was I a *gilgul*? Was I destined for the Rav? Was I going to serve him as a wife? I sat on the step. Leaned against the doorjamb. I had to think that the Rav was right. He was there…in the next room…he would read my mind. See that I was doubting him. I didn't want that. I closed my eyes. And what did I have to do to purge the evil out of the smaller children? Which smaller children? I didn't hear voices, I didn't know anything. The Rav would show me the way.

Close to midnight, we left to walk home. Daniel hurried ahead, but I was tired. Tired and confused. Suddenly Eran was standing beside me. I ignored him, quickened my pace toward Daniel.

"You need to watch him," Eran called to me.

Watch him? Watch who? I turned around.

Eran had caught up with me.

"Daniel. You need to watch Daniel," he said. "The Rav has seen darkness in his soul."

Darkness? In Daniel? It couldn't be. Daniel was good. Daniel was pure. And yet…the Rav knew everything. Daniel had told me that the Rav could read minds. And…why…why had the Rav sent Daniel to seven *kivrei tzaddikim*? And if there was darkness in Daniel's soul…there was all the more reason not to tell him what the Rav had told me…that I was going to be his wife.

"Daniel…" I called him, but he didn't turn his head. I began to run toward him. How was I going to keep such a big secret from him? It was such a load! When Rav Tzefanyah had told us that I was destined to marry him, Daniel and I had at least had each other to lean on…but now I was all alone. Now all I had left was the Rav. And I had to trust him. Put all of my trust in him… just like we had been trusting him for the past five years.

***

Rav Natas had been at our house for two days. The *hillula* for the *tzaddik*, I don't remember which *tzaddik*, had stretched on and on. There were only three boys in the circle now. And it was easier to cook for them. It was almost morning of the second night when Daniel fell asleep. In his place at the end of the table. He'd never moved back to sit beside the Rav…even after Emanuel had been thrown out of the circle.

I watched Daniel's head tilt back, rest against the wall behind him. His jaw dropped and his mouth opened. I could see the glint of light on his fillings.

Rav Natas told Shimmy to bring him his staff. But this time, he didn't unwrap it. "Brainless, an ignoramus who will never put together the *kavanot* for Hashem's name, an *am haaretz* who has never learned a page of Gemara," he said.

Yigal rubbed his eyes. The end of his nose. He nodded.

The skin around his nostrils had turned white, I noticed.

Rav Natas adjusted his turban. It was one that Daniel and I had bought for him. But it was small. Every time he wore it, he had to keep adjusting it. And when it moved, I noticed a thin red line caused by the pressure. "An evil man. A man without hope," he said. Then, for a fraction of a second, he looked at me.

I looked away.

Daniel slept on. I was glad he hadn't heard the Rav. His words would have hurt him. In that spot in my chest where the feelings I could never name lived, I felt...anger. I was angry. Daniel had to change. Why hadn't he asked the Rav what he had to do to fix himself? Why hadn't he used the powers of the *tzaddik*?

Finally, when the sun was already rising, the Rav stood up. He went into one of the bedrooms. Shimmy shook Daniel. I watched him start, blink his eyes, and stumble to the bedroom. I curled up on the couch.

I'd barely fallen asleep when I heard Yael calling to me. "I'm going out." Yael stood in the doorway. Her hair was pulled into a ponytail, but she hadn't brushed it. Her shirt was wrinkled. I didn't iron anything anymore.

We slept for hours and hours. I heard the children getting up. Opening the fridge. I had to wake up. Take care of the kids. But I couldn't. My head was hurting. Worse than ever before. In the afternoon, I heard the men getting ready to go to the mikveh and to shul. I had to cook. In case they came back.

It was already dark when they came back. "Where are the little boys?" Daniel asked as soon as he walked in.

I pointed to the bedrooms. I had bathed the children, scrambled eggs for their supper, and put them to bed. Daniel walked to the bedroom. He woke up the children and seated them beside Rav Natas at the table.

Aharon and Hillel slipped off their seats. Eran caught them and pushed them back.

The Rav began to ask them questions, one after the other, so fast that there was no time to answer. Which animal is dangerous? What does a lion eat? Where do birds sleep? Three-year-old Hillel began to cry. Aharon stared at the Rav.

"Why aren't you answering?" he said. "Why can't you think?" He looked at Daniel. "Simple questions that they cannot answer." It was a statement. "There is an evil spirit inside them that is eating their words."

Answer, I begged Aharon in my heart. They were children…surely there was no evil inside them?

Aharon began to cry.

The Rav stared at me. "Why are you thinking that?" he asked.

I looked away. Suddenly, I was too afraid to look at him. Maybe he would see the evil within me.

The Rav took out his pendulum. He raised his head slowly, looked at Daniel. "Leave the room," he said. "Go out of this house. You…you have evil forces within you. And because of the evil that darkens your soul, I cannot help the children when you are in this house."

Eran moved toward Daniel.

He would drag him out of the house if Daniel didn't listen to Rav. But of course Daniel would listen to the Rav. We always listened to the Rav.

Daniel shuffled to the front door and walked out.

Yigal picked up the notebook that was beside the Rav.

The pendulum swung in circles. "The evil spirit will leave them. They will become successful," he said. The pendulum was still swinging when Eran reached for Aharon and shook him. Hard. Yigal shook Hillel. Up and down. Side to side.

And I watched them.

***

Dina called me one day soon after. It had been three years since we'd last spoken. She and Avi had finally had a baby boy after four girls, and she wanted to get my advice. I pitied her baby, coming into the world without the spiritual protection of a *tzaddik*.

For some reason, when I told Daniel about the new baby, he told me that we should go to the bris. Dina seemed surprised to hear that Daniel and I would be coming, but she was happy. Especially when I offered to drive her to the mother and baby home after the bris. Avi even asked Daniel and me to be *kvatter* and *kvatterin*, to bring the baby to the mohel.

Dina was scattered before the bris began, fussing over her four little girls, giving out lollipops for the kids to suck during the actual bris so that they'd keep quiet. I had given her that idea. She kept asking about lollipops and sweet wine, but she wasn't focused on the only important thing.

"There are forces of evil out there, trying to latch on to the pure. You need a *kameya* to protect the baby," I told her.

"Um, hi, mazal tov?" Dina said. And then she asked me unimportant questions about wrapping and unwrapping the baby.

I needed to help her see what was important. "I can ask our Rav to write him a *kameya*. But you need to tell me his name," I said.

Dina looked around. "Yeah, sure," she said and began unwrapping the swaddling blanket.

"All my kids have *kameyot* ," I said. "It purifies them. Purges the darkness."

"Well, this baby here is eight days old, and he hasn't had time to do anything evil that needs purging," she snapped.

I sighed. I had to make her understand. She was leaving her child so vulnerable to the forces of darkness. She needed a *tzaddik* to guide her. A *tzaddik* like we had.

Later, as we drove to the mother and baby home, I tried to help her understand. To know what she must do. "There are deep things going on in the world," I said. "And only a few people can see them. *Tzaddikim*. We have *tzaddikim* who can guide us. They can give us the *tikkun* to fix us up." It was hard talking to her when she was sitting behind me, but I had to make her understand.

"All I want is to get to the mother and baby home in one piece. Maybe slow down, Racheli? You're driving like a maniac!" Dina said.

I swatted her words away like a fly. "You need *tikkun*, Dina. The baby needs *tikkun*." I slowed down for her.

"No *tikkun*, thanks. I'm already doing enough running a home for five kids. I don't have time for a *tikkun*," she said, and then added, "You didn't bring the kids."

"They don't go out to places like this," Daniel said.

"Places like what?"

I could see her face in my mirror. "There's darkness out there," I said.

Dina sighed. "This is not good, Racheli," she said.

She looked afraid. Because she didn't have anyone to help her.

"You need to root out the evil," I said.

Dina muttered something, and I thought I heard the word *cult*. How little she understood about holiness, about purity. When she got out of the car, she didn't look at me. Maybe she didn't have the strength to see her own evil reflected there.

I waited till we were back on the road, and then I turned sideways to look at Daniel. He was engrossed in his *sefer*. "Daniel?" I waited to make sure that he was listening. "We're so lucky," I said. "We're not clueless to what's going on in the world. We know about *tikkunim* and we have a *tzaddik* to guide us."

***

In the middle of the summer, Rav Natas sent Daniel to Chatzor with Eran and Yigal. And he called me for the first time.

"Daniel isn't at home," I said when I recognized his voice. Why was I telling him where Daniel was? The Rav himself had sent him to Chatzor to the *kever* of Choni Hame'agel. That was why I didn't have the van.

"I don't need Daniel. Daniel needs to get rid of the evil that darkens his soul. We need to meet in Geulah," Rav Natas said. "Rechov Amos, near the end, at ten tonight."

I was there. Leaning against a low stone wall. Behind the wall, two cats chased each other and howled. It was ten fifteen. The Rav wasn't going to come.

And then he was there. Walking toward me. He was wearing the long black frock of a Rosh Yeshiva. On his chest, the pendulum swayed with each step. He didn't look at me. "If you listen to me, you will be blessed. You cannot pity the children. I will clean the evil out of them, make them pure and holy, but you must not stand in my way." He turned and began to walk away.

But what about us? What about our lives together? He had told me that I was going to be his wife.

The Rav stopped. He didn't turn to face me. But I heard his words. "At the end of summer, you will divorce Daniel."

The words floated through the darkness toward me. If I peered closely, I would see them, I was sure. I sank against the wall. Scratched my nails against the rough stone. I couldn't do it. I couldn't divorce Daniel. We were married, weren't we? And I still loved him. I watched the Rav walk away, and I knew. I knew that the Rav had told Daniel that he was going to divorce me. That was why he had sent him to Chatzor with Yigal and Eran. They would make sure that he didn't come back before the Rav had spoken to me. Not that Daniel would have come back before the Rav allowed him to.

I was so confused… Who could I ask? Who could I confide in? Since I'd married Daniel, I'd always turned to him with anything I didn't know. Could I ask Abba? My brothers? Once I'd thought that they knew everything. Could I ask Ima? But they weren't in the circle. There was no way that they could understand anything about the holiness of the Rav. I watched the people hurrying by. Didn't they realize that there was a whole world that they knew nothing about? Who was going to help me?

If only I could share this with Daniel. Daniel always knew what to say. But the Rav had said that there was so much evil in him. He'd told him over and over again. Till I wanted to put my hands on my ears. Why…why couldn't Daniel fix the evil inside himself? Why? If he got rid of the evil, maybe we could change the situation. I had to divorce Daniel…even Rav Tzefanyah had seen that we weren't destined for each other. But it was only Rav Natas, who could speak to angels, who could see my real *zivug*. My soul mate. Was I worthy of being his wife? The wife of the Rav? And what about Tiferet? The Rav was married to her.

After Daniel came back from Chatzor, he no longer looked at me. When he spoke to me, he would look at some point beyond my shoulder. Part of me wanted to scream. To tell him that I was still his wife. That he had to fix himself up. But part of me knew that our paths were parting.

Months of total confusion and sadness followed. I was in mourning. I knew that I was going to divorce Daniel. I knew that when the Rav told him to give me a divorce, he would do it. He hadn't refused to take Shimmy to the yeshiva. He wouldn't refuse to divorce me. But Daniel and I had built something together. Would he let go of it? Would I allow him to? I hated it when I had these thoughts. Maybe the Rav would read them. Maybe the angels would carry my thoughts to him. I had to think about the great merit. The wife of a *tzaddik*. When I went shopping, took the children to the park, prayed at the Kotel, I watched the women walking by. I wanted to tell them that I was going to be the wife of a *tzaddik*. I was going to be a faithful servant. Do whatever he told me to do. When I thought about this, my heart would begin to pound, my breath would catch in my throat. Sometimes I would feel a headache coming on…but I ignored it. I was filled with excitement, delight, elation. And yet…fifteen years cannot be thrown to the wind with the words of one man.

Unless that man is your leader. Unless that man has been telling you how to live your life for more than five years. Telling you when to eat, when to sleep, when to pray, where to go.

***

That summer was the hottest summer that Israel had ever seen. From the Golan in the north to the Negev in the south, every man and beast sweated and panted. The sky was an enormous, upturned oven…heavy as the oven the Arabs used to bake pita. Every spear of sunlight was trapped beneath, reflected back a thousand times. We longed for a breath of breeze, but the hot air mocked us. We prayed for a cooler day, but every day, the sun rose, hotter than the day before. The jasmine on my porch drooped and shriveled despite the water the children splashed on it when they played in the inflatable pool that Yael had bought for them.

Daniel was often away. Sometimes for a week at a time. The Rav sent him to the north, with Eran and Yigal, each time to a different group of *kivrei tzaddikim*. He was praying, I knew, that the evil inside him would go, leave him clean. When Daniel was at home, the Rav would come to the house. Sometimes it was for a *hillula*, sometimes not. But every time, we sat around the table for hours. Yael, Shimmy, Yaakov, Ahuva, and even seven-year-old Meir knew that they had to sit at the table. Watch the Rav read from the Siddur Hakavanot. Watch him read from his book on Kabbalah. Until they fell asleep on their chairs.

But four-year-old Aharon and three-year-old Hillel were too young to sit. Too young to watch the Rav in silence. After an hour, they would slip off their chairs, run to this bedroom or that, hide behind the washing machine or in a closet, creep out of the house. And when Eran and Yigal would find them, the questions would begin. Questions that they could never answer.

The Rav would swing his pendulum, speak to the angels, and Yigal would record what they had said. The Rav would unwrap his staff. Then Eran would shake Aharon, and Yigal would shake Hillel. We never said a word against the Rav. Because what he was doing was for the good of the child.

When Daniel was away, the Rav would call me. I would leave Yael to look after the children. She was old enough to do everything. They were usually up until after midnight. It was late, unhealthy for young children, something inside me, a tiny part of me that was still thinking rationally, cried out. But it didn't matter, because it was vacation time, and anyway, even before vacation, they had been going to sleep at that time, because they rarely went to school. I would meet the Rav in our usual spot at the end of Rechov Amos. We never met for longer than a few minutes, and he never looked at me. He always spoke about the darkness in the world, the blackness that surrounded us, the evil that we had to get rid of. Sometimes, he would berate Daniel. Two or three times, he spoke about our marriage. Before every meeting, I wondered if this time, this time it would be the night that he would tell me that it was time to divorce Daniel. I would come back home, crying with relief, crying with frustration. I didn't want to divorce Daniel, but I did want to.

Finally, at the end of October, Rav Natas called Daniel and me to the yeshiva. We both knew that the call meant it was time for our divorce. But we didn't speak about it. Not after the Rav called and not during the short drive to Mekor Baruch. We arrived there just before two o'clock in the morning. Like five years earlier, the streets were quiet, bathed in warm, yellow light. Again, there was one white lamplight on the street. Again, Daniel parked beside it. Again there was a cloud of tiny moths fluttering around in never-ending circles, pulled by the bright light.

Rav Natas sat at the head of the same long, heavy table. "Perhaps…" he said to Daniel as soon as we walked in. "Perhaps…when the evil has been purged completely, you will remarry your wife. It is a mitzvah, stated in *Ketubot,* to remarry your divorced wife."

Daniel nodded. Rav Natas had told him about this mitzvah several times. There was a chance, then, a chance that Daniel and I would remarry one day.

I glanced at Daniel. Did he want to tell me something? Now…before we were severed apart? Daniel was staring at the embroidery on the Rav's robe. Look at me, I pleaded. As soon as the plea left my heart, my mind squashed it. The Rav would hear it. I couldn't think like that. I was going to be his wife. The wife of a *tzaddik*. Quickly, I glanced at the Rav. Surely, he would look at me? Send me a message? But his gray eyes were still. Pools of clear water without a ripple moving across the surface.

And then I saw the *get* on the table. Twelve lines of Aramaic that were going to separate Daniel and me. The Rav nodded. Yigal and Eran signed beneath the last line. Yigal rolled up the thick paper. And Daniel handed me the *get*.

He began to shuffle backwards. I could hear his feet scraping against the floor tiles. Now the Rav would look at me. Now. But he didn't.

I followed Daniel up the steps, pulling my weight up by clutching the banister. There were no moths fluttering around the white lamppost when we got into the car. Perhaps they had died.

No one – except for the Rav, Yigal, and Eran – knew that Daniel and I had divorced. Since Daniel could no longer sleep at home, he spent his nights in the shuls in the Old City. I hadn't known that emotions could give you a physical pain. But now I knew. Whenever I thought about Daniel, my chest throbbed with pain. I tried to push the pain away. To focus on the new role that was waiting for me. But I still missed him. The children thought Abba was in the north. They didn't ask me why he wasn't coming home, when he would be back. They already knew that we never knew the answers to these questions. Daniel did come home sometimes. I could tell by the food that was missing, the wet towel lying on his bed, the dirty laundry on the floor. A few times, I found him asleep on the couch in the living room. I would hurry the little children out to the park for breakfast. Before I gave in to the urge to wake him up and talk to him. And when we would come back, Daniel was no longer there. And Rav Natas didn't call me. When I finally called him, he didn't answer my calls.

Somehow, at the end of October, we got ready for Shimmy's bar mitzvah.

***

"What's this nonsense about *hechsherim*? Why can't we just bring in a caterer instead of having you run around like a chicken without a head? A bar mitzvah, especially your first one, should be catered."

Abba picked up Aharon and kissed him on the head.

"Careful of your back, Abba!" I loved to see him enjoying the kids.

"It's too much for you, Racheli."

Abba walked into the living room. But he couldn't sit on the couch. One boy from the circle was sleeping on the couch. Two more were sleeping on the floor. The boys often came here to sleep. Sometimes one, sometimes more. I took a few steps toward Abba. There were blankets thrown all over. Yael should have tidied up better. I couldn't stop to pick up the mess. There was so much still that I had to prepare before the Rav arrived. I went back into the kitchen.

A bar mitzvah is supposed to be a happy time. But I was tense. So tense that I could feel the stress radiating off me. My family was making me feel tense. Yossi and Dov were on the porch with their families, waiting for the whole thing to start and end. Gila was here and there, nowhere really. Ima was fussing over the tables. Where were the chocolate tefillin that I had bought? I wanted them scattered over the tablecloths.

"Where's he learning, anyway?"

It was Abba again.

I felt the tension getting worse. As if it could.

"He's learning in the Rav's yeshiva," I said.

"So where are his friends? The other kids that learn with him. Why aren't they here yet?"

Questions. So many questions. All my family did was ask questions. "Ask Daniel," I said. Abba would never ask Daniel. I knew that. The familiar pain started up in my chest. Daniel and I were no longer married. What would happen when my family found out?

"What's going on, Racheli?" Abba asked me. "You're exhausted. This rabbi and his goons…"

I looked around quickly. Checked that no one had heard Abba. He shouldn't talk that way about Rav Natas.

"It's okay, Abba. It really is," I said. "Putting a bar mitzvah together is a feat."

"Especially when you need to deal with a crazy rabbi. And his entire yeshiva."

Where was Daniel? Abba would never talk that way around Daniel.

***

A week after Shimmy's bar mitzvah, Rav Natas called me and told me to meet him on Rechov Amos. The time had come. It was early Thursday afternoon. I left the children with fourteen-year-old Yael and told her to prepare all the food for Shabbat, because I had to go out and would be back only the next day.

I left to meet the Rav. The Rav was waiting at our usual spot on Rechov Amos, but this time, Yigal and Eran were with him. The Rav got into the front seat, while the boys got into the back of the car. The Rav told me to begin circling through the streets of Geulah. Where were we going? Where were we going to get married? Had the Rav arranged for a hall and a caterer? I didn't know, and I didn't ask. The Rav knew what we had to do. I would do what he told me. I would be the wife of the Rav.

"Stop."

There were three boys standing at the corner, huddled over something one of the boys was holding. Eran jumped out of the van and said something to them. They climbed in.

The Rav nodded. He rubbed his fingers over the smooth stone of the pendulum. We circled some more.

I stopped outside a men's clothing store. Eran ran in and came out with two more boys. We circled and circled until we had ten boys in the van. Ten boys so that we could say the *sheva berachot* of our wedding. The Rav and I were married in the Ramot forest, just before sunset.

When I returned home the next day, I smelled the chicken and the cholent cooking. The aroma of a freshly washed floor. Yael had fulfilled her task as she was supposed to do. But then she ruined it. She told me that since she had prepared everything for Shabbat and I had done nothing, she wanted to go to visit a friend after I lit candles. I slapped her across the face.

Finally, I was married to a *tzaddik*. Then why did I feel so sad? I shoved that sadness deep, deep inside me. So deep that I was almost sure that I'd never felt it. That was probably the last feeling I had before I stopped feeling anything.

CHAPTER ELEVEN

Into the Devil's Den

December 2008

The children and I didn't move into the Rav's house until two months after we were married. Traveling back and forth between the house that Daniel and I had shared for so many years and the Rav's house had exhausted me.

Early one morning, I packed a suitcase for myself and told my eldest daughter, fifteen-year-old Yael, to pack for herself and the children. I looked into ten-year-old Yaakov's room. He had already left the house for yeshivah. I had to remember to call him and tell him to come to the Rav's house. Our new home. Meir, Aharon, and Hillel, my youngest three children, aged seven, five, and three, were still sleeping. When had they gone to bed? I didn't know. Routine and schedules were a thing of the past. Lost in the mists of time. I didn't mind. No, we were involved with something so much bigger than breakfast at seven thirty and bedtime at eight. We were part of the elite. A royal family. Rav Natas was a *tzaddik*, and we had been granted the honor to serve him. In his great wisdom, he was going to purge the evil out of my two youngest sons, Aharon and Hillel.

Suddenly, the house was stifling. Too small for my mission. I strode to the enormous living room windows that faced the street and yanked open the blind. I stepped onto the porch. The Jerusalem air was crispy, sharp as shards of glass, so early in the morning. I breathed in deeply. It was filled with promise. A promise that had nothing to do with Daniel and everything to do with Rav Natas. His wife! Like Tiferet, I was now also his wife. I was going to help him, this hidden *tzaddik*, to get rid of the evil in the world. I spun around and headed back into the house. I could hear Yael banging open closet doors. Slamming drawers as she looked for pajamas, sweaters, socks. If I had spent more time on the porch, instead of rushing ahead like I always did, maybe I would have noticed the geraniums that were wilting, the pots filled with crinkled, brown leaves. Maybe I would have smelled the rot in the air.

I drove quickly. By now, I could have driven to the Rav's house with my eyes closed. But maybe it was simply that the Rav was guiding my car toward him with his spiritual powers. I pulled into a parking spot alongside the building where Rav Natas lived. I was finally home. I turned around to face the three boys strapped in the back seat. Hillel was sleeping again. I shook him awake. Had he been sleeping for long? I had to wash his hands when we got in. "Be good children," I told them. "Try to behave like Yehoshua, the Rav's son. Make the Rav proud." Hillel rubbed his eyes. "Don't touch your eyes before I wash your hands," I said sharply. The Rav was so careful about things like that. Now that we were in his house, our new home, we would have to be more stringent. Suddenly I couldn't wait. I had to see him. "Bring the luggage in," I told Yael. I slammed the door and ran into the building and up to the first floor.

Tiferet, the Rav's first wife, opened the door. White blobs of something stained the front of her robe. Black bags, swollen like miniature eggplants, hung under her eyes. She didn't invite me in. I didn't expect it. After all, we were two wives sharing one husband.

"Where's the Rav?" I asked.

"Gone to the mikveh," she said. "We didn't sleep all night. He went before sunrise, for the *neitz* minyan."

I didn't ask when he would be back. We never knew. The ways of a *tzaddik* are hidden. I knew that.

"The Rav has given you the room near the bathroom," she said. She stared at the children standing behind me, but made no move to welcome them. "The children can share the beds."

"Where are Shimmy and Avner?" I asked. I hadn't seen my two eldest sons in days.

Tiferet shrugged. "At the mikveh. Maybe. We need to clean the walls today."

I peered into the semi-darkness behind her shoulder. The walls. I would scour off every scuff mark, every fingerprint. The Rav would be proud of me.

The children spent the day in their room. I wanted Yaakov to be at the mikveh with the Rav, but Tiferet didn't know where the group had gone. There were hundreds of mikvehs in Jerusalem. Besides, maybe they had gone up north, to the graves of holy rabbis. Maybe they had gone to Netivot. We didn't know. We never knew.

Yael unpacked the suitcases and repacked them, stacking every child's clothes in neat piles. "Hillel doesn't have socks," she said when I stopped my scrubbing for long enough to peep in.

I shrugged. I had given her plenty of time to pack.

Hillel pulled at my skirt. He was hungry, but too young to translate his hunger into words.

"Wanna eat something," Aharon, two years older, said.

I shrugged again. Aharon was always hungry. It wasn't good to be so hungry all the time. It meant there was something evil lurking inside him. The Rav had told us so, just over two months ago, the last time he had come to our house, when Daniel and I were still married. "Later," I said. "You'll eat later."

The morning passed. The afternoon began and passed. And still the Rav had not come home. In the early evening, I lay on my bed. My shoulders ached from scrubbing the walls, and the skin on the edge of my right thumb had split. A tiny papercut that burned like fire every time I knocked it. I closed my eyes. I heard Aharon going to the bathroom. He was drinking water from the *netilat yadayim* cup.

I must have fallen asleep, because I woke with a start when Hillel banged into my side. And then I heard him. The Rav was back. I jumped up. I had to wash my hands. Fast…before he saw the impurity that had settled on them as I slept. I ran to the sink outside the bathroom, but the *netilat yadayim* cup was gone. I remembered Aharon drinking. I turned on the faucet and washed my hands without a cup.

The Rav was in the living room, sitting at the head of the table. Yigal stood on his right, Eran on his left.

I stood at the end of the table. Waiting for him to notice me. He didn't look at me. It was the impurity on my hands. I was sure of it. Then he looked up. Even from the end of the table, I could see the glint of the silver in his eyes. My heart beat faster. He knew. Like he knew everything else. Fear coiled around and around me, squeezing out the breath inside me.

"Bring the food," he said. "Today is a *hillula*. We must honor the *tzaddik*."

I wanted to hurry to the kitchen, to have the honor of serving the Rav his meal, but my legs were glued to the floor tiles. Because Tiferet was the wife who always cooked at the Rav's house. Sheets of fire flickered over the Rav's eyes. He was in a different place. Seeing things that we could not see. How lucky I was to be part of his greatness.

Tiferet brought out platters of chicken and roast potatoes. Peas in red tomato sauce and spiced with cumin. I could smell the spice. It tickled my nostrils, reminding me that I hadn't eaten all day. I ground my teeth together. Food! How could I think of food when there was such spiritual greatness around me? I had to focus on the darkness, the evil that we were purging out of the world.

At a nod from the Rav, Tiferet pulled out the chair at the end of the table. The hard edge banged into my knee, but I didn't flinch. It was for my good, I knew.

The men ate. Tiferet chewed on the bones of a chicken leg. Loud sucking sounds that barely broke the silence. Then the singing began. The men sang and sang, and I stood and stood. When, when would the Rav notice the walls that I had worked so hard to clean? Finally, Yehoshua brought a bowl of water for the Rav to wash his hands. The Rav patted his lips with the damp napkin. "Bring the children," he said.

Eran and Yigal went to my room and brought Aharon and Hillel to the table. The Rav waved his hand. Eran pushed Aharon into a seat. Yigal pushed Hillel into a seat opposite him. "He cannot eat," the Rav said pointing to Aharon. "He is a *rasha*, and we must purge the evil from him."

I knew this already. The Rav had told Daniel and me many times. And many times he had tried to purge the evil from them. In different ways. Painful ways. I slammed shut the door in my mind that led to these images. Everything was decreed by the Rav, and I must not question it.

"He must eat," the Rav said, pointing to Hillel. "This is the only way to his *tikkun*."

Eran put a plate piled with chicken and potatoes in front of Hillel. He poured the peas over the mountain.

"Eat," the Rav said.

Hillel was hungry. Finally…food. He liked chicken, so he tore at the meat and stuffed it into his mouth. When he'd finished with the chicken, he started on the potatoes. He was going slower now. Please, Hashem, help him finish it all.

"Eat the peas," the Rav said.

Hillel stopped eating. The fork hovered over his plate.

He hated peas.

"Eat the peas."

The fork fell onto the plate.

"Feed him."

Yigal pushed Hillel's head back and began to shovel peas into his mouth. When Hillel refused to open his mouth, he slapped him.

I kept quiet. I was already used to the beatings. I was made of stone, wasn't I? Stone didn't flinch. Think, think of the evil that you are purging, I told myself.

Hillel finished the peas on his plate. He finished the peas in the pot. And we all watched.

Finally, the Rav looked at me. "We will purge the evil out of him, and you will thank me," he said.

I nodded. I would thank him. The Rav knew everything. And if he wasn't thanking me for cleaning the walls, it was because I didn't do a good enough job. Tomorrow I would do better. I glanced at Aharon.

The Rav pushed his empty plate toward Aharon. A pile of chicken bones was piled neatly on the side. "Eat this," he said. And then he looked at me.

I lowered my eyes. My shoes were scuffed, I noticed. I would have to buy a new pair. The Rav liked me to dress well.

We spent two, three, or four more hours at the table. Listening to stories, an occasional quote from the Torah. Hillel fell asleep at the table.

At some point, the Rav stood up and walked out of the room. Yigal and Eran followed him. I didn't move. I was too tired to make my legs obey me. After a while, Yael came to stand beside me.

"Where are Shimmy and Avner?" she asked.

"Why did you come out of the bedroom?" I stared at her without really seeing her. I couldn't think of the children. I didn't know if Ahuva and Meir were still in the bedroom. I didn't know where Shimmy and Avner were.

All I knew was that the Rav knew that I hadn't washed my hands. That was why he hadn't welcomed me into the house.

***

Our marriage had been a secret for the two months that I had still been living in the Old City, but now, now that I was living in the Rav's house, I could serve the Rav, the *tzaddik*, with my whole heart. A few days after we had moved in, I was ironing the Rav's shirts in the kitchen, when Aharon threw a piece of Lego at me.

The red piece of Lego hit my arm and dropped onto the ironing board.

"Want Abba," he said.

I pushed it off. Daniel? He couldn't ask for Daniel, couldn't mention his name. Daniel was bad. The Rav had said so. "Abba isn't here." I pushed the iron close to the row of buttons, to press out the tiniest wrinkle.

"Want Abba." Hillel crawled under the ironing board and pulled out the Lego.

He mustn't ask for Daniel. The Rav would hear him. "Abba isn't here. You mustn't think of Abba. Don't speak about him." I put the iron down and glared at Aharon.

He glared back.

Suddenly Yael was standing in the doorway. Hillel was balanced on her hip, chocolate smeared across his cheeks. Why couldn't she keep him clean… the Rav liked us to be clean. Aharon clenched his fists. I could see the red Lego peeping out between his white knuckles. He opened his mouth. He was going to scream.

"Don't speak about Abba." I kept glaring. Why couldn't he be like Yael? Yael understood. She didn't make trouble like Aharon and Hillel. There was no evil in her. None in Yaakov either. None in Meir. The Rav didn't have to work on them.

Aharon closed his mouth. He was still glaring.

Why were Aharon and Hillel so bad? Why were two of my kids evil? What had I done wrong? "Don't speak about Abba. You hear me?" My voice was quiet, but forceful.

Yael stroked Hillel's head. Backed out silently.

Aharon, still sitting on the floor, began to scoot out of the kitchen.

And then he banged into the Rav's legs.

The Rav didn't move. Didn't look down. He stared at me. His eyes were the color of clouds. "Daniel is evil, filled with so much darkness that even when he isn't here, he can still influence the children." A sheet of fire fell over his eyes, turning the clouds into molten lead. "We must rid them of the evil that they carry around in their hearts."

I knew what that meant. Something inside me clenched tight. But I had to serve the *tzaddik*. I tried to breathe. Make my thoughts pure. Think, think of the great merit.

"We must get rid of the evil."

I was made of stone. I didn't feel anything. I had to prove that I was worthy of being the Rav's wife.

Flashes of silver lit up the Rav's eyes. He turned and walked to the living room.

Of course we had to rid them of evil. We were lucky to be in the house of the Rav. He knew how to do things that no one else could do. Because he was a *tzaddik*. How many times had Daniel told me so? And then I smelled something burning. The Rav's shirt. Smoke. I lifted the iron. I had burned a brown triangle into the fabric.

From the living room, I heard Eran ordering Aharon to stand in the corner. I grabbed the shirt and stuffed it into a bag, just as Tiferet came into the kitchen.

Her nostrils flared. She could smell it. Smell the smoke.

She would tell the Rav. I didn't want that. I didn't want him to be angry with me. He would stop talking to me. "I'm going to the store," I said. I was responsible for all the shopping, taking care of all the errands that had to be done outside the house. I hurried through the living room, making sure not to turn my head toward the corner by the sliding doors that led to the porch. When I came back, two hours later, Aharon was still standing in the corner.

***

The next day, Eran told me to get ready. We needed to go to the north…to the *kever* of Shevuel ben Gershom. My first trip as wife of the Rav. I should be excited. Was I? Of course I was. I had to be. It was an honor. I had to get everything ready. Make it perfect. But what was the blackness looming in the back of my mind? I hurried to the kitchen. Opened the cabinets. I would make rice. Rice mixed with lentils and chopped vegetables. The blackness. It was creeping forward. It was an evil blackness. I had to stop it. Stop it before the Rav would see it. Meatballs. I had bought ground meat last night.

I heard someone behind me. The Rav's voice. "Leave the cooking for Tiferet to do. You need to be at the table."

The Rav was there. Dressed in a black robe. His staff in his hand.

Had he seen? Seen the darkness in my mind? It was an honor. An honor to serve him. Help me, help me clear my thoughts, Hashem.

Eran and Yigal were at the table, sitting next to Aharon and Hillel. The Rav opened his book on Kabbalah. For the next three hours, we sat there. Every time Hillel's head dropped onto his chest, Eran shook him awake.

There were gold flowers and buds embroidered onto either side of the robe. When I stared at them for long enough, the buds opened up. The smell of frying onions wafted into the living room. Aharon licked his lips. He was hungry again. He was always hungry. It wasn't good.

Finally, we were in the van. In the back seat were Eran, Yigal, Tiferet, and Yehoshua. Aharon and Hillel were on the floor in the back, squashed between their legs. The older children had been sent to the park.

We were in the car, waiting to leave, when I realized that I hadn't seen Yaakov that morning. Where was he? Had he gone to the mikveh that morning with the Rav like Shimmy and Avner? I didn't know. Maybe he had gone again to his yeshiva in the Old City. Why couldn't he stay with us? With the Rav?

Yael came out of the building. Why wasn't she in the park? Why were all my children so rebellious?

She handed two bags of Bamba to Hillel and Aharon.

I didn't ask her where she had gotten them. "Where's Yaakov?"

"Yeshiva." She kissed the boys. And then she began to walk away. Toward the park. It was beginning to rain. Fat drops that bounced up when they hit the ground.

Why wasn't Yaakov with his brothers? Why couldn't he stay near the Rav? Why wasn't he serving the *tzaddik*? I watched the raindrops smash into the windscreen. Race down the glass and disappear into the little holes at the front of the hood of the car. Where was the Rav? Should I go and find him? Maybe I could help him?

I turned to the back. Tiferet's head was back against the seat. Her eyes closed. A blue vein in her neck pulsed.

Eran was picking his teeth. He held the toothpick up to the gray light coming through the car window. "Shevuel ben Gershom was a priest for the idol of Micha. He was a false prophet in the time of Shlomo Hamelech."

A false prophet. How many hundreds of years had Shevuel waited for this day? This day when Rav Natas would finally purge the evil in him? Elevate his soul. The rain turned into pellets of ice. They hit the roof of the car, slid off the hood. I didn't think about the children in the park. I was focusing my thoughts. Getting ready to help the *tzaddik* achieve this lofty goal.

It rained all the way up to the Banias Falls. It was a good sign, I decided. Rain was a sign of blessing. The Rav didn't talk to us as we drove along. He was reading from the Siddur Hakavanot. The children were hungry. They were always hungry. It wasn't good to think of food all the time.

I heard Hillel whimpering. Aharon was quiet. He had learned that it did no good to cry out.

The Rav told me to stop long before I turned onto the road that would take us to the *kever*. He took out his pendulum. The pendulum swayed very slowly. The Rav directed me according to the swinging of the pendulum. Eventually, we drove into a moshav, past the houses with patches of green grass and piles of wet irrigation pipes, old wood, and children's bikes. Past the sheds filled with black and white cows and out a back gate. It was drizzling softly, and I drove slowly. The wheels of the van weren't gripping the wet, muddy track. I felt the van slide, heard Aharon's head… or was it Hillel's…hit the car door. I turned a final bend, and there we were…in front of a small reservoir. Tall reeds grew around the entire edge. A narrow path cut through the thick grass and led to the edge of the water. Was the *kever* of Shevuel here? I didn't ask. The Rav's eyes were closed in concentration.

Eran and Yigal climbed out of the car. They used a foot pump to inflate a small rubber boat and carried it to the edge of the water. The Rav opened his eyes. "You will push me in the boat to the other side of the reservoir," he told me.

The thick grass was wet. My pumps, the new black pair with a bow on the front, were soaked within seconds. I hesitated at the edge of the reservoir. The water was brown. Dark. I couldn't see what was on the bottom. Couldn't see where to put my feet. Eran nudged the boat toward the Rav. As he lowered himself into it, the boat tilted and tipped. Then it was stable. I took my shoes off, edged forward. Cold mud squelched up between my toes. The water rose toward my knees. It was cold, so cold that it hurt. But it wasn't deep. I began to push the boat. The Rav closed his eyes.

Suddenly, someone was splashing next to me. Tiferet. Her hands were on the boat, next to mine. She pushed hard and the boat began to slip away. I lunged forward. The water hit my chest. The cold took my breath away. I gasped.

"Go back," the Rav shouted. "Stupid woman. Evil woman. Go back."

I had never heard him shout.

Tiferet backed away. She tripped on her wet skirt. Fell into the water. Her arms sank into the water. And then she was up, stumbling toward the car.

That night, when we finally got back to Jerusalem, the Rav went to the mikveh. He was there all night. In the morning, he called me. He was standing by the sliding doors that opened onto the porch. It had snowed in the night, and the porch was covered in a thin layer of snow.

"You are holding up everything," the Rav said. He rubbed the stone of the pendulum between his fingers. "You are making it impossible to remove the evil."

I was trying so hard. What else did I have to do? I looked at my feet. I was wearing my old shoes again. I had ruined the new pair.

"You cannot talk to Aharon and Hillel." The Rav stared at me.

He was looking into my mind. I had to agree. I had to think it was good.

"If you talk to them, you will ruin my work. It will take much longer." The Rav pushed the sliding door. A gust of freezing air blew in. "Eran and Yigal are now responsible for the children."

Of course it was good. If I didn't talk to the children, soon they would be pure.

That afternoon, when the Rav had gone to the mikveh, I went for a walk. I didn't have a coat...it was in my old house in the Old City. The cold rushed up my sleeves, wrapped itself around my chest. Where was Daniel? I missed him. A low-hanging branch snatched at my snood, trying to yank it off my head. No, I didn't miss him. I couldn't think about him. Besides, he hadn't come to the Rav's house. To look for me, for the children. He knew that the work the Rav had to do was because of the evil inside him. I was alone. And I had to make sure that I didn't stand in the way of the Rav.

***

We fell into a routine over the next three or four weeks. Every night was a *hillula* for a different *tzaddik*. At the end of the meal, the Rav would tell Eran and Yigal to stand beside Aharon and Hillel. If they couldn't answer the questions, Eran would shake Aharon, and Yigal would shake Hillel.

When the first light of dawn was staining the black sky a charcoal color, we would fall asleep. One morning, Hillel crept into my bed. His pajamas were wet. I could feel the wetness against my legs. He didn't speak to me. I didn't speak to him. Even though everyone was sleeping, we didn't talk. Because the Rav could hear through the walls, hear things when he was sleeping.

One day, when I came back from shopping, I didn't see any of the children. I dropped the groceries on the kitchen floor and walked to my bedroom. Our room was a mess. All the clothes that Yael kept neatly folded in piles in one of the suitcases that we had brought with us were spread over the beds and the floor. The suitcase was zipped closed, thrown on its side in a corner of the room.

Rav Natas was reading from his book on Kabbalah. Finally, he looked up. He didn't speak. He beckoned for me to follow him to my bedroom. He pointed to the suitcase.

"Aharon is evil. And we must clean him," he said. He walked toward the suitcase and unzipped it.

Aharon was in the suitcase, tied up, a *kippah* stuffed into his mouth.

"Tell him to behave…to be good," the Rav said.

I looked at Aharon. The Rav was staring at me. His eyes the color of water. I looked at Aharon. Why was he making this so hard? "I can't help you," I said. "You must behave better. You must help the Rav take out the evil." I was doing something holy…and that belief made my voice steady. There was no pain. I could feel no pain. I was a stone.

The Rav zipped the suitcase closed. He told me to leave the house. To go for a walk.

I drove to our house in the Old City. Wandered through the house, looking for our coats. Why weren't my kids normal? Why did Rav Natas have to clean out the evil inside them? What could I do to make them better?

The next day, I had to take care of a problem with the water bill. When I came back, I saw Aharon standing in the corner near the sliding doors. Eran was watching him. A pile of sunflower seeds were on the floor around his feet.

The Rav was leaning on the doorjamb of the kitchen door. "He must stand there…until the evil leaves him."

Aharon stood there for hours and hours. I went out of the house. Took food to the children who were in the park. When I came back, Aharon was in the bathroom. I went into the bedroom. I lay on my bed. I heard Aharon pleading to go to the bathroom every half an hour. He was resting his legs.

The Rav began to shout. He was shouting about darkness, about the evil that he had to chase away.

I stood up, ran into the living room. "Ask the angels. Ask them if it is nearly over. If we can stop."

The Rav took out his pendulum. Yigal brought a notebook to the table. He sat beside the Rav. The Rav's forehead creased as he concentrated. He whispered words and the pendulum swung back and forth. Slowly at first and then faster. Eran was scribbling in the notebook, recording exactly what the Rav said. Finally, he looked up. "It's going," he said. "Like a tumor, the evil is shrinking."

Something moved in my chest. I suppose it could have been a glimmer of relief. But I couldn't be sure, because I was made of stone, and stones don't feel anything.

***

One night, a few days later, I came back from doing the shopping when it was already dark. The house was quiet. The older children were out again. The Rav, Eran, Yigal, and Hillel were in the living room. The table had been pushed back, and Hillel was standing in the center of the room. Yigal held a half-empty bottle of arak in his hand.

"Jump," the Rav said to Hillel.

Hillel jumped. Up and down. He jumped many times until his face was red and he crumpled in a little heap.

"Give him more arak," the Rav said.

Hillel drank arak and jumped. He drank more arak and jumped some more. When he threw up, Rav Natas told me to clean the mess. I didn't talk to Hillel.

***

The next time I went out, Aharon fell against a heater. He had burns on his legs. Eran sent me out again. This time to buy burn ointment and bandages.

When I came back, Rav Natas was yelling at Aharon. He was supposed to be standing in the corner. The evil was almost out. The last shadows had to be removed. He had to remain standing in the corner, but he wasn't obedient. He wasn't listening. Why couldn't he listen?

Rav Natas was yelling louder. From the corner of my eye, I watched Yael take the other children into the bedroom.

Eran propped Aharon up, but he flopped down to the floor. Rav Natas was enraged. He pulled open the sliding doors. He yanked Aharon to his feet. He was going to throw Aharon off the porch.

The first time I had been proactive with my children was when Rav Tzefanyah had wanted to marry Yael. Six years earlier. Now, when Rav Natas was about to hurl Aharon off the porch, something inside me woke up.

I stood between Rav Natas and the porch. "I'll take him away," I said. "I'll take him to a friend in the south. She'll look after him." I reached out for Aharon's hand.

Rav Natas stared at me. Before he could tell me not to go, I pulled Aharon out the front door.

More than seventy kilometers to Migdal Yam. I drove fast. Aharon was asleep in the back of the car. The land stretched out on either side, green and lush. Full of promise. Just as it had been when Daniel and I had left nine years earlier. But this time, the longer I gazed at the scenery, the more sure I was that it was mocking me.

It was dark by the time we reached Tikvah Goodman's house. She opened the door. Looked at me, looked at Aharon, who was reeling beside me. She picked him up. She was strong, surprisingly strong for a woman as old as she was. She laid him on the couch.

"He needs to stay here," I told her. "One day, two, three. I'll be back for him."

Tikvah stared at me. "Where's Daniel?"

I stared back at her. How many times had she asked me where Daniel was? What had I always answered her? "Daniel is learning," I said.

Aharon began to whimper. Tikvah moved toward him. The leg of his pants had lifted up. The skin was red, blistered, swollen. "What happened?"

"He fell against a heater," I said. That was what the Rav had told me. I had believed him. But Tikvah didn't believe me. Tikvah, who had never believed me when I had told her that I was fine, didn't believe me now.

"A heater?"

What was she questioning? A heater had fallen on him. I had seen the heater in the corner of the room when I handed Eran the bandages and burn ointment. It had been a mistake to come here. I grabbed Aharon's arm. He was too heavy for me to lift. I pulled him onto his feet. Rav Natas would be angry with me. Angry that I had taken Aharon away.

"Leave him here," Tikvah said. "His burns need to be treated. They're infected. He could die."

I pulled Aharon toward the door.

Tikvah moved to stand in front of the door. "If you don't leave him here, I'm going to call the police," Tikvah said.

I pushed past her.

Maybe she was right. Maybe Aharon had to go to the hospital. I had to ask the Rav what to do. He could put his staff on Aharon's legs. That would cure the burns. Why hadn't he done that?

I heard a choking sound coming from the back seat. Aharon was crying. He hadn't cried for months. Since we moved into Rav Natas' house. Why was he crying now? I had to take him to the hospital. But I had told the Rav that I was going to Migdal Yam.

My phone rang. The Rav. The Rav knew that I was thinking of doing something without asking him. I answered the phone. "I'm coming home," I told him, even though I knew I was going to the hospital.

"Go to your house," he said. "The children are at your house. With Yigal and Eran. If anyone asks you why Hillel isn't moving, tell them that he fell off the climbing bars in the park."

I didn't want to go to my house. I wanted to go back to Rav Natas. I could hear Tiferet in the background. She was shouting. Tiferet never shouted. I wanted to tell Rav Natas that I would be home soon, but he had put down the phone.

Aharon was still crying. I had to take him to the hospital. But I wanted to go home to Rav Natas.

PART FOUR

Whoever does not see God everywhere does not see Him anywhere.

– Kotzker Rebbe

CHAPTER TWELVE

Shackled

Early February 2009

It was the smell in hospitals that made people ill. Always those smells of disinfectant and medicines. And now there was also the breezy lemon-lime smell of someone's perfume. Who wore perfume to come to the hospital?

Aharon was lying on a bed, his eyes wide open, his lips shut. What was he looking at?

There was a nurse with a chart, a bald doctor standing at the side of the bed. Huddled together, whispering.

The curtain around the bed billowed. Another doctor came in. More whispering.

I called the Rav again. He hadn't answered my call five minutes ago. Did he know where I was? Had the angels told him? Was he angry? I had told him that I was taking Aharon to Migdal Yam.

This time the Rav answered.

"They want to operate," I said. "Should I let them operate on Aharon?"

"What did you tell them?" the Rav asked.

The nurse with the clipboard stepped toward me. The scent of citrus came with her.

"What should I tell them?" I asked.

She tapped her pen against the papers.

"Tell them yes." The Rav cut the connection.

Funny how I could pick out the soft tap-tap of her pen.

"We need to operate," the nurse said. "The heater burned him badly."

Why was she looking at me like that?

"Why didn't you bring him here before…when it happened? You *are* his mother?"

I stared back at her. Why was she looking at me like that? I told her what the Rav had told me. Tap, tap. Tap, tap. She didn't believe me. I could tell by the way the corner of her lip curled upwards to the edge of her nose. I looked away.

The doctor stepped forward. The top of his head was shiny under the bright lights. He should be wearing a *kippah*. I didn't want a man who wasn't religious to operate on Aharon. Had I told them they could operate? I couldn't remember. "When will you operate?" I asked. I needed to tell the Rav when it was happening. Maybe he would go to the *kever* of a *tzaddik*. Pray for Aharon.

The doctor stared at me. He didn't answer. He turned away.

"I need to talk to her."

A woman with long, black hair pushed forward. Black eyeliner.

I didn't want to talk to her.

"You need to tell me what happened," she said.

Tell her? I'd already told them. Aharon had fallen against a heater. "He fell," I said. Maybe she would leave if I told her.

She folded her arms across her chest. Pink nails. Tiny diamonds on the tips. "Where's the heater now?"

The heater? How could I know? I had to think. Think fast. "We threw it out. It was broken."

She scratched her lip with the tip of a nail. Looked at me. "Do you want a drink?"

I wanted her to leave. Leave me alone. It was a mistake to come here. I should have gone back home to the Rav. He could have cured the burns with his staff.

"How did a broken heater burn him?" A light blue shirt. A policeman. Two policemen.

Why were two policemen here? This was an emergency room. I didn't answer. Just stared at the dark blue badge on their shoulders. "I want a drink," I said.

No one moved.

My phone rang.

Everyone watched me. The policeman, the woman with black hair, the nurse.

My phone was in my hand. It was the Rav. "Tell them you are living in the Old City," he said. "With the children."

They were all looking at me. Looking at me like I'd done something wrong. Me. Something wrong.

"Give me your ID," one of the policemen said.

I didn't need to give him my ID. But he had black eyes, evil eyes. So I looked in my purse. It was there. The blue plastic peeped out between five or six notes that the Rav had given me. I handed it to him. Moved away…to Aharon's bed. I felt around his neck.

"Where's your husband?" the policeman said.

The red string with the *kameya* was missing. Aharon had lost his *kameya*. I had to tell the Rav to write a new *kameya*.

Someone was pulling away the bed. They were taking Aharon away. He couldn't have an operation without the *kameya*. I held onto the bed.

Someone pulled me back. I pushed away the hand. I ran after the bed. But the hand was there again. Holding on to my arm. They took Aharon away.

And the policeman was talking to me again. I didn't like his voice. It was cold. Mean.

"Where is your husband?"

I stared at him. My husband. My husband was Rav Natas. But he didn't know that. Couldn't know that. It was a secret. Only those in our circle knew it. He meant Daniel. He was evil. He had put evil into the children. I turned to face him, stared into his black eyes. I wasn't afraid of him. "He did bad things to us. To me and the children," I said. "We had to run away from him."

Anat…I had heard the policeman calling her Anat…she looked angry. Was she angry with me? Maybe she was angry with Daniel?

My phone rang. It was Yigal. "Hillel is blue," he said.

The people around me were whispering. All whispering again. I turned my back to them. Walked away so they couldn't hear me. "Call an ambulance," I said. The ambulance would bring him to the hospital. I didn't want him in the hospital. They were making trouble for me here. "No, call the Rav." The Rav would tell him what to do. But Hillel was blue. "Call an ambulance," I whispered.

"You need to come and answer more questions," Anat told me. "We'll give you a drink. Are you hungry?"

I looked at the top of my phone. It was three o'clock in the morning. I was hungry. "I need to see the *hechsher*. I want Badatz," I said.

She nodded.

I followed her to a room upstairs. The policemen were already there. The same policemen who'd been in the emergency room.

Questions, questions. More questions.

Where was Hillel? Did Yigal call an ambulance? Did he tell the Rav? I needed to tell the Rav about the *kameya*.

The policeman's phone rang. He answered it. The other policeman watched me.

Anat's phone was ringing. Anat answered, but she kept watching me. Like a cat watching a bird that's pecking for worms.

Suddenly I was afraid. Afraid of all these people. Help me, Hashem. What did they want? Why did I come here?

"There is another child in the emergency room," the policeman said.

I watched Anat sitting up straighter. Flicking her hair over her shoulder.

"He was brought from your house in the Old City."

So Yigal had called an ambulance.

"You must come and see him."

First I had to tear up the notes that the Rav had sent me. I stood up. "I need the bathroom," I said.

The policemen and Anat stood up. They were looking at me strangely. Was it pity? Was it horror? I didn't know.

Anat followed me down the corridor. Waited outside the door. I tore up the notes into minute pieces. Stuffed them deep into the garbage, under the soggy tissues, under the dirty diaper. I had to protect the Rav. I knew that these people belonged to the forces of evil. I had to make sure that no one got to the Rav. I had to serve the *tzaddik* and make him proud of me.

***

In the emergency room, in the cubicle, there were so many doctors and nurses around Hillel…is it Hillel…he was a strange blue color. I tried to reach under his shirt to check if he had a *kameya*, but the policeman blocked my way. I turned around, hurried to the furthest corner in the emergency room, quickly dialed my mother's number. It was the first time in many, many years that I had thought of my family as a source of light. It was late at night in New York. Ima wasn't used to hearing from me at all, except for when I needed money. And I never called at odd hours. "Ima, I'm in trouble," I whispered into the phone before the policeman came over to stop my call.

"Racheli? Are you okay? Where's Daniel? Where are the children?"

"I'm in the hospital with Aharon and Hillel. The police think I hurt them. Please, Ima…find me a lawyer."

The policeman reached me. The conversation was cut. He made me go back to the doctor.

The doctor looked at me. "He's unconscious. Beaten badly. He may never open his eyes again."

Hillel was pulled out of the tiny cubicle. I already knew that it was pointless to try to run after his bed.

The policeman was standing in front of me. He was saying something about an arrest. Who was being arrested? Was the Rav arrested? Daniel? He was telling me that I could call one person. Why did I have to call someone? He stared at me. Anat stared at me. I was tired of all these people staring at me. He told me that I was being arrested. What for? What was I being arrested for? Criminals are arrested. I wasn't a criminal.

I was in a police car. We were driving to…to where were we driving? They were taking me home. Home to the Old City. Because they didn't know that I lived in Mekor Baruch. I was going home. Tomorrow I'd go to see Aharon and Hillel in the hospital. I'd take them gas balloons. They liked gas balloons. We were getting closer to the Old City. But they weren't going in the right direction. They weren't continuing on Rechov Haneviim. They were turning onto Shivtei Yisrael. I told them they had taken a wrong turn. They weren't listening to me. We were in the Russian Compound. I knew all about the Russian Compound. Sometimes, I used to pass by when I walked from the Old City to Geulah. But why was I here?

I walked through a large metal door. There was a policeman on either side of me. I walked up two steps. There was a loud buzz, like a million bees gone crazy, and we walked into the next room. The heavy door closed behind me. I had to undress so that the guard could check that I wasn't carrying anything. Undress? I didn't want to undress. What was I carrying, anyway? They had taken my purse, my phone. More metal doors opened and slammed shut. I entered a cell.

In that moment, everything changed. I was no longer a wife and a mother. I was no longer part of society. I was no longer a human being. This was the beginning of my death.

***

The first thing I noticed was that there were no windows. Everything was made of stone. Stone bunkbeds with a thin mattress on both sides of the cell. No windows. A half wall jutted into the room. Two girls. I couldn't look at them. They weren't our kind of people.

"What are you doing here?" one girl asked. She walked toward me. Her sweater had slipped off her shoulder. There was a row of tiny blue butterflies tattooed over her shoulder, fluttering toward her collarbone.

I didn't answer. I was tired. So tired. And where was I supposed to sit? Everything was grimy. I couldn't lie down on that mattress. Ever. It wasn't just grimy. It was full of an impure spirit.

"Nice jewelry, nice makeup," the other girl said.

Of course I dressed nicely. The Rav liked us to dress nicely. And I was his wife.

"You look like a nice religious woman. I know because we have neighbors like you." She came closer too. Too close.

Her glasses were so thick that I couldn't see her eyes properly behind them. Or was I just tired? I sat on the very edge of one of the mattresses. Felt the cold of the stone creeping through the fabric of my skirt.

The girl with the glasses bent down and pulled a plastic water bottle out from under the bed I was sitting on. "There was a mistake, *geveret*," she said. "Happens all the time. They'll let you out soon. And you'll go back to your house and your kids. You have kids, right?" She looked at her friend. "They have lots of kids. No joke. Ten, fifteen, at least." She pushed the bottle into my hand. "Drink," she said. "They never give you enough to drink."

I drank the whole bottle. I was tired. But I couldn't lie down on this mattress. I stood up. Walked to the half wall. There was a toilet behind the wall. No door.

***

Later that morning, I was called out of my cell. Handcuffs? I backed away. Finally, I told them that only a woman could touch me to handcuff me. After the handcuffs came the shackles. It was hard to walk with the shackles. One step, two, three. I waddled as if I had a gym band around my legs. But this gym band clanked.

It took three minutes to walk to the police station. Out through a series of heavy doors, turn right, walk past blue metal barriers. A three-minute walk. And it was heavenly. I was breathing the air of Jerusalem, my city. This was my home turf…maybe I would see someone that I knew? My home turf. That made the pain even greater. What was I doing like this? In handcuffs and shackles? And why, why was I going to the police station? I had to go home. Maybe the Rav needed me.

Questions, questions, questions. This was an interrogation, and it was endless. Two policemen. One with a belly that ballooned the fabric of his shirt, stretched the slits of the buttonholes into ovals. One whose forefathers had been part of the rabble that came out of Egypt. I lied and lied some more. I told them that Daniel was evil. He had hurt us. The evil policeman yelled, cursed, used words that I'd never heard before. Rude, obnoxious, and vulgar.

"I want to call my mother," I said. Where was Ima? I had told her last night…or was it a year ago…time trickled past so slowly…that I needed a lawyer. I didn't want to listen to these men shouting at me.

"No more calls. You can speak to your lawyer. Only to your lawyer. If you get one."

What was he talking about? Ima would get me a lawyer. If I was still in jail. The Rav could free me at any time that he wanted. He could walk through the walls and take me home if he wanted. I just had to wait, and it would happen. Even now, now, he was watching. Watching how well I was protecting him. Keeping him safe from these evil men.

Suddenly the chubby officer stood up, walked around to my side of the scratched table. "You have two kids in the hospital. One could die." He stepped closer, until his belly almost touched my nose. "Who is Natas?" he asked.

The Rav. How did they know about the Rav? I stared out the window. At the patch of sky I could see.

"We checked your phone. We saw you called him. From the south. From the hospital. What's your connection?"

The evil one stood up. Walked around the table. Looked at me with disgust. "How could you let it happen?"

The chubby one leaned closer. I stared at his buttons. Another second and they would all fly off.

"Why didn't you leave?" he said.

Leave. How was I supposed to leave? Of course the Rav knew more than me. He was a miracle worker. Where was I supposed to go? Who would have helped my children if I had left? Who would have cleansed my children? Were these men mad?

"What kind of a mother are you?" the evil one yelled. "What kind of a mother lets someone do these kinds of things to her children?"

What kind of mother? I was a good mother. I was doing the best for my children. Then why was he looking at me like I was a piece of garbage? I closed my eyes. The forces of evil were so strong. So strong that they could hide the truth from people who weren't worthy enough to see it.

The Russian Compound is a pit stop. Drug dealers, thieves, white-collar crime suspects...after their arrest, they're all held in the Russian Compound for two or three days. Usually that's plenty of time to gather enough information about what they've done. The judge then decides if the case will be thrown out of the court system or if the suspect can be released on bail, put on house arrest, or sent to jail. Within a day or two, anyone who has been arrested knows where he's heading. But that didn't happen with me. I was in the Russian Compound for three weeks, because it was impossible for the investigators to piece together what had happened.

***

My lawyer, Joanne Meyers, came to me for the first time in the afternoon... sent by Yossi. An older woman. A friend of Ima's.

It was that bond of friendship that pushed her to take the case. A case she'd have normally run from. Joanne finished her speech and looked at me.

She wanted me to thank her. Well, I wasn't going to thank her. I wasn't a criminal, to be pitied by everyone. "I want a siddur. A Sefer Tehillim. A cup to wash my hands," I said. "I can't stay here without those."

Joanne took out a purple Parker pen. A thick folder. She put her hands flat on the folder. "You'll be staying here with or without those. So I suggest that you tell me what happened...from the beginning."

Ima should have found me someone normal. Someone nice. I stared at the wall behind Joanne's head. I couldn't tell her. I couldn't tell her the secrets of our circle. Secrets that we had never spoken about between us, the members of the circle. She wasn't worthy. She would never understand. I blinked. Poor Joanne was waiting. "Daniel did it all," I said. "He's evil…"

Joanne looked at me. "You'll have to tell the truth, Racheli."

The truth. Of course I was telling the truth. What did she think? That I was making things up?

Joanne clicked the top of her pen. In, out, in, out. "Natas left the country this morning," she said.

She was lying. He was in Mekor Baruch. Waiting for me. Waiting for the right time to come and take me out. She couldn't scare me.

"You're not talking about your kids, Racheli. Why aren't you talking about your kids?"

My kids. "Where are they?"

"Shared between your brothers. Daniel has been arrested."

They couldn't be there. My brothers had TVs in the house. They didn't dress right. "I have to tell them to leave. They can't stay there," I said.

Joanne pinged the elastic that was holding her file closed. "You're going to be here a while, Racheli. Till you come straight. So make it easier and start now."

"I want clean clothes. Four skirts, four shirts, ten pairs of underwear. That's all they allow. I want them. I need to change my clothes."

Joanne put her hands on top of her file. They were speckled with brown age spots. Blue-green veins ran from her wrists and stopped at the knuckles. Where did they disappear to?

"I'll see what I can do about your clothes."

Joanne left. More doors opening and closing. No one to talk to. The girls in my cell had left. I lay on the mattress, the mattress that I thought I'd never touch. What had happened to me? The Rav had to come and get me. I watched a spider crawling along the slats of the bed above my head. I needed a *kameya*. I would make myself a *kameya*. When the guard came to bring me supper, I asked him for a pen and a piece of paper. I got a piece of card. He came back with a pen and a piece of card that he'd torn off a box. I tore the card into two so that I could write on four sides of paper: *Everything that happens to me is for the best. Please, Hashem, plant happiness in my heart so that I can make You happy and everyone around me. Please, Hashem, for Your sake, save me and help me to subjugate myself to You. In this world a person has to work hard to do what is expected of him.* I fell asleep holding on to my *kameyot* .

The next morning, I didn't wake up until the guard banged on the door of my cell. Another investigation. I had to take my *kameyot* with me. But he was yelling at me from the door. Where were my *kameyot*? I pulled back the thin blanket, lifted the pillow. There...under the pillow.

But it wasn't an investigation. I was taken to see Ima. She had arrived from New York the night before. I hadn't seen her since Shimmy's bar mitzvah. Ima wasn't part of our circle. Anyone who wasn't part of our circle couldn't understand. Ima hugged me. But I didn't hug her back. The Rav wouldn't want me to hug her back. But there was that smell...rosewater...and I was a little girl again. Sitting beside her on the porch. Listening to the click-clack of her knitting needles. Waiting to tell her what the rabbi in *gan* had told me. That I was a soldier in the army of Hashem. I hadn't found the words that night, when I was five years old... Ima was looking at me.

She pulled me to the table...pulled the two chairs next to each other.

My fingers stroked the *kameyot* in the pocket of my skirt. Ima was staring at me. As if she wanted to read my mind. But she couldn't read minds. Only the Rav could do that.

"Racheli..."

She was a bad person. "I'm not Racheli. I'm not your daughter," I said. She didn't want to serve the Rav. "I belong to a different generation. I'm a *gilgul* from a different generation."

She was crying. Wiping away the tears with the back of her hand.

"I have a role to play. Something that you can't understand. I'm a soldier. A servant of the *tzaddik*."

She didn't understand. She wasn't in our circle. "One day, you'll understand."

"Racheli...they said you did things."

Ima...only she wasn't really my Ima...was choking. As if something was stuck in her throat.

"They said that you...hurt the children. Racheli...tell me that it isn't true."

The guard yelled, a roar that made me jump. "No English. You speak in Hebrew. You hear me?"

Ima glanced at him. "I can't speak to her in Hebrew. I always speak to her in English."

How could I explain to her about the evil, the darkness? The need to make the world pure. The need to make the children pure.

The guard walked toward us. The door opened, and my children spilled into the tiny room.

Why were my children here? Had the Rav sent them? Did they have a message for me? Seven-year-old Meir ran to me. He tried to climb on my lap. "Ima, I want you to come home. When are you coming home?"

Ahuva. Quiet. Big eyes.

Yaakov. Avner. Watching me. My children. They ran to me, all trying to touch me, to hold on to a piece of me at the same time. Something inside me, some long-forgotten instinct suddenly twitched. And then, just as suddenly, stilled. I saw Yael.

Why was she wearing a loud, pink shirt? Why wasn't she wearing tights? She was fifteen years old. Much too old to let the whole world need to see her legs. I stood up. Shuffled toward her slowly. Heard the clank of the shackles. Pulled her toward me. "You need to be *tzanua*. More modest," I said.

Shimmy. Shimmy was wearing jeans and sandals. "You can't stay with Yossi and Dov," I told them. "This isn't how we dress. The Rav doesn't allow it. No socks? How can you walk in Jerusalem with no socks?"

"Natas has gone," Shimmy said.

Natas? Just Natas? "What do you mean Natas?" I asked. "How can you call him Natas? He is the Rav. You must call him Rav Natas." Meir cuddled against me. When had I sat down? The children couldn't stay with Yossi and Dov.

Shimmy looked at the floor. At his sandals. "Natas is in Australia."

Rav Natas in Australia. It was ridiculous. Of course Rav Natas wasn't in Australia. He would never leave the holiness of Eretz Yisroel. "Don't tell them anything," I warned Shimmy. I stared at all the children one by one. "We have to protect the Rav."

He stared at me. Didn't answer.

My brothers. They were already putting nonsense into his pure head. Destroying the work that Rav Natas had done. "You can't stay with Yossi and Dov," I said. I had to control the children.

The guard moved out of the corner. A gray shirt. He was a prison guard. Not a policeman. I knew the differences between the uniforms already.

Ima pushed a bag toward me. "Take your clothes, Racheli." She was crying again. "You didn't ask about the little ones," she said. "What about Aharon and Hillel?"

Aharon and Hillel…what would happen to them now that they weren't with the Rav?

The guard yelled.

I stood up. Meir clung to my legs. His *kippah* was smudged with something…cream cheese? Ahuva was crying. She stretched out her arms. But it was too late. Ten minutes, fifteen minutes. The meeting was over. I couldn't stay. I began to shuffle out. Turned around for one last look. Heard a loud crack. No one moved. Hadn't they heard the crack too? Something inside my chest was hurting. A dull ache. Was it my heart? For the first time in so long, I felt some kind of emotion stirring within me.

Back in my cell, I sat on the mattress. The children. Who would tell them what to do now? Who would guide them? What was going to happen to Shimmy? What about Aharon and Hillel? I was alone. So alone. I'd been surrounded by people for so long. Always busy. Rushing here, rushing there. There was nowhere to go, nothing to do, no one to talk to. What do you do when everything that makes you into you has been taken away? I didn't know.

Nothing to do. Nothing to clean, cook. I pulled my pen out from under the mattress. I could write. I walked to the door. "Hey, I need a notebook," I called to the guard.

He was rocking on a chair, his legs against the wall. He didn't move. "A notebook? You think this is the Ramada?"

I tried again, and again. A sheet of paper. A receipt. But he ignored me.

The day wasn't over. An hour later, I was taken out and put in a room with Daniel. We faced each other across the table. He had circles under his eyes. His beard was scruffy. How did I look? I wanted my makeup. I stared at Daniel. His green eyes were dull. Something flickered inside me. Anger? I'd never been angry with Daniel. Did I miss him? "You know I didn't do anything," I said. "It was all the Rav."

Daniel glanced at the guard. "Don't talk about the Rav here," he said. "They want you to talk. They're listening. Don't say anything."

I stared at Daniel. He didn't know that I had married the Rav. Only those in our circle knew. And he had been thrown out.

Ten minutes. Ten minutes and the visit was over.

I shuffled back to my cell. Lay on my bed. It had become my bed. The cold slab of stone with a dirty mattress had become my bed. I wanted my home in the Old City. I thought of Daniel. We had been in the room for ten minutes. How many minutes had we shared together? I saw us planting flowers together. Building a sandcastle together. No. I mustn't think like that. Daniel was evil. Was I angry with him? It was his fault that we were here. He had brought Rav Natas to the house. I'd never been angry with Daniel. And the Rav…he wasn't in Australia…Shimmy was lying…he had to be lying… the Rav was going to come and take me out of here. Thoughts spun in my head, faster and faster, around and around like the cotton candy machine I'd once seen in a park. But nothing came of the thoughts. They were one blurry mass…they never turned into a fluffy cloud of sweetness.

In the middle of the night, the door of my cell swung open. The guard switched on the light. A short, withered woman, with a face as dark as milky chocolate, stood in the middle of the room. A black scarf was wrapped around her head and neck. A gray shawl around her shoulders. She was wearing two skirts. Underneath the brown skirt, I could see the hem of a black skirt.

"You're on my bed, *motek*," she said. She smiled. One front tooth was chipped so badly that only a sliver of tooth remained. "But you can stay there for now." Two steps, three, and she was standing by the other bed. "I'm Bruriah," she said. "This is my fourth time here. I'll be in prison for a few years, and then I'll be out for a few, and then I'll be back here. Like always. I know how things work here." She poked a very pink tongue through the gap in her teeth. Bruriah kicked off her shoes. One skidded under my bed, and she giggled. She giggled and giggled until the giggle turned into a throaty laugh. "In prison, you learn to laugh," she said.

Bruriah was taken out of the cell first thing in the morning. For an investigation, I knew that already.

I was alone. I took the toilet paper out of the toilet and began to write. *Hashem, Abba, I'm so tired here. I'm so hungry. Hashem, give me the strength to carry on. It's hard here.* I tore off the squares that I had written on and put them in my shoe.

When Bruriah came back, she was in an even better mood than the night before. She was going to prison. For two years. "You need to wear a shawl," she said. "If you wear a shawl, Hashem will help you more. Like He helped me."

A shawl? I'd stopped wearing a shawl after I married the Rav. But I was dressed modestly. I didn't need a shawl.

Bruriah pulled the bag that Ima had sent me out from under the bed.

"You can't touch my stuff," I said. I tried to grab it back.

Bruriah shrugged. "Show me what you have. You have another skirt? They let you have four skirts here. You can wear a skirt over your shoulders. Poke your head through the waist." Bruriah kicked off the shoes again. This time both shoes made it under my bed. She began to laugh. When the tears were rolling down her cheeks, she stopped. "I'll be out of here tomorrow," she said. "When you come to Neve Tirtza, tell them you want to be with Bruriah."

Neve Tirtza? Where was that? I wasn't going anywhere. The Rav was coming to take me out. He could walk through walls.

***

The investigations continued. But I didn't get used to the evil policeman, and the shirt buttons of the second policeman never popped off. One week ended. The second week ended. And then one morning, I was walked to a car standing in the car park outside the prison. Eran was sitting on the back seat.

"In. You're going for a polygraph," the guard said. He moved a few steps away. Stood next to the second guard. Took out a cigarette.

Eran looked at me. He put his finger on his lips. "No polygraph. It's an excuse. There are cameras here," he said. "They want to hear what we will say."

"Where is the Rav?"

Eran shrugged.

"Who else is with you?"

He shrugged again. "They released Daniel," he said. "I heard the guards talking."

Released Daniel. That meant he had gone back to our house in the Old City. Had the children gone back too?

Beit Mishpat Hashalom

I knew that my case would go before the Shalom Court, Beit Mishpat Hashalom, across the road from the Russian Compound. Joanne had told me, when she had brought me a notebook. Some days, I wrote only a short paragraph. Some days, I filled an entire page. Always I thanked Hashem. Begged Him for the *emunah* to continue.

And then, not long before Purim, three weeks after I'd been arrested, Joanne told me that the case was scheduled. It was a sign from Hashem, I knew. I was a modern-day Queen Esther, and I needed to fast for three days and three nights. If I completed the fast, it would be a great merit for me. Did I drink? I don't know. I'm sure not. My body was working on a different level. I was on a different level. I had peeled away layers and layers of evil.

I was taken by truck to the courthouse across the road. It took longer to get in and out of the white truck than it would have taken to walk there. I struggled to climb in because of the shackles. Thirty seconds later, I had to jump out. It was too high to jump out. A prison guard, part of the Nachshon Security Team, gray shirt, emblem with two crossed rifles, stood a few steps away, a gun in his hands.

I waddled into the windowless, stone waiting room to wait until I'd be called to the courtroom. I sat on the small stone bench in the cell and started to cry and pray to Hashem to save me. Suddenly, I heard a man singing. The men's holding cell was next to mine. He was singing "Tov l'Hodot la'Shem," it's good to thank Hashem, in the sweetest voice I'd ever heard. I joined in, singing softly. The words and the melody carried me away, for a tiny fraction of time, from inside the cell.

Move. I had to move. The guard pushed open the wooden doors. I was standing at the end of a long corridor. On one side of the corridor, tall windows, with tens of tiny square panes, opened onto a courtyard where people were sitting around tables drinking coffee. So people still did normal things like drink coffee. Pushed, jostled, shoved. How fast could I walk? I stumbled on the peach and cream stone floor. Why did I stumble? The stones in the floor were as smooth as polished marble...worn even by the hundreds and thousands of feet that had shuffled along them. There was half a bottle of Coke on the green wooden benches that lined the wall. I was dizzy, weak from my fast, but I knew that I wouldn't touch it. Cameras flashed. The press was here. Questions. People yelling at me.

"Don't speak to them," Joanne reminded me.

Her hand was on my arm. I saw the blue-green veins pulse. Speak to them? I giggled. I wasn't in prison, but I giggled, like Bruriah told me I would. Speak to the press? When did I tell anyone anything? I knew how to keep quiet. We walked past courtroom after courtroom.

And then Abba was there. Shouting at the guard to take off my shackles. Telling him that it was degrading, dehumanizing. Abba was there, in front of me. Telling me something. I strained to hear. But I didn't need to listen to him. Because Abba wasn't part of our circle. Because anyone who wasn't in the circle didn't understand. Abba was pushing people aside. Trying to get closer. Telling me something. Everyone was shouting. And for the first time since I'd been arrested, I wanted to cry…because I couldn't hear what my father was telling me.

Hours and hours later, Joanne told me that there would be no bail, no house arrest. The case was too big. It still wasn't clear what had happened, but there was enough evidence to send me to prison. Any time that I spent in prison would count toward my eventual sentence. I was going to Neve Tirtza, a prison for women in Ramle, central Israel. The only person I knew of who had gone to prison was Rabbi Meir Kahane.

CHAPTER THIRTEEN

Neve Tirtza

Late February 2008

Together with the other prisoners, I shuffled toward the huge, gray truck that bused prisoners back and forth from prison to the courthouse. A prison warden, some sort of gun strapped in front of him, was watching us.

"Enjoy your last moments in Jerusalem," he said. "You'll be in your new home for a very long time. I wonder if you'll see any of your kids' weddings. For what you did, you deserve to rot in prison." His words were the first of a constant barrage that I was going to be hearing over the next few years.

I climbed in. If I stood on the metal bench of the prison truck, if I pressed my face close to the grating on the slit of window, if I ignored the glare of the guard, then I could glimpse the hills of Jerusalem. I was leaving the city I loved. Heading to Neve Tirtza. For how long? No one could tell me. There were the hills of Ramot, trees, rocks, tiny houses filled with people living their lives. I could see the tomb of Shmuel Hanavi, which I had visited so many times in the past. We had cut Aharon's hair there when he turned three. How many days of *hillula* had we celebrated there? When would I ever be free again to come back here, to come and go as I pleased?

I was like Yosef Hatzaddik heading for Egypt. Forced to travel to a place that he didn't want to go to. But I wasn't like Yosef. A bus sped past the window. Full of people going where they wanted to go. No one had told Yosef that he had done something wrong. But everyone was telling me that I was going to prison because I did something very wrong. What did I do that was wrong? I didn't do anything wrong. I had simply obeyed the Rav's words. After all, a *tzaddik* is like a doctor who knows what is best for anyone who is ill. Rav Natas was only trying to save my children from the evil forces.

At the Ramle-Lod junction, the van turned right. Then left and then right again. We stopped outside the solid white metal gates of Neve Tirtza. Neve Tirtza, Joanne Meyers had told me, was one of four prisons in a complex of four. The other three prisons were for men. I saw a watchtower.

Built like a windmill. Stunted palm trees. A sandbank outside the prison wall.

The truck drove on. Stopped outside high gray gates topped with barbed wire. Lurched forward through another two sets of gates. Then we stopped.

The guards started shouting immediately. "Out of the truck quickly... we're late. We have to get you inside, already. Move faster. This isn't Disney Land."

I felt like I'd left planet Earth, entered a different life. We walked through a big metal door, walked for five endless minutes. My ankles were aching from the metal shackles. I was trying to hold on to the few bags that I'd brought from the Russian Compound with just a few of my fingers because my wrists were handcuffed. I needed to go to the bathroom, but I didn't know if the guards would let me.

Finally we reached the main entrance of the prison. Glass doors opened and then closed behind me before the doors in front of me had opened up. I was taken to a side room. I undressed. I was checked to make sure that I wasn't bringing into the prison anything that wasn't allowed. These humiliating checks were carried out every time a prisoner came back to the prison. Constant humiliation became a part of my life...from the wardens, the inmates...humiliation was far more prevalent than fresh air.

Finally, I was given back my own clothes. So...I could wear my own clothes in prison. I moved into a waiting room. A guard stood outside, his face sprinkled with pimples, talking on his phone. I waited there forever. I still had to go to the bathroom. I tried to catch the guard's attention so that he could take me. It had been such a long day.

"Wait," he said. "Soon you'll be in your cell. And you'll be there for so long that you'll be begging me to take you out. Enjoy the open space while you can."

What open space? I was closed up in a room with a tiny window through which I could see only him, the guard. I wondered where Rabbi Kahane had been imprisoned. He had been fighting for Israel, and everyone loved him. But it wasn't like that with me. My court case had been high profile. Covered in the papers and on TV. People didn't love me. They called me a monster, the abusive mother. Everyone in Neve Tirtza was waiting to see the mother who had hurt her own children. Except that I hadn't hurt them.

Suddenly, I remembered Bruriah. "I want to be with Bruriah," I shouted to the guard outside. "Please, please, can you put me in the same room as Bruriah Cohen?"

The guard picked at a pimple. Stared at me. "Shut up, you idiot. This isn't a hotel."

I wasn't an idiot. I was Racheli. A nice person. But no one could see that anymore. I sat very still on my orange plastic chair. The guard was too deep in the darkness. He would never understand. I stared at the wall opposite me, where the scraping of chairs had gouged a long slash into the plaster. Why wasn't I getting used to the insults? Why did they still hurt so much? I began to cry. Again. Since my arrest, I'd been crying all the time. I'd never cried so much. I hadn't cried when I'd isolated my whole family from me. I hadn't cried when my kids were being abused. I hadn't cried when Rav Natas had presided over my divorce from Daniel. I hadn't cried at all! I'd been made of stone. But now, slowly and painfully, I was beginning to feel again. Feel the emotions that a human being feels.

A second warden came in. Finally, the first warden walked me through the building. Past a grassy area, past more buildings. There was the smell of detergent, clean laundry. And then there was the isolation ward.

"Isolation"? I was going to be in isolation? Why?

The warden looked at me with disgust. "You have to be here till we decide what to do with you. Your case isn't like any of the other inmates. It's much worse. We have to see how the other prisoners react to you. Everyone here wants to hurt you...just like you hurt your kids."

I wanted to tell him that I didn't hurt my kids. But I'd told so many people so many times, and no one believed me. No one believed that Rav Natas was a *tzaddik*, and that I had to, *had to* listen to him.

Isolation wasn't strictly isolation. I was put in a cell with a small hill of fabric. The door slammed shut. The smell of sweat wafted around the cell so thickly that I could rub it between my fingers. The fabric shifted. There was a top and a bottom to the hill. The top was a head. I peered more closely. Underneath a veil, I made out two eyes, the color of the sky. They belonged to someone.

It was a good sign. The Rav had sent someone...a shawl lady...to be in my cell. From afar, he was taking care of me. I was in prison with a *tzaddikah*. Someone that I could learn from. Eventually the shawl lady moved and began to talk. We talked and talked. There was nothing else to do. When she told me to put on more clothes, I began to feel anxious. Anxious and glad. Maybe I was in prison because I hadn't been doing things the right way. I put on another skirt, used my third skirt as a shawl, like Bruriah had told me to do. Then I wrapped my fourth skirt around my head. These extra clothes made me feel more secure, more holy. I was lucky the shawl lady was here. She was showing me a way to get close to Hashem.

Two days later, the prison administration realized that they had made a mistake by putting me together with the shawl lady. The shawl lady was moved to another cell in the isolation section. Another woman came in. Short, spiked blond hair. "It's not fair," she yelled to the warden, sticking her foot out to try to block the warden from shutting the door. "I don't want to be here in isolation. It's not faaiir!"

"Who's there?" A voice called out. Women were always shouting from cell to cell. Trying to make contact with the new inmates…anything for a whiff of the world outside.

"Who cares?" Another voice.

My new cellmate held on to the bars of the window in the door. The back of her neck was fleshy. The skin sat in folds, and out of these folds a row of tiny black moles protruded. "Yolanda. Call me Yolanda."

"Who'd they put you with?" someone else shouted.

Yolanda half-turned to stare at me. Icy blue eyes. Not the blue eyes of the shawl lady.

I shrugged, kept on saying Tehillim. What was I supposed to tell her?

Yolanda hitched the strap of her tank top higher onto her shoulder. "She has a skirt around her shoulders. Another one on her head."

"The mother who hurt her kids." One voice.

"Who could do that, anyway?" Another voice.

Yolanda turned to look at me. This time fully. "That was you?" she asked.

I bent my head closer to my Tehillim.

"Yeah, you better pray. What kind of a mother doesn't look after her kids?" Yolanda kicked the door with the back of her boot. "Take me out of here! I'm not staying in isolation, and I'm not staying with her. Guaaarrrd!" Yolanda screamed over and over.

The next morning, she was taken out. Put in some other cell, where she began to scream again. Demanding to be let out. Until the other women told her to shut up. And then she screamed louder.

In the afternoon, a woman my age was brought into my cell. The same interrogation started up when the women heard the door of a cell opening and closing. Who was here? Whose cell was she put into? This time I answered for myself. But it didn't help. Two minutes later, the shouting started. I heard once again how evil I was. How I wasn't fit to be a mother. And that was how it was. Every few days, someone new came into my cell. Part of their acclimatization was hearing about me.

The next day, the woman was moved and Yonit, a Moroccan who was mentally impaired, was put into my cell. She didn't care who I was. She wanted me to braid her hair. Over and over again. Yonit loved music. She brought with her a small transistor radio and listened to music all day long. When she danced and sang to herself, she didn't see anyone else...she was in her own world. Sometimes, I would just watch Yonit. Seeing her enjoy herself made me feel happier. Sometimes, when the cloud of depression fell over me, I'd join her singing and dancing. It helped me to push away the apathy of depression for another day.

The worst part of being in isolation was the loneliness. I had been the master of my ship. For nine years, I had taken care of my family. For another six years, I had been busy day and night with the circle. And now...nothing. I had nothing to do, nowhere to go. I didn't even have the horror of investigations to break the monotony. The minute I had walked through the doors of the Russian Compound, I had begun to die; in isolation, stripped of everything, my death was completed.

When a person dies, his body dies, and his soul lives on. In prison, I felt like my soul had died. Weren't souls supposed to be eternal? But my soul was dead, and my body had to keep living. And at the same time, there was the ultimate paradox...there was a physical pain in the center of my chest, as if I were getting punched. As if my soul was crying day and night. How could a dead soul cry?

I spent a lot of time writing. The same sentences over and over again. I was dying. I was so, so lonely. *Please, Hashem, help me overcome this sadness. Please, Hashem, send me candles for Shabbat. Please, Hashem, send me someone, anyone to talk to.* Pages full of self-pity. How had this happened to me? I was the wife of a *tzaddik*.

My first Friday in prison drove home the reality of having been stripped of everything. It was getting closer and closer to Shabbat. I wasn't sure that I'd have Shabbat candles to light. How could it be that I wouldn't light candles? How could it be that this simple mitzvah had been taken from me? When I told the guard that I needed two candles for Shabbat, he laughed.

"You… What kind of a mother are you? You didn't look after your kids… and you want to light candles?" He straightened the badge on his shoulder. He cursed me using the same kind of vulgar language that the police investigators at the Russian Compound had used.

So I made a sign. Each day, I received my Badatz meals in a cardboard box. I tore open the box and made an enormous sign that I held up when the guard came in. It had to be big, large, easy-to-read letters. People who weren't religious, who used such vulgar language…surely they couldn't read.

"Why so big?"

"Because you're not religious, so you don't know how to read."

The guard looked at my sign, looked at me. This time he didn't curse. He looked at me with the same expression that Shimmy had when he had brought home that stray cat. "You have to wait until the head warden comes," he said. "I can't authorize your candles."

I couldn't wait for the head warden. "I need to light now. It won't help me if the head brings me the candles in an hour, it'll already be Shabbat. I need to light now."

The guard shrugged.

I couldn't see the other women in the other cells in isolation. But we could hear each other. So I pleaded with them to join me in begging Hashem to send us Shabbat candles in time for us to light. They weren't interested in lighting Shabbat candles, but there wasn't much else for them to do, so they agreed. We all shouted to Hashem. When everyone had stopped, Yolanda kept going. And then, after ten minutes, the head warden appeared with two handfuls of candles.

"How did you do it?" A young voice. Atarah. She was part of the hilltop youth, the shawl lady had told me. "I want to light too," she shouted.

"She needs candles too," I told the head warden. It felt good to do something for someone. Later, when I was staring at my candles, watching the tiny flames with blue centers, I thanked Hashem for the candles. And asked Him to take me out of prison.

I got used to the voice of young Atarah over the next three months. She never agreed to put her hands out to be shackled. Every time the warden came to take her out for something, to see her lawyer, or to go to a court case, there were screams.

"Put your hands out," I'd yell to her when I heard the guard approaching.

"Never! You think I'm going to let myself be handcuffed?"

And then the shouting would start.

"Put out your hands, Atarah," I'd yell.

The shouting would get louder. Soft thuds. Pushing. Dragging. And the guards would carry out Atarah with her hands shackled.

***

After that first Shabbat in prison, I was given permission to use the phone for an hour a day. The phone was an old payphone mounted on a plank of wood screwed to a set of wheels. The wardens wheeled this little phone from cell to cell. The phone stood about half a meter off the floor so that we could use it by putting our hands through the small slit that was carved low into the door of the cell. The phone had a short cord, which meant that to use the phone, I had to sit on the floor. We all wanted to use the phone. But the warden passed the phone first to whomever he liked best. The rest of us waited and waited. Finally, it was my turn. One hour. What a joke. I had so many calls I wanted to make…the kids…I missed my kids so much and wanted to get back to them…my lawyer, Rav Natas, Daniel even. I hadn't spoken to Daniel since I'd moved into the Rav's house. Now I wanted to hear his voice. I was terrified that I'd have to stay in prison for a long time, like the guard had told me. I knew that the phones in prison were tapped and that every word I said could be held against me in court. And I wanted to hear the voice of the Rav. The love I felt for him was so strong that I took my chances and dialed his number anyway.

Why wasn't he answering? He was at the *kever* in the north. Davening for me to get of prison. Or maybe he was at the mikveh. I tried Yigal. Eran. Had they been arrested as well? Was only I arrested? Maybe they'd already been released. I'd heard bits and pieces of news from the guards when they spoke amongst themselves. I'd heard that the Rav had flown away to hide from the police, but I wasn't sure of anything. I had to talk to the Rav. To hear him tell me that everything was going to be okay. But there was no answer. I had only this one hour to call. Someone had to answer. Please, Hashem. My fingers ran over the buttons. And then I was dialing Daniel's number. "Daniel?" Was I allowed to talk to him? What would the Rav say?

"Hi."

"It's me." Didn't he recognize my voice? Didn't he want to talk to me?

"I know."

I'd missed Daniel's voice. Suddenly, I even missed the way he drummed his fingers against everything. "I miss the kids. It's a nightmare here." Daniel had never been a talker. And he didn't know how fast the units on my phone card were running out. No one told me they'd go so fast. With every word I said, the numbers fell lower. Talk, Daniel. Talk. I glanced over my shoulder. Could the Rav hear us? "Do you miss me, Daniel?" I wanted him to miss me. To tell me that it was all going to be okay.

Daniel didn't answer. I could hear him breathing. "Did you marry him, Racheli?"

"No."

"Eran told me you married him."

When had Eran told Daniel? Yes, I had married the Rav. Had I wanted to? "I married him...but I didn't want to," I said. Of course I hadn't wanted to. And now I knew what I wanted. I wanted to stop feeling this awful loneliness. I wanted my life back. I wanted to share it with Daniel. Even if Daniel had never really shared much.

I could still hear Daniel breathing. He hadn't cut me off.

"I have to find out...find out if...Racheli...it's complicated. A man can divorce his wife. And he can remarry her..."

Rav Natas had said that Daniel could marry me again. It was a mitzvah.

"You don't know halachah...," Daniel continued. "A man can divorce his wife. And he can remarry her...but if she marries someone else in between, he can't marry her again."

Suddenly my hands started to shake. I slumped against the wall. I was already crouched on the floor, but I began to keel over.

"Racheli...maybe...it wasn't a real marriage... I...I have to speak to the rabbis."

Who would he speak to?

Yonit wanted the phone. She pulled at my arm. She was wearing socks on her hands. Telling me to get off the phone. Did I have to wear socks on my hands? Would it make me better so that this would work out? So that the Rav wouldn't ever find out that I wanted to remarry Daniel. Did I want to remarry Daniel? Did I want to stop being the wife of a *tzaddik*?

***

In isolation, the cell door was opened only when the head warden was present. The head warden was present four times a day, when we were counted. Sometimes, he came by at other times. If he was there at mealtimes, the door was opened to deliver our food. If he wasn't present, the food was pushed through the small slit at the bottom of the door. Laundry was usually sent out and thrown back to us through this small slit. The inmates in isolation were considered to be the most dangerous prisoners, so if we ever needed to leave the cell, we had to first be handcuffed. For this to happen, we had to kneel on our knees and put our hands through the slit. Once we were handcuffed, the door was opened.

When you're isolated to this extent, any visitors bring with them the breath of life. My parents had prolonged their stay in Israel, and they came to visit me every week. During these short half-hour visits, visitors were allowed to bring me two calling cards that they would buy in the prison canteen right outside the gates. The cards were expensive. For sixty shekels, you got fifty minutes calling time. When you ran out, there were no more phone calls. Toiletries and anything else I needed also had to be bought there.

Aside from these regular visits, since I was an American citizen, once or twice a month, two representatives from the American consulate would come to visit me. They would bring me newspapers. When I complained that I wasn't being given paper, they made sure the wardens supplied me with notebooks. I also had regular meetings with a representative from the Rabbanut. He was helping me to sort out my marital status. Was I married or divorced? Who was I married to? I welcomed these visits, because they were an excuse to get out of my cell. But it was the visits from the children that I longed for most.

On their first visit, the warden walked me to one of those little rooms on the right, beyond the entrance to Neve Tirtza.

"Your kids don't know anything about how to behave normally," the warden said before he unlocked the door. "They hammered on all three doors like wild animals. Couldn't wait to be buzzed through like normal people."

I didn't tell him that my kids missed me. That they wanted to see me. I was their mother. I didn't tell him because I wanted him to take off my handcuffs before the kids saw me. I put out my hands. "Please…before I go in…" I begged.

The warden looked at me. "Are you crazy? It's against the rules."

I stepped inside. And then he took off the handcuffs. And then Meir ran to me. A social worker was there. She had brought the kids to Neve Tirtza. Six of them. Hillel and Aharon were still in the hospital. I wished that they could have come.

But the children weren't dressed right. Not one of them. Yael and Ahuva…I couldn't look at them. How could good girls walk around without tights? Daniel and I had worked so hard to give them the right values. And Shimmy…Shimmy was still wearing jeans and sandals without socks. Even after I'd told him not to when he'd come to the Russian Compound. "This is the way you dress?" I asked him. "Why can't you dress right? You know I'm not there…you have to do the right thing on your own."

Shimmy didn't answer.

I sat on one of the couches, lifted Meir onto my lap. Patted the seat next to me. "Sit next to me," I told the kids.

Ahuva jumped onto the couch.

"Show Ima what you brought for her," the social worker said to her.

A phone card. Maybe it was a phone card. I needed a phone card.

Yael held out a small photo album.

I took it. "You need to wear tights," I told her. "This isn't the way to dress."

Yael tugged at her skirt.

It didn't hide her legs. Her skirt was too short.

She smoothed her ponytail. "Look at the photos, Ima," she said. "Gila took us back to our house one day… I chose photos…so that you…" She stopped.

She rubbed her palms over her eyes.

"Yael wanted you to have the photos so that you won't feel lonely," the social worker said. "Your sister took them back to your house. Helped her find photos of each of the kids."

Photos… Gila knew how I wanted the kids to dress… Why didn't she try to make sure that they were doing the right thing… She could help…but she wasn't helping. She couldn't see…because she wasn't one of us.

The social worker came closer. "You didn't hug the children," she said. "Don't you want to hug them before they go?"

I stared at her. What did she know about being a mother? She wasn't even married. I hugged the children. I had seen them once in the Russian Compound. This was the second time in over a month that I was seeing them. And when I hugged them, I realized how very much I had missed them. How much I wanted to get my children back. How much I missed being a mother. I hugged each of them and whispered messages into their ears. "Don't watch the TV. Remember to say Shema before you go to sleep. Daven for the Rav."

"Finish up," the warden said. It was the same warden with the pimples. How could he be so mean? So mean that he would never let us have an extra minute.

The social worker took Meir's hand. "You didn't ask about the other children," she said.

The other children. If I thought of them, I would die. How much they had suffered! The pain! And I had done nothing. How had I done nothing? I tried hard to push these thoughts away. These thoughts were killing me, and I wanted to survive. The social worker didn't know what it was like in prison. Prison was death, I wanted to tell her. I was so miserable that I had to fight to remain alive. Thinking of Aharon and Hillel, what had happened to them, was agony. Somewhere in the turmoil of endless misery inside my chest…I missed my children. But if I thought of them…thought of Aharon and Hillel…I would die. Die again and again. Could a dead person die? Was that what hell was?

The warden walked me back to my cell. He unlocked the door to my cell. "What kind of a mother hurts good kids like that? Poor kids. *Miskenim*," he said.

I sat on my bed. Opened the album. Looked at the children. I had taken these photos. But Yael had added four more photos. Of her, Shimmy, and

Ahuva in Yossi's yard. Her sleeves were too short. Ahuva's skirt didn't cover her knees. Maybe it belonged to one of Yossi's kids. I took out a pen and carefully colored in all the places that should have been covered. My children weren't following the Torah, and it hurt.

***

That week, I also began having weekly meetings with a private psychologist, Rotem Beller. Ima had hired her. But I couldn't thank her because Ima was a bad person. Someone that Rav Natas wouldn't want me to talk to. Rotem was the only psychologist who was willing to travel to Neve Tirtza and endure the wait until she was called in to see me. We met in one of the rooms just inside the main entrance. She wasn't part of our circle. I didn't want to talk to her.

Rotem looked at me. Looked at a blank piece of paper on the table in front of her. And back at me. "What do you think about everything that has happened to you?" she asked.

Think? I didn't know how to think. Didn't want to think.

Rotem just sat there. Looking at me.

So I spoke a lot about the darkness in the world, the evil in people. The evil inside all the members of my family. But I didn't speak about Rav Natas or about Daniel. Rotem listened. When she shook or nodded her head, her blond-gray curls shook. Knock-knocked against the silvery frame of her glasses. I watched the bump in her throat bob up and down, waited for her to say something. But the bump in her throat was the words that she was swallowing. Rotem didn't say anything more.

The guard came in.

"Do you write?" Rotem asked.

I nodded.

"Keep writing," she said. "Write it all down. Everything that you think."

I was already writing to Hashem. Now I began to write long letters to Daniel. *Why aren't you willing to forgive and forget? I was always there for you. You know that I only did it for you. Remember how I was there next to you when Rav Tzefanyah told you all those crazy things to do? Why can't you be there for me? I was so sad that I had to do all those things. I thought it was all for Hashem. Daniel, please, remember me…* Suddenly all the words that had been inside me all those years came flooding out, caught in the ink of my pen.

Thanks to Rotem's recommendation, I was going to see Hillel. I hadn't seen him since the night in the hospital when I'd been arrested. This time I traveled in a prison van instead of the truck. Finally, we got there. I was hurried inside through a back door so that nobody other than Hillel and the social worker at this home would see me. The home staff was disgusted with me and didn't want to ever see me. I had made Hillel handicapped.

I was shackled, but it didn't matter this time. My feet felt light in spite of the heavy metal around my ankles. There was light and laughter in Hillel's new home. Home. This was where Hillel was going to live for the rest of his life. A wide, clean corridor with pictures of animals, children playing in a field, flowers in bloom. Open doors that led into bedrooms with neatly made beds. And bedrooms with special beds. I looked at all of these things. And then we reached Hillel's room. Hillel was here…instead of building a tower of Lego in *gan*. Instead of chasing a friend down the slide in the playground.

The warden unlocked my handcuffs, and the nurse put Hillel into my arms. For half an hour, I held him, rocked him, sang to him all the songs that I used to sing to the children. Hillel didn't move and didn't open his eyes. He never did. But he had to be listening. I knew he was listening. He would wake up. He must. Please, Hashem, wake him up.

***

About two months after I arrived, Yemima and her husband Netanel came from Migdal Yam to visit me. The guard took me to the visitors' room. Yemima was wearing a flowered head scarf. It smelled of the sea. She was expecting. I looked away. That used to be me. They were waiting for me to speak. I wanted to ask them if they had spoken to Ima. If they had brought me phone cards. All calls had to be made using cards with prepaid units. But instead, I said, "Thank you for coming." As if I was thanking them for coming to a Shabbat *seudah*, even though I knew that I would probably never do that again. Even though I didn't want to talk to them. But I did want to talk to them. I was lonely. So lonely. Part of me, my soul, maybe, was dead. Dead from the pain. Anyone who spoke to me gave me the feeling that I was alive. Netanel and Yemima used to be my best friends… Were they still my friends? I'd lost everything…but maybe I hadn't lost their friendship?

Netanel talked first. "How are you?" He didn't wait for a reply. "The children miss you," he said.

How did he know about my children? They were living with a family that the Welfare Ministry had set up for them. A young foster family. For the time being. Daniel was trying to get the house ready, organize help so that he could bring them together again.

"I have a letter from Ahuva. And one from Shimmy," I said. I wanted to show him the letters. Ahuva wrote that she loved me. That she was waiting for me to come out. Shimmy wrote that he was counting the days for me to come out like he counted the days for *sefirat ha'omer*. I didn't think about how many days he would have to count. I didn't know.

Netanel nodded. But he didn't ask to see the letters. I told myself that it didn't matter. The main thing was that they were here, Yemima and Netanel. They were here and they were talking to me. If they were talking to me, it meant that I was still alive.

"Do you need anything?" Netanel asked.

I wanted to tell him that everything in this world needs some kind of nourishment. A flower needs sunlight, water, and nutrients. A dog needs food and attention. A person needs food, attention, and acknowledgment. But in prison, you are no longer a person, so no one has to talk to you like you are one. But Netanel and Yemima were talking to me, so that meant that I existed.

Yemima sighed. She tugged the corners of her headscarf to tighten it. Her face crumpled.

She was sorry for me. We'd been neighbors...walked into each other's homes, and now...I was a prisoner...and for something so horrible...

"What do you think about?" Netanel asked.

I stared at him. Think? I didn't know how to think. My father and brothers knew how to think. So did Daniel. So did Natas. I blinked. He knew that he had gotten through to me.

"Don't you think something...anything?" he asked.

I was silent. And then I shook my head. I laughed. A sound came out. A jerky sound. Like the scraping of a bicycle chain that was left in the rain. But it was a laugh. So I laughed again. I could think enough to know that I could not think. Did that mean I was thinking?

Netanel leaned forward till his stomach was pushing against the edge of the table between us. "You are still there, Racheli," he said. He stared at me like he had stared at Daniel in Migdal Yam when I had invited them to a Friday night meal and Daniel spent half an hour making Kiddush. Daniel never let me invite them again. "Your head is still with that *rasha*. You have to choose a side," he said.

Yemima sighed and put her hands on her belly.

"Who are you, Racheli?" Netanel asked.

And then the guard stepped closer. "This isn't a coffee bar. Time to go."

I didn't want them to go. There was something so warm and loving in their visit. They cared about me and about what I was going through…even though I had distanced myself from everyone who wasn't in the circle of the Rav. They made me feel alive…and I wanted this feeling to last forever. Quickly, I pushed a notebook that I had filled into Yemima's hands. "Take it," I said. "Give it to my parents. I can't keep it here. The wardens mustn't find my notebooks."

Yemima looked at the notebook, opened to the first page. "Why? Why can't you write?" she asked.

Why? Didn't Yemima know that everything had to be a secret? I wanted to tell her that in the circle everything was secret, but the guard was shouting again.

Yemima hugged me. I didn't ask them about the phone cards, because she hugged me. The warmth and caring I felt in that hug chipped away another piece of my heart of stone. A deep, deep part of me remembered, in a fuzzy kind of way, like when you're driving down a misty road at night, that there were other kinds of people in the world. People who didn't hurt other people. People who could fix others without hurting them. My world had shrunk and shrunk over the years in the circle. But here in prison, where I was living in a tiny cell, my world began once again to open up very, very slowly.

***

"There's a lawyer here to see you," the warden told me. "Do you want to go?"

I swung my legs over the edge of my bed. Stood on the stale popcorn that one of the other girls had been eating the night before. A lawyer? I had spoken to Joanne on the phone a few days ago and she hadn't told me that she was coming. But it didn't matter. Any reason to get out of my cell was a celebration. A reason to walk around, move about. Of course I wanted to go.

It wasn't Joanne waiting for me in the little meeting room.

The woman had a short, black bob. A perfectly straight part showed her white scalp. She smiled. "I'm Natas's lawyer," she said.

I didn't have shackles on. But my legs wouldn't move the right way. I shuffled to the chair. Held onto the back.

"I went to see Natas in Australia," she said.

So Shimmy was right. The Rav had gone to Australia. Were there *kivrei tzaddikim* there? Had he gone so far away to pray for me? For us?

"He sent me here to talk to you. Maybe there's a way for us to work this out so that it will be good for all of us."

What did she mean?

"Maybe we can be together in this…remain united against everyone else."

I heard her words, heard them through a fog of emotion. The Rav was still thinking of me. He wanted us to be together. Could we be together after everything that had happened? Of course we could be together. We were married.

"Natas wrote a letter to you and asked me to give it to you," the lawyer said. She bent down and unzipped one of the compartments of her briefcase.

A pull-along luggage bag. Much larger than the briefcase suitcase that Abba had given Daniel. I watched her rummaging among the papers. She unzipped another compartment.

She looked up. "I can't believe I forgot it," she said.

"How could you have forgotten such an important thing?" I stared behind her at the warden. He was listening to us. There was always someone listening to you in prison.

"I'm sorry," she said. "Is there anything that you want me to say to Natas?"

Natas. He was the Rav. Why didn't she address him with respect? What had the Rav written in that letter? Had he explained to me why he had gone to Australia? How could he leave me? I was his wife. Did he still love me?

The lawyer was waiting. I leaned close so that the guard wouldn't hear me, opened my mouth, but no words came out. Did I still love him? How could I still love him? My children were hurt. Hurt from the ways that he had tried to take the evil out of them. But…he was a *tzaddik*. "Tell him…tell him that I don't hate him," I said.

The District Courthouse

The guard woke me up at four in the morning because I needed to be in the District Court, Beit Mishpat Mehozi, in East Jerusalem at ten. Again, it was the same hard bench in a van with a tiny slit for a window. This time, the guard did not let me stand on the bench to look out. In Jerusalem, I didn't jump out of the truck straight away. To see things…I never knew what it meant to look around and see things. The walls of the courthouse were the color of sand. Across the parking lot, I saw a low house with a stone veranda. The metal shutters were open and pinned against the walls. The laundry was blowing in the wind. I moved from the truck into the waiting room at the back of the court. Until I was walked to the courtroom.

People rushed at me. Cameras.

"Don't talk to them," Joanne told me.

I looked at the white marble tiles. Polished. Marble steps. Dark marble pillars. A smell of wood. Paint. Toasted cheese sandwiches. There was a cafeteria somewhere. Abba was there. He hurried toward me. Pushed past the reporters. He wasn't allowed to talk to me. The wardens tried to push him away. I was so lonely. What joy to see someone familiar. To see Abba. Did I still think that Abba was evil? No, he wasn't evil. Could I think things without the Rav seeing them? Maybe. Maybe he was too far away to read my mind.

Then Abba was there, in front of me. And this time I could hear him. "Make your own relationship with Hashem," he told me. "You don't need some idiot telling you how to talk to Hashem."

I wanted to tell Abba that I always spoke to Hashem. That I wrote Him letters. But the warden shoved Abba aside.

I sat on a bench at the side of the courtroom. The windows were open. They were covered with bars and a grid. Like our home in the Muslim Quarter. The judge sat higher up, on an enormous black chair, behind one, two, three computer screens. The lawyers sat in front of her. Spectators behind the lawyers. In rows of wooden benches. Like in a shul. There in the corner of the room was the flag of Israel. The national emblem in bronze. I closed my eyes. Saw the flag waving at the Israel Parade that I'd so often enjoyed as a child in America.

And then I saw Tikvah. Tikvah Goodman. I breathed in deeply. I could smell the antiseptic smell that was hers. I was sure of it. I thought back to the last time I had seen Tikvah. When I had taken Aharon to Migdal Yam. She should have looked after Aharon. She was a nurse. She'd always bandaged the cuts and scrapes of the kids.

And then she was telling the court about me. That all the kids from Migdal Yam would get together in our yard to play on our swing set. That I sat with the kids in the park every afternoon. That I was an aerobics instructor and a lifeguard. That I gave a parenting class.

I stared at Tikvah. I was there, in court with handcuffs and shackles, because of her. She could have healed Aharon's burns. But instead, she'd called the police. I sat for hours and hours. Words washed over me. What were they saying? Where was Natas? He wasn't in Australia. He couldn't be. Would I see him?

I didn't listen anymore. I had to daven. Say Tehillim. Hashem would decide everything. He had already decided. My *kameyot* were in my pocket. Their holiness passed through the fabric of my skin, into my blood, making me strong. I was dressed all in white. White was the color of purity. The color of purity would help me. I listened to this one talk and that one talk. The judge raised her hand. I saw three stripes of black ribbon on the sleeves of her black robe. I needed the bathroom. Even though I hadn't drunk all morning. Would they let me go the bathroom?

The judge was talking. *Modeh, v'ozev, v'rucham. Admit to your sin, leave it behind, and you will receive mercy.* What was she talking about? People were standing up. Abba was trying to get to me. But the warden was pushing me forward. Joanne was next to me.

But the warden was still pushing me forward.

And finally we were in the truck going back to Neve Tirtza. I was too tired to stand on the bench and look out the window. What time were we going to be back? *Please, Hashem, let us arrive back before four or after four.* We were counted four times a day: at 4:00 a.m., 12:00 a.m., 4:00 p.m., and at 10:00 p.m. When we were being counted, we weren't allowed to move until the counting was completed. So before every counting, you had to make sure that you were in a place you wanted to be for the next half hour. I didn't want to be in the waiting room. *Please, Hashem. Please, Hashem, make Joanne understand that I'll never speak against the Rav.*

***

The day after I'd been to the District Court for the first time, the social worker brought the kids again.

Five kids. Avner wasn't there. "Where's Avner?" I asked Yael.

She didn't answer. I looked at Ahuva. She had to know.

"Avner didn't want to come," Ahuva said.

Didn't want to come? Of course Avner wanted to come and see me.

"It's going to take time. Time and a lot of work on your part," the social worker said.

I turned to face the social worker. "What did they say to him? Why won't he come? Why didn't you make him come?"

"He's fourteen. He's starting to think for himself. We can't make him do anything. I hope that no one will ever again make him do something he doesn't want to do," the social worker said.

She was talking nonsense. We all had to do things we didn't want to do. It was part of life. But I didn't answer her. She knew how to say things better than I knew how to.

When the warden took me back to my cell, I took out my diary. *Hashem, I'm so lonely here. Give me the strength to keep going. Give me the strength to stay happy. And please, please, send me more calling cards. My card is almost finished. Two days ago, when I called Dov's house, it took Meir three minutes to find Yaakov. Why, why can't they understand that every time I have to wait for someone to come to the phone, my units disappear into nothing? No one can understand what it's like to hold on…only You can understand, Hashem.*

***

Dina was my next visitor. "Never thought I'd see the inside of a prison," she said. I was happy to see her. Even though she complained a lot about how hard it was to get there and how she had to wait hours to see me. "Drive past Neve Tirtza's white and pink brick wall along the main road. Turn right. Park. Walk down the red brick path. Knock on the blue door. Ignore the barbed wire running along the wall above. Focus on the earthenware pot lying on its side in the pebbles along the path. Someone actually planted a white flower in there. Ha! And then I had to wait for hours and hours until they brought you in. Well, I'm glad you're not wearing a skirt wrapped around your head anymore."

I didn't laugh. I still had one on my shoulders. But Dina wouldn't understand.

"Anyway, no time for sweet talk. Half an hour isn't a long time. What happened wasn't just weird. You were in a cult, Racheli."

"Dina, don't…" I said.

"You have to hear it. You have to listen to me this time. You were brainwashed. Do you know that? He did something to your mind. You were brainwashed to love him, and you have to get yourself deprogrammed."

I looked at the warden. Could I ask him to take Dina away?

But I wanted Dina here. She was a friend. Someone who looked at me like Racheli, not an evil person. Only it was so hard to listen to her talking. Dina went on and on about the Rav, saying terrible things about him, about the circle.

"Can't we just talk about something nice?" I finally begged.

"You had better join every program they have here so that you can straighten yourself out. You have to do everything to get your kids back. You hear me, Racheli?"

"How are your kids, Dina?"

The guard yelled that half an hour was up. Dina had to leave.

***

Three months after I arrived, I was moved out of isolation, together with Yonit, into the main branch of the prison. We moved into a cell with four other religious women. Six women in one tiny room was a different kind of nightmare. I quickly learned that there was one rule in prison: make someone else's life more miserable in any way you can. In the morning, women either went to school (to complete their high school diploma or one of the courses that were offered) or to work. Both ended at one o'clock. The whole afternoon stretched out, and it was filled either by watching TV, waiting for the phone, or snitching on each other. The women reported every infraction to the wardens. Maybe someone had more shirts than they were allowed, maybe they made too much noise.

I tried to keep away from everyone. I stayed on my bed most of the day. Davening from the books that the *rav* of the prison had brought me. *Shir Hashirim*, a book of supplications. When I wasn't davening, I was swamped in my misery. Thinking nothing. Thinking about the Rav. Thinking about what I had lost. Thinking about the children. Daniel…it hadn't been all bad with him. We'd had so many good times together. But I couldn't think of those times. Because the Rav would know if I thought of those times. And I was married to him. He was all I had left. Unless Daniel found a way for us to remarry. No house. No children. Just waves and waves of pain, washing over me, stopping me from breathing. Physical pain in my chest. Every breath brought more pain into me. Shards of glass driving into my heart. Pain and more pain. How much could it hurt? A dead person couldn't feel pain. Why was it hurting so much? I was more tightly wrapped in my agony than a caterpillar in its cocoon.

I was lonely. I didn't want anyone near me. What did I want? I wanted Chagit to leave me alone. Chagit, in the bunk above me, was a woman I couldn't avoid. She had eyes as black as the darkness that looms in a crack between rocks. The day that I came in, she complained to the warden that I didn't shower often enough. A few days later, she complained that I didn't know how to wash the floor in our cell. I had missed the skirting boards. I tried to laugh. Bruriah had told me that in prison you have to laugh. So I laughed. But it was a silent sound. A dead sound. Because I was afraid of Chagit. When was I ever afraid? Racheli who used to hustle her children through the Arab Quarter in the Old City. I felt that flutter of fear. It was a horribly exquisite feeling. Fear. If I was afraid, it meant that some part of my soul was alive.

The next time I met Rotem, I told her that I was afraid of Chagit. "Tell the warden he has to move me. I can't sleep with her in the bunk above me."

Rotem bent back the clip on the top of her pen. "So you're afraid?"

I nodded.

"What other feelings do you have? Can you tell me how feel about what happened?"

What had happened? Months had passed. I'd been in prison for several months already. How many times had the other prisoners yelled at me for what I had done? Shunned me? How many times had the wardens degraded me? How low had the constant humiliation of handcuffs and shackles brought me? I stared at Rotem.

"You can talk, Racheli. You're not in court. This isn't an interrogation. No one is going to read my notes."

"You don't know what it was like there. You don't understand who he was. What he did. He was our leader. Our *tzaddik*." I stopped.

"This is between you and me, Racheli. I'm here to help you. Do you want to tell me what happened?" Rotem's curls bobbed against her glasses.

What happened. Where should I begin? Migdal Yam? The skiing trips with Daniel? Rav Tzefanyah? The outing to Sea World? The meals that lasted for hours and hours? The suitcase? Where should I begin? "Do you know how it feels to serve a *tzaddik*?" I asked her. "Can you imagine how it feels to know that you are part of a select group? That you know something that no one else knows?"

Rotem swallowed. She didn't say anything. But I knew that she understood. I knew that she was there to help me. And I knew that Ima, my Ima, had sent her. I began calling Ima once a week on Friday just to wish her *Shabbat shalom*.

***

A few days later, Yonit and I were moved to a different cell. Two of the women in our new cell were Arabs. Every day, I got a box of food – airplane meals, really – with a Badatz *hechsher*. The box drove Samira mad. The day after I moved in, she told the warden that I took apples, oranges, carrots, and cucumbers from a different box of food that was allotted to the other women in the cell.

I didn't deny it, I just tried to ignore her. If she was busy talking to the warden, it meant one less person in line for the phone. I had to call Daniel. I huddled into the wall. Tried to disappear into the cracks between the tiles. Daniel had spoken to many people, tried to get a clearer picture of where we stood. Where I stood. Was there any chance of getting back together?

"Daniel?" Across the hall, in a room with turquoise walls, a young mother, a prisoner like me, played with her baby. Rocked him up and down on a curved pillow. Why wasn't Daniel picking up the phone?

"There's nothing to do, Racheli. You married the Rav, and that means we cannot get remarried." The young mother was still rocking her baby. He slipped sideways, almost off, but she steadied him.

"I can't talk to you anymore. It's not modest for men and women to talk to each other if they aren't married," Daniel said.

I knew that. Daniel had told me that back in New York, when we'd lived in Queens, next to my parents. When we'd gone to Mr. Bornstein's store to buy milk.

***

A week later, I was in court again. This time it was to the Jerusalem Family Court in Givat Shaul to decide where the children were going to be. The court handles divorces, traffic offenses. Most people who come here aren't in prison. Which means that there is no assigned holding area for prisoners. I waited in the truck in the parking lot. Then walked in with two guards, handcuffs, and shackles when my case came up. Utterly humiliated.

Daniel was there. Joanne called him up.

Daniel didn't look at me, because we weren't married. He stood behind a *shtender*. Only it wasn't a *shtender*, and he wasn't learning. He leaned on it. But he didn't have the footrest that he was used to. Joanne asked him where he'd been learning all the years. Questions and more questions.

Everyone in the court was talking about the kids as if they weren't mine. As if they were someone else's children. I was disconnected from being their mother…from taking care of them…had I lost the chance forever? I wanted to get out of prison, take care of them like I used to before the Rav came into our lives.

There were more questions, but I didn't listen anymore. I wondered if the kids had come with Daniel… Maybe they were waiting outside for me. Maybe, maybe, maybe. Hashem had already decided everything.

When I got back to Neve Tirtza, I made a poster. I stuck together three sheets of paper and wrote: *Modeh, v'ozev, v'rucham.* Big letters in Hebrew. *Admit to your sin, leave it behind, and you will receive mercy.* How many times had I heard those words in the court? Who had said them? The judge? The lawyers? I didn't know.

Samira was painting her nails.

But I knew that I had heard them. Maybe it had been a voice from heaven. Tzaddikim had heard voices from heaven. I knew that the words were meant for me. And so I made a poster. Hung it up on the wall beside my bed. I stared at the letters. Stared at Samira. She painted her nails twice a week. On

Mondays and Thursdays. Today was Monday. But it didn't really matter what day it was, because my soul was dead.

Samira pushed the nail brush into the jar and stared at my poster. "You think those words are going to help you?" she said. "Let's say you admit what you did. Then what? How are you going to leave it behind? And who is going to have mercy on you?" She pulled out the brush and began to work on another nail.

I spent all night crying until my eyes were as red as Leah's. I wondered if my lashes would fall out. *Modeh, v'ozev, v'rucham. V'ozev. Leave behind.* I had been taken out of the circle. I was physically disconnected from the bad. There was no way for me to serve the *tzaddik*, to complete my mission, free the world of evil spirits. *Modeh. Admit.* I had to admit that I had been wrong to let the Rav work with the children. How was I going to do that?

The more I formulated my thoughts, distilled feelings into words, the more I began to think. And thinking led to feeling. I couldn't let myself feel. I had to stop feeling. It was agony. But I was so lonely that I had to write. Writing helped alleviate the pain. But it also made the pain worse…because if I wanted to write…I had to think…and if I had to think…I felt. The misery got worse and worse. The more I woke up, the more I realized what I had done. The more it hurt. And the more it hurt, the more I was able to admit why I was behind the prison gates. What I had allowed to happen. Behind the prison gates, the gates of teshuvah opened.

***

It was almost Elul. The children were coming to visit in two groups. One of the social workers had decided that I couldn't give the children enough attention if they all came together. The guard walked me into the visitors' room, and I saw Shimmy, Yael, Ahuva, and Abba. Abba should have been back in New York. Why was he here?

Ahuva handed me a bag.

I could see the shampoo and chocolate through the thin blue plastic.

"You're here?" I had to talk to the kids. I had only half an hour. Ahuva was trying to give me something.

Abba smiled.

He had a sad smile these days.

"Yossi got them for you," Shimmy said. He pushed the bag closer to me.

I had told Yossi that I needed shampoo. Was the chocolate Badatz? "Where are you learning, Shimmy?" Every time that I asked him on the phone, he didn't answer me clearly. I took the bag. Everything that was brought to me had to be purchased in the canteen outside the prison. And they didn't stock Badatz chocolates.

Ahuva tugged at my hand. Gave me a piece of paper. Probably a picture. She was good at drawing.

I looked at Abba. Held on to Ahuva's hand. Smiled at Shimmy. Half an hour. Not enough time to give each of them enough of myself to last till the next week.

"Ima and I are moving back to Israel," Abba said.

"What about work?"

"We'll find a manager. Or retire."

Leaving New York. Abba and Ima were leaving New York for me.

Abba leaned closer to me. His eyes were red. When had he flown in?

"It's Elul, Racheli. You've been crying and crying. Now it's time to add teshuvah to your tears," he said. "Remember what I always told you? The world was created with the letter *heh*. Like a house with three walls. So you fell through the bottom, but you can climb back up through the window that Hashem left in the *heh*. Climb back up, Racheli, climb up."

I stared at Abba. Could I?

"You can't go back up through the same opening that you fell through. You have to find a different route."

Abba was talking fast. He knew that I wanted to talk to the children.

"Go through the window. That means you need to change yourself. But you have to take the first step, Racheli. Hashem runs the spiritual world with spiritual laws, just like He runs the physical world with physical laws. The spiritual laws of the universe say that the first step of teshuvah has to be taken by the sinner. Take that first step."

I stared at Abba. "I've cried, Abba. Cried and cried." Enough tears to fill an ocean. I couldn't do more.

"You can't just cry tears of self-pity. You have to regret what you did. Feel real bad. Real bad, Racheli. And then…you know what? Then the hand of Hashem will reach out, under the *malachim* that surround Him, and pull you close."

"Ima…look!" Ahuva was tired of waiting. But Abba had come from New York to tell me this. I had to listen. Because Abba loved me.

"Why does Hashem have to reach under the *malachim*? I'll tell you why, Racheli. Because the *middah* of *din*…the attribute of justice…that *middah* tells Hashem that He cannot accept sinners. But Hashem loves you, Racheli. He loves you, and He'll put out His hand secretly to accept you."

Abba was crying. I was crying. I didn't want to cry when I was with the children. I wanted to be happy for them. "Show me what you made for me," I told Ahuva.

Ahuva unfolded the paper she had brought. It was a letter. A letter to the judge. *To the judge. I want my mother to come out. I think she knows that she did the wrong thing. If I want, I can see that maybe she has changed. And I will be happy if she comes out.*

***

That first year in Neve Tirtza, I fasted all of Elul, breaking my fast every night. On Rosh Hashanah, I blew the shofar. On Yom Kippur, I was the chazzan. Samira cooked her lamb kebabs in the room while I sang every prayer I could remember and made up tunes for the prayers I couldn't remember. Like water dripping onto a rock, all the things that had happened to me – being in prison, the loneliness, the humiliation, the realization that I could never get back together with Daniel, the pain of missing my children – everything was slowly, slowly making its mark on my heart. I had been taken out of the circle of evil. Now it was up to me to take the circle out of myself. To walk through the gates of teshuvah.

Would I be able to do it?

CHAPTER FOURTEEN

Waking Up

2009

"You're facing years in prison, Racheli," Joanne told me, about a year after I'd arrived in Neve Tirtza.

We were having another meeting in the prison. Preparing for another session in court.

"Natas is here in Israel. Brought back from Australia. Your only chance for a shorter sentence is to turn into a court witness. You have to stand up and tell the judge what Natas did."

A court witness? I stared at Joanne. She was crazy. Stand up and testify against the Rav?

"What's the problem?" Joanne asked.

I didn't answer her. I saw the Rav. His eyes, the color of water. I saw him speaking to the angels. The pendulum. Swinging.

"What's the problem, Racheli?"

Joanne's voice was louder this time. The warden looked up.

"You want me to stand up in court and speak…tell them what the Rav did?"

"Correct."

Joanne didn't know who the Rav was. Of course she didn't. Only we knew. The Rav was a *tzaddik*. And then I saw Hillel. Hillel didn't move. Didn't smile. I mustn't think of Hillel. I would die if I thought of him. Die again. The Rav had made a mistake. He would do teshuvah. And…I was married to him. "I…I can't."

Joanne stared at me. "You can't?" She stood up. "You can't stand up and tell the court what he did to your kids? Think of your kids. You need to think about this, Racheli. Think hard."

I didn't answer her. Because six years of living in the circle couldn't be cancelled out easily.

Joanne picked up her bag.

She had a small briefcase. Much smaller than the one Natas's lawyer had.

"Maybe everyone was right," she said. "Maybe I was crazy to take this case."

The warden took me back to my cell. "You're crazy," he said. "Only crazy people let their kids get hurt. And then won't do anything about it."

There was a new woman in our room. Pants and jacket. Stalking up and down the cell. She was shouting. "Prison…I get sent to prison and they're still walking around. You hear? They were the ones who convinced me to do it. I didn't know a thing about fraud till I joined them."

She stretched out her arms as she spoke. As if she could pull the others, the ones who were really guilty, into prison with her.

"That's how this system works…throw the innocent into prison and let the guilty slip away!"

She had a Parker pen in her pocket. I needed to write. Rotem had told me to write. It would help me. Moriah was sweeping the cobwebs from the corners of the room. "Your day is Wednesday," she said to the new woman. "On Wednesdays you clean."

The woman thumped onto her bed. Pulled her legs up and hugged her knees. She watched Moriah. "No," she said. "I don't clean. I'm a lawyer."

Moriah brought the broom down close to the lawyer's nose. "On Wednesday, we'll see."

I fell onto my bed. Turned to the wall. My back was a shield that kept everyone away from me. A lawyer. Smart people like her could say no. I stared at the poster I had made. *Modeh, v'ozev, v'rucham.* I had to leave him behind. I had to forget about him. What was wrong with me? Why did I still believe that Rav Natas was a *tzaddik*? Why couldn't I stand witness against him? I began to write a letter to Natas. *Yitzchak…* He would want me to call him Yitzchak…Yitzchak Luria…the Ari Hakadosh…the Rav was a *gilgul* of the Ari…he told us…when had he told us…I couldn't remember when…did Daniel know? It didn't matter now…

Yitzchak, I know you so well. I know what you are capable of. You must not remain on the path that you chose. You have two choices: You can either remain where you are and sink in the quicksand that you are standing on, or you can come in front of all of Am Yisrael to acknowledge and to confess to all the evil you did. Listen to what Shimmy told a reporter who questioned him. The reporter asked him how it could be that you are denying everything. And he answered that lots of people say that the Holocaust didn't happen, but there are people who have numbers on their arms to prove it. Shimmy said that he and the other kids also have marks on their bodies to prove it. You cannot continue to deny it. Hashem rescued me and my children. Took us out of your control and brought us under His wings. It's not too late, Yitzchak, you can still admit to it all and say sorry and come back into Am Yisrael. Hashem will judge between us and the end will come… Amen.

I read and reread the letter. Would it get to him? How would it get to him? I had done so much bad. I was climbing up through the window of the *heh*. I was coming back to Hashem. So why…why was it so hard to stop loving him? Why couldn't I make that complete break? Was I really crazy? *Hashem, Hashem, help me. I can't bear thinking that I still have feelings for the Rav…for Natas. Why can't I believe that he is Natas? Just Natas. Not a rabbi at all.*

It was late…I wanted to go to sleep…but the lawyer…her name was Amanda…was still shouting. "Innocent…you hear me?"

Only Yonit was listening. Sitting on the end of the lawyer's bed and nodding. As if she understood everything.

Yonit. Poor Yonit. With a mind that never grew, thinking that never got her anywhere. Except into Neve Tirtza. Yonit couldn't say no to the drug dealers. But the lawyer should have. Lawyers were smart. I should have been smart too. Smart enough to take my kids and run. Why hadn't I? What was wrong with me?

The next morning, the warden came to wake me at four. It was another court day. It was cold. Too cold to get out of bed. The warden began to yell. Moriah and Samira told him to shut up.

"Get out of your bed," the lawyer shouted at me. "Get out, so we can go back to sleep. You don't get out and I'll tell the head warden. Make sure your visitation rights are cancelled. Who wants to visit you anyway?"

So she had heard… I had to find my *kameyot* . I had to find my Tehillim. My siddur. I couldn't go if I didn't have them all. Why couldn't they all stop yelling? My *kameyot* were under my pillow. A few more seconds and I'd have all of my stuff together. As I pulled my *kameyot* out, the letter that I had written to the Rav fluttered to the floor. Behind me I could hear the boots of the warden coming closer. I had to get out. I pushed the letter under my bed with my foot.

Doors buzzed open and closed. I climbed into the truck. And there, on the bench opposite me, was the Rav. How had it happened? How had he arranged for us to be in the same truck? Was he going to say something to me? Why, why hadn't I brought my letter? Was he going to tell me that he still loved me? The Rav looked at me. Looked away. An hour and a half from Ramle to Jerusalem. For an hour and a half, I waited for a message from him. A hint. But there was none.

Prisoners were forbidden from speaking to each other. I was terrified to speak to him and get caught. But this was most likely my last chance to say something, anything to him. I had so much to say to him. So much time had passed since we last spoke. My mind and heart were racing…we were driving up the mountain to Jerusalem…the ride was almost over. If I didn't speak now, I would lose my chance, and who knew if and when I would ever have another chance.

The guard was looking out the window.

"The Rav…can you hear me? Do you still love me?"

The Rav didn't look up. The guard turned his head. Stared at me.

My hands were shaking. My heart was pumping. Had I really said those words? Were those the only words I wanted to tell him? My eyes were burning. I wanted to tell him so much more…I wanted to tell him that he was wrong…that I hated him…but instead I had asked him if he still loved me. I was a fool…I had lost the chance to help him see that he had done wrong… lost the chance to persuade him to tell everyone that it was all his fault…lost the chance to get my kids back.

***

The next day was Tuesday. I couldn't get out of my bed. I was crying. Crying and crying. And Samira was getting more and more angry. She didn't have to do her nails on Tuesdays. Tuesdays were for plucking eyebrows. I didn't know that Samira had finished until she threw the tweezers at me.

"You should go and work in the laundry. Or go bind books. Or go to that stupid learning program," she told me. "All day you lie in bed and cry. It drives me crazy."

The learning program. The *midrashah*. Yonit had told me about that. Every morning, the guard came to walk her there. Like he walked Moriah to the laundry. Samira to the class where they studied for a high school diploma. The *midrashah*. I could not go there. I could not learn Torah.

Amanda looked up from her crossword puzzle. "Stop complaining and let her cry," she said. "It would do you good to be more like me. I don't judge someone from what others say about him, I judge him by figuring out for myself who he is."

Samira stared at Amanda, but she didn't answer.

"It all depends on who your friends are," Amanda said, clicking her Parker pen against her teeth. "Look at me…a decent lawyer until those crooks got hold of me. Like Racheli…a decent mother until that rabbi got hold of her. And what about you?"

Samira opened her mouth.

"Even you were probably decent…once long ago." Amanda turned back to her crossword puzzle. "Butterfly of temperate regions with dark purple, yellow-bordered wings…any idea?"

Samira snorted. The learning program. The *midrashah.* I would never go there.

But the next morning, when the warden came to get Yonit, I told him that I also wanted to go to the learning program.

"Only idiots go there," he told me. "So it's a good idea for you to go there."

There were nine women in the program. In Neve Tirtza, there were about two hundred women. Only nine women went to the *midrashah*. Lag ba'Omer was coming up, so they were drawing bonfire pictures. I didn't want to draw a bonfire. I sat. I remembered Abba learning. I remembered the Shabbat songs that he sang with my brothers. That afternoon, I asked Yonit why she hadn't told me about the Rabbanit. The Rabbanit had been coming for a few days already. Yonit said that since I didn't come anyway to the *midrashah*, it didn't matter that a new Rabbanit had come to teach.

I came the next day and the next. Because finally, finally, I had found a place in the prison where there was some holiness. The first few times I came into the classroom, I didn't speak. I sat and watched. I enjoyed leading the davening, though. In the mornings, we spent about twenty minutes reading all the names of people who were sick, or who needed to do teshuvah or who needed an *ilui neshamah*. I liked reading out the list. But I didn't say anything to the Rabbanit.

There was a window here, and I could feel the hot air blowing in. I sat. The lawyer had told me that I could be sentenced for years. So I had to get used to sitting. The girls were still busy with their pictures. I didn't want to draw and color. The Rabbanit, Rabbanit Shlomit, who led the learning program, was tall. As tall as a building, maybe. When she sat down, she collapsed neatly, story by story, until she had folded her tall frame into the plastic chair. Her face was sharp and angular. The light coming through the window fell onto her face and made shadows. The longer I looked at her, the more beautiful she became. Until the thing called beauty lost its meaning and all I saw was the beautiful angles of her cheekbones and jawline.

And then the Rabbanit talked about Rabbi Akiva. It happened one day, when the girls were coloring their bonfires. She talked about Rabbi Akiva. How he'd lost all his students and started again with five. I knew the story, but I listened to her anyway. Because the Rabbanit was looking at me as she spoke, and if she was looking at me, talking to me, it meant that I was someone. And it meant that I was alive.

The Rabbanit finished the story. The girls carried on coloring their bonfires. And I carried on doing nothing. Thinking. I was trying to think.

Then the Rabbanit walked toward me. She sat down next to me, leaned forward, and touched my arm. Rubbed it up and down. Asked me my name. Asked me about my family. Asked me what I was thinking. I didn't answer her.

And then she said, "Rabbi Akiva started again. Anyone can start again."

Ha! Rabbi Akiva could start again because he hadn't done what I had done. But I didn't want to tell her. Maybe she hadn't heard. Maybe that was why she was talking to me. Being nice to me instead of yelling.

The Rabbanit pulled her chair closer to mine. "Do you believe that Hashem created the world?"

Of course I did. I nodded.

"Do you believe that Hashem created the power of teshuvah?"

Yes. I nodded. The Rabbanit's headscarf covered all of her hair. Not a strand peeped out.

"Put those thoughts together. Recreate yourself with teshuvah and recreate your destiny."

I stared at the Rabbanit. I was trying. I was really trying. But I still had those feelings…those feelings that I shouldn't have. I couldn't tell her about them. No. But I wanted to talk to her. Not to just nod my head. So I told her it was hard. So hard.

"Teshuvah isn't as easy as flipping a light switch," she said.

A light switch. It was so true…teshuvah wasn't about flipping a light switch. I looked away. Stared at the yellow and orange in Yonit's picture.

One of the other girls was calling the Rabbanit. I didn't want her to go. I wanted her to talk to me for longer. But she stood up. Went to the woman with the long gray braid that reached all the way down her back. Sat next to her, passed her crayons, and told her about the power of *modeh ani* in the morning. How every single deed that we do affects the Upper Worlds, which, in turn, makes an impact down here. "Hashem gave us the power with our words to build and destroy," the Rabbanit said. "When we wake up in the morning and say the words *modeh ani*, we have already accomplished more than we can imagine."

I started going to the *midrashah* every day. The Rabbanit spoke to me, made me feel like I was a person. Most women in Neve Tirtza were here for dealing in drugs or for white-collar crimes. A few were here for murder. Yet the Rabbanit poured out her love to everyone.

After a week or two, the Rabbanit spoke to me about how easy it is to slip into depression. "It's easy to be sad," she told me. "But you have to have good thoughts."

Good thoughts. What kind of thoughts were good thoughts?

"Good thoughts are thoughts that are positive. Thoughts that make you happy. That give you the strength to carry on."

I wondered if she knew what I had done. The Rabbanit told us that she never did research on the background of the women who came into her classroom. But it was impossible not to know about me. It had been all over the media. I didn't open up that day. Or the next. But I kept coming to the classroom.

***

"You need to do everything you can to get your kids back," Dina had told me. "That means taking every course that they offer in the prison." Dina was right, which was why I started taking part in a parenting course. A parenting course…I used to give a parenting course. When I'd been a mother. But mothering was a role that I had lost. Like I had lost everything else. The more I listened to Tali, our coach in the parenting class, the more her words drew me back into the spectrum of normalcy. The more I moved back into the spectrum of normalcy, the more I wanted to belong there. The children became my focus. My reason for living. I had to prove that I could be a normal mother so that I would be allowed to mother them again.

There were twelve to fifteen women in the group. Some of the mothers had been involved in drugs, one had robbed a bank, two were accomplices to murder, one had killed someone. But I was the worst mother. Because I hadn't done anything to protect my children. This fact was established at the end of the very first class.

Tali closed her file, threw her ponytail over her shoulder. "Who wants to share something that happened to them when the kids came to visit this last week?" she asked.

The women began talking, but I didn't hear anything they said. I was thinking about Shimmy. The three older kids had come to visit. I'd prepared rice for them to eat. I had wanted to make a cheesecake, or an ice cream cake, but the fridge in the kitchen had stopped working. There had been nowhere for me to store it, so I'd made rice. Shimmy had refused to eat it. Yael and Ahuva had eaten his share while he'd complained that he was hungry, had come all the way here, and there wasn't even anything to eat.

Tali looked at me. It was my turn to share.

"I was hurt," I said. "One of my kids complained about the food I served when they came. He's an older kid…he should be able to understand that the fridge wasn't working. He –"

"And where were you when they were getting hurt…why didn't *you* understand things?" Nurit yelled.

"Yeah, you're a mother? How did you let all that stuff happen?"

That came from a new prisoner. I couldn't remember her name. My stomach slid up into my throat. Why had I opened my mouth?

"You think you're religious? You're as religious as I am! I know all about religious people. I have neighbors who are religious. Religious people don't do things like that." Shulamit didn't shout. She never did. But she always managed to link anything bad to religion.

Tali was looking at me. Waiting for me to answer them.

These women had also done things wrong. They were here for a reason. I didn't have to be afraid of them. "You don't understand…"

Nurit stood up. Her hands were on her hips. "*You* can't understand. You're not fit to be a mother. And you can't complain if your kid doesn't like rice. You can't complain about anything."

I didn't have to listen to them. Let them talk to me so…so…not nicely. "You weren't there. If you had been there, you'd have realized that I didn't have a choice. I didn't know how to –"

"You had a choice. Every time something happened, you had a choice, and you chose not to do anything. You're a crazy person. Even cats take care of their kittens," Penina said.

Penina had adopted one of the cats that roamed around the prison – an enormous black cat with white socks – and no one was allowed to touch her cat. No one touched the cat, because Penina was in Neve Tirtza for murder.

I stood up because there wasn't any way I could defend myself. My legs weren't holding me up. I stumbled toward the door. Hammered hard. The warden had to open up. Open up and take me back to my cell.

They hadn't been there…alone…with no one to talk to…for six years. There was no way, absolutely no way that I could have chosen differently. I had to hold on to that excuse. Because without it, I would go insane. Or die from the pain.

But the following week I came back. I had to show the prison authorities that I was taking the course. And I continued attending the classes. A few weeks later, the new prisoner in the group – her name was Carmel – complained that her twelve-year-old daughter wouldn't come to the phone when she called home.

It was a problem I had. Shimmy and the girls were still living with Yossi. Avner and Yaakov were living with Daniel, who had moved back into our house. The last time I had called the house to talk to them, Yaakov had refused to come to the phone. "I have one kid who won't come to the phone too," I said. "I feel that –"

"Ha! Your kid doesn't want to come to the phone? Why should he come to the phone after what you did?" Nurit yelled.

"I didn't –"

"Don't tell us that you didn't do anything. You *chose* to do nothing," Nurit yelled louder.

Loud enough for the warden to open the door to check that everything was okay.

Tali nodded at him to let him know that everything was okay.

"You don't understand," I said. "Natas was a *tzaddik*." I stopped. I had called him Natas. For the first time, he wasn't "the Rav."

"You chose!" Nurit yelled.

I stared at her. "I thought that I had to listen to him because he knew everything. I didn't have anyone to ask anything. I didn't *do* anything…"

Tali put up her hand. "Enough," she said. She looked at me closely. "Choosing is an action," she said. "Choosing is doing *something*. You chose. You chose to listen to your rabbi. You chose that obedience above your kids."

I didn't say anything more. I wanted the class to be over. So that I could get to my cell. Into my bed. Far away from anyone in this parenting group. *Why?* I wrote in my notebook. *Why did I choose Natas above my kids? How did I become a yes-man to such an evil person?* I stared at my writing. He was Natas. He was no longer the Rav. I closed my notebook. I couldn't write more. There was no way out. The result was all mine. Hashem had sent me the children, and I should have protected them. I was supposed to have looked after them, raised them to be good Jews. But look what I had done!

I had chosen not to do what Hashem wanted. I had heard it from others. And, now, from within myself, a voice screamed out at me. I had chosen. I had chosen, and the results were before me. They would be before me for the rest of my life. And now, I could go insane. I could die from the pain. Or I could grow. I had to choose.

***

I suppose it was because I was religious. Or maybe the prison authorities wanted to see how I'd cope with the responsibility. Or maybe the prison rabbi just felt sorry for me. Whatever the reason, I was given a job as the *mashgichah* in the kitchen. The job kept me busy until three in the afternoon, which was great. What wasn't great was that Shulamit was also working in the kitchen where we would prepare the food for the prison staff.

There were six other inmates in the kitchen. Four cooked for the other prisoners, one cooked for the officers, and I was put in charge of checking the chickpeas, rice, flour. I was also responsible for turning on the fire if there were any non-Jews on the shift. Working in the kitchen was a big privilege given only to the most trusted prisoners. There were knives here. You couldn't find knives anywhere else in the prison. And there was also access to all the offices on the second floor and the officers' dining room.

Most of the women here were old-timers serving ten to twenty years for violent crimes. But my crime was unforgivable. And to top it all…I was religious.

I'd checked the rice and was sifting the flour when Shulamit said, "I've been working here for twelve years, and you can't tell me what to do. We're not Badatz here."

I ignored her. Even though she was an accomplice to a murder crime. I wanted to work here. The familiarity of kitchen work was soothing. And I had access all day long to the fruit and vegetables in the prison fridge.

But Shulamit wasn't finished. "People shouldn't ever talk to you. You should be shot in the head."

I should yell back at her. She wasn't here because she was a *tzaddikah*. But I didn't. What was the point? I didn't have anything to say to defend myself.

The following day, Shulamit changed tack. Since yelling at me hadn't worked, she decided to rope the lawyer who shared my room, Amanda, into her cause. "It all happened because she's religious," she said. "Religion makes you crazy."

Amanda was using a wet towel to pull a tray of potatoes out of the oven. Quickly, she set the tray on the counter. "I don't know if religion makes you crazy. There are plenty of religious people who aren't crazy. And there are plenty of people who aren't religious who *are* crazy."

Shulamit stared at the lawyer, trying to figure out if she agreed or disagreed with her.

The lawyer picked a potato from the edge of the tray. She blew on it and popped it into her mouth. "Needs more salt," she said.

Shulamit turned to me. "There's no way you can do teshuvah," she said.

"Leave her alone."

It was Simi. Simi was also an old-timer. She was forty years old, but she'd been in and out of the prison since she'd turned eighteen for drug dealing. Her face was as lined and wrinkled as a raisin. That was the first of many times that Simi stood up for me. I needed Simi…not only because she protected me from Shulamit, but because she acknowledged that I was person. If she acknowledged me, it meant that I was alive.

I carried on checking the beans that I had soaked in water the night before. *There's no way you can do teshuvah.* I *can* do teshuvah, I wanted to scream. All my schooling had taught me that. Abba told me I could. The Rabbanit told me. But maybe…maybe teshuvah was for people who'd done things that you could fix up. Like lying. Hurting someone's feelings. Eating something that had the wrong *hechsher*. Maybe there were limits to teshuvah. How could you do teshuvah if you'd done something that had changed someone's life? Changed the lives of a lot of people…of your kids…in ways that could never, ever be repaired? Was Shulamit right? Maybe there was no way that I could do teshuvah.

***

Sometimes, the Rabbanit got permission to take us into the yard for a class. I enjoyed these classes because we were outside. In the air. I could see the sky beyond the barbed wire on top of the wall. On one of these afternoons, I was stroking one of the stray cats that lived around the prison when the Rabbanit asked a question that I couldn't answer.

"Everyone has something good about them. I want you to think for a moment and each one of you will speak about one of her good qualities, her good *middot*," she said.

Was she looking at me?

Did I have a good *middah*? What were my good qualities?

The Rabbanit went around the group. Everyone was finding something to say. Yehudit had worked for two years binding books in the prison workshop before she started coming to the learning program. She'd been the best book binder.

"That is a skill. That isn't a good *middah*," the Rabbanit said gently. That was a skill she had.

Yonit, dear Yonit, had such a long list of good qualities that we joked that every *shadchan* would be calling her.

Soon it would be my turn. What was my good *middah*?

Shifra said she never yelled. Never screamed.

That was a good *middah*, the Rabbanit said. A person should always talk calmly.

What about me? I didn't have a single thing to say about myself. I wasn't a good wife. I wasn't a good mother. I wasn't a good daughter. I couldn't even say that I cooked well. I had used my cooking skills to cook for bad people. Could I say I took my kids to the park every afternoon? What did that count for now? Could I say that when I woke up in the mornings to daven, I tried not to make noise in the cell so that the other five girls could sleep longer? Where had that sensitivity for others been when I'd been in the Rav's circle?

The Rabbanit was looking at me. "Racheli?"

I looked away. There was nothing, absolutely nothing, good about me.

The Rabbanit handed out sheets of paper. "Write your good *middah* at the top of the page. And then think about how you can use that *middah* here in prison," she said.

I took my sheet of paper. Crumpled it into a ball.

The Rabbanit came and stood in front of me. "Who is Racheli?" she asked me. "There's a wife, there's a mother. And there is someone called Racheli. You have to find her," the Rabbanit said.

Find her. How was I going to find her? Did I want to find her? Would I like her if I found her? All these thoughts spun through my head. But they were feelings. Horrible feelings that made me feel like a heavy, wet blanket had wrapped itself around me, making it impossible for me to move a limb. How could I find a way to take these feelings, condense them into thoughts, give them words?

In Neve Tirtza, I had plenty of time to think. From my window, I could see the top rows of windows in the warehouses across the street. I counted and recounted those windows, hundreds of times. From the counting of the windows, I moved to counting the lights on top of the building. My mind wandered to other things. I began to think about what I was feeling… Thinking was horrific. It became even worse when I tried to write down what I was thinking. Tried to make sense of the feelings.

The week I met with Rotem, after the Rabbanit had challenged me to find one good *middah* and I hadn't managed to, I spoke about the Holocaust. "People in the Holocaust were victims. Their pain was imposed on them from the outside. They were persecuted for doing good things, for just being," I said.

Rotem nodded. She didn't say anything.

"It's different with me," I said. "My pain is self-imposed. I've done the bad things." I took a deep breath. Could I say it? Could I tell her what I'd been thinking? Say the words, the phrases, the sentences, that I'd jotted down in my notebook? I laced my fingers together. Pressed the knuckles hard against each other. "I destroyed my home and my children with my own hands. My misery is something that I made. My Holocaust is self-made." I said it.

Rotem nodded.

She was supposed to say something. But she didn't. She let my words hang between us. I imagined that the words molded into one, became a pendulum. A pendulum swinging back and forth between us. I asked those words if they could find a good *middah* inside of me. But there was no answer.

***

Gila visited me again. She had come a few times. This time I took some cookies with me to the visitors' room so that she would have something to nosh on.

"Remember the necklace you gave me?" I asked her.

Gila laughed. "You expect me to remember a necklace from a million years ago?"

"Not a million. Maybe twenty. It was a little pendant. A heart. It had *Number One Sister* engraved on it."

Gila shook her head.

Why couldn't she remember? "I'd wear it now, if I had one like that."

"I'll look for one like it. Will that make you happy, Racheli?"

Happy? I would never be happy again. But I didn't tell Gila that. Instead, I sat still and let her massage my neck and shoulders. And I talked. It was good to have someone to talk to. "Shimmy is counting the days till I come home. Just like he counts the day for *sefirat ha'omer*," I told her. I told her about the other children too. But I could tell that she wasn't listening. Not really. She wanted me to talk about the cult. About what had happened. About how it had happened. But I couldn't tell her. Because I still didn't know. I couldn't put into words the threads of thought that were beginning to come together in the dark hours before dawn when I woke up and couldn't fall asleep. If I'd known how to put my thoughts into words, I'd have told her that some awful things happen in a second. Like a terrorist attack. I'd have told her that other things, like rot, take time to happen. The rot starts slowly, in one small spot. Then it spreads surely…until all you have left is a putrid mess.

***

Every afternoon, the Rabbanit walked through the cells visiting whoever wanted to talk to her. Sixty women. Even the girls who never came to the learning program wanted to talk to her. I always talked to her. It wasn't like talking to Rotem. Rotem had a way of making me think about what had happened even if she didn't say much. But the Rabbanit…well, she was a Rabbanit. Connected to holy things. I could see it in the light that shone from her face. I liked Rotem. I waited for our weekly sessions. When she spoke, I listened. But Rotem wasn't religious. And since she wasn't religious, she couldn't understand me completely.

But the Rabbanit…she spoke. She spoke about hope, how we could all become better people. And when she spoke to me, she spoke about Hashem and how much He loved me. I wanted to believe that Hashem could still love me. I wanted so much to be loved. I could put aside the horror of my deeds and think instead of coming closer to Hashem. It was this longing that stopped me from killing myself. Irony of ironies: I was in Neve Tirtza for doing things that I had thought would bring me and my children closer to Hashem. This very desire to come close to Hashem stopped me from ending my life.

One afternoon, the Rabbanit came into our cell. I was lying on my bed. But I didn't move. It was already the middle of Elul. I was fasting all day, every day, breaking my fast only at night. So I felt weak. I hadn't gone to the *midrashah* that morning.

Samira was reading a magazine. She had a pile of fashion magazines that she flipped through every afternoon. One after the other. When the warden let Rabbanit Shlomit in, Samira stood up. The magazine slid off her lap and flipped closed. A woman with a red hood that covered one eye stared at me.

Rabbanit Shlomit hugged Samira. "*Mah shlomech, motek*?"

Samira held out her hand. Shiny, blue stars glittered at the tip of every red fingernail.

The Rabbanit held Samira's hand at an angle. Held it up to the fluorescent light. "When you leave here, you'll open up a salon," she said.

Samira looked at me. She didn't pull her hand out of the Rabbanit's hand. "You have to stand up," she said. "Even a fool knows that you stand up for your teacher. She's your teacher, right?"

"Don't stand up," the Rabbanit said. "You don't feel well."

I nodded. Someone had noticed I was weak. Someone was taking care of me. I sat up slowly. My head spun. I had to drink, but I couldn't drink. It was Elul. Elul was the month to come close to Hashem.

The Rabbanit sat on my bed. Reached for my feet and rubbed them.

"What about teshuvah?" I asked her. "I need to do teshuvah."

She rubbed my foot harder. Pressed her thumb against the ball of my foot. "Hashem isn't standing over you with a whip, waiting to punish you," she said.

I didn't answer her. I'd never stopped believing in Hashem. I had lost everything, but I hasn't lost my relationship with Hashem. I had never stopped trying to come close to Hashem. Wanting to serve Him better. Rabbanit Shlomit put that relationship in a different light. *Hashem isn't standing over you with a whip, waiting to punish you.* I wasn't used to thinking of Hashem as my Father Who loved me. My concept of Hashem had become mangled in my mind. Warped. Natas had instilled so much awe and fear into me that those feelings spilled over into my relationship with Hashem. Rabbanit Shlomit reminded me that there was a different way.

Her words weren't a magic wand. But I thought about what she had said. Like I thought about everything she said.

And I kept going to the classes. One day in class, I found a magazine with a picture of an old man smiling. The camera had caught him in a moment of joy. I could hear him laughing. I cut out the picture. He looked so happy and so holy. I put the picture with my *kameyot* . Whenever I felt the pain overwhelming me, I would look at the picture. I was dying from the pain, and I knew I had to help myself survive. So I used anything spiritual to help myself.

***

"Life is going on without me," I told Rotem, a few days after the Rabbanit had come to visit me in my cell. "I try to feel connected, but I'm totally disconnected. No one needs me. No one is waiting for my call. I'm not a part of my children's lives. And no one is telling them that it'll be different when Ima comes back."

Rotem jotted something on the yellow pad she always brought with her and rarely wrote in. She nodded.

She'd pulled her hair into a ponytail. Without the curls around her face, she was…different. I'd been thinking, thinking so much that my head hurt. I had to tell her what was on my mind. For so many years, I'd kept all my feelings and thoughts stuffed away. Now I was finally learning to express myself.

"Do you have children?" I asked. I didn't know anything about Rotem. And she knew so much about me.

She nodded.

"My children are leaving the path of Torah," I said. "I try to tell them what to do, but I've lost control. I can do nothing. I don't know if they're learning, if they're davening. If I say something, they won't come to the phone. They won't come to visit."

Rotem nodded. "How do your parents feel?" she asked.

My parents? I stared at Rotem. "Why isn't your hair loose?" I said. "It suits you better loose."

Rotem smiled, but she didn't answer.

"Why are you smiling?" I asked her.

"Because you like my hair loose," she said. "Isn't it less modest that way?"

She didn't wait for me to answer. "You're starting to heal, Racheli. It starts with little things. You're seeing that things aren't black and white."

I picked at a loose thread in my skirt. Wound it around my finger and tugged till it tore off. The guard banged on the door. Our time was up. I walked back to my cell slowly, trailing my fingers along the wall, letting the cool of the concrete seep into me. How did my parents feel? I didn't need Rotem to tell me. I could begin to imagine how they felt.

I was learning to think for myself. Just as I was hurting because I hardly had any contact with my kids, my parents were hurting from not having any contact with me. They were there for me. They weren't bad people. My parents wanted to help me. Maybe even Yossi and Dov wanted to help me. They'd taken the kids. Faygie and Ayelet.

That afternoon, when it was my turn to use the phone, I called my parents even though it wasn't Friday.

"Are you okay, Racheli?"

I always called on Friday. "I'm fine, Ima," I said. "Can you please ask Abba to come on the line as well? I wanted to talk. I want to ask for your forgiveness...because I haven't treated you nicely. Can you both forgive me?"

Ima made a funny sound. Like she was choking. And I could hear Abba crying.

"Hashem picked a family for me," I said. "You were picked to be my parents. I have to focus on what you can give to me and on what I can give to you."

"Thank you, Racheli," Ima said. "We finally got you back. I thought that we had lost you forever. I love you...never stopped loving you..."

Ima was crying too. We were all crying.

***

The head warden, Boaz, wanted to talk to me, the warden told me as he walked me to the prison offices. What was it about? He had no idea. I tried to think of something I had done wrong. Who had complained about me? Were they going to take away visitation rights, like they had done when Gila came to visit and we had tried to exchange shoes under the table? That had cost me a month of visitation rights. My breath caught in my throat. Refused to enter my lungs. But ten minutes later, I started breathing again.

"You want me to change the bandages on the shawl lady's legs?" I had to get this right.

Boaz nodded. He rubbed his hand over his smoothly shaven head. "She has a name. Neta. She can't take care of it herself. And she won't let anyone else near her. But she's agreed for you to do it."

I thought of what the Rabbanit had told us not so long ago. How we had to try to help the other women in prison. Helping others would make us become more giving people. More loving. We could lend others our phone card. Talk to them when they came back from a court case. Smile, even. I could do this. Change Neta's bandages.

Ten minutes later, another warden walked me to the infirmary and then to isolation. Neta was still in isolation. "She doesn't talk," the warden said. "*Taanit dibbur*. A religious nut."

He held his nose and unlocked the door. A sour smell filled the cell. Cheese. Sweat. Something older than old. Neta was on her bed. I knew that somewhere in that pile of beige, brown, and black fabric, there was a person. She turned her head when I called her. The smell worsened. If that was possible. And I spotted her blue eyes. Like pieces of a summer sky.

"I'm changing your bandages," I told her.

She nodded. But didn't move.

There was barely room for me to crouch down next to her bed to work. I began to peel off her socks and stockings. Three, four pairs. The skin of her legs was dark brown. Greasy patches with crusty flakes that fell off as I pulled at the fabric. Large boils weeped out something yellow. My stomach heaved. I stood up and ran to the door. Pushed my forehead against the bars to try to fill my lungs with clean air. And then I came back to swab her legs. Rub in the creams. I rubbed gently. Neta grunted. Waved her hands about. But she didn't push away my hands. I left Neta's cell in a good mood. Because finally, after four months, I had found a good *middah* in myself. I was able to take care of someone. I could care for someone.

2010

I was feeding leftover chicken to the ginger cat that I had adopted when I decided that life was like a big puzzle. Different parts of our lives, the various roles we played, were all separate puzzle pieces that could be fitted together to make a big picture. When I was arrested, my puzzle was broken apart. The pieces were separated, and there was no longer a full picture. In 2010, the pieces began to fall back into place. And the picture that they made was horrific.

At this stage, seventeen-year-old Yael, sixteen-year-old Shimmy, and fifteen-year-old Avner were officially boarding in institutions. The four younger children, Yaakov, Ahuva, Meir, and Aharon, were living with Daniel, who brought in daily household help to keep things more or less running. Every afternoon, when I called the children, I hoped that Daniel would answer the phone, speak to me for a moment. He'd told me that there was no hope of us getting back together, but irrationally, I still held on. Maybe some rabbi, somewhere, would find a way for us to remarry. One afternoon, Daniel did talk to me.

"We need to get an official divorce with a *beit din* at the Rabbanut," he told me.

A divorce. I clutched the phone harder.

"What we did with Natas isn't enough. It has to be official."

I knew that. That was exactly what I was holding on to. I wanted to get back together with Daniel. With my kids. Have a normal family again. Why was he talking about a divorce?

"I'm getting married, Racheli."

Married. Daniel was getting married? Why hadn't he told me earlier? Why hadn't the kids told me? Daniel was still married to me. "But…what about us?" Someone was hitting me on the shoulder. She wanted to use the phone. I shrugged her away. "What about the family?"

"I already told you, Racheli…we can't remarry. You married Natas after he divorced us. We can't do anything. Do you know how many rabbis I spoke to?" Daniel's words came out in a rush. And then he stopped talking.

Was he still on the line?

"Once we're divorced, it'll be good for you too," he said. "You'll have so much merit. I know it'll help you with the children…to get them back."

I didn't want merit, I wanted Daniel back. I wanted my family back. I wanted my family whole…even though it hadn't been good…it had had a semblance of wholeness. And now there was no more hope.

"You'll have all of that merit," Daniel said again.

I couldn't think about the merit. All I could think about was that I was losing Daniel. Again. Forever.

Two weeks later, I was taken to the Rabbanut. Plenty of people go to the Rabbanut to get divorced. But they aren't prisoners. They don't waddle in with two guards, hands and legs shackled. The room was full of people. Why was Joanne here? The *toen rabbani,* the clerk from the Rabbanut who had visited me so many times in prison? And there were so many rabbis there. Why were there so many rabbis?

I could barely stand. The storm of emotions inside me was making me rock back and forth. I was going to faint. I wanted to close my eyes, but Daniel was there…right in front of me. And he looked so kind and warm.

He was going to get remarried in a few days, and he was glowing. But…this was what he had looked like when we got married…kind, warm, glowing. It couldn't be…he wasn't about to cut the connection between us…it couldn't be. I was sobbing. An ocean of tears poured from my eyes.

"Pay attention," one of the rabbis said. "You need to concentrate. This is important."

His words came at me through a mist…I was fading away…as if I was being slowly, slowly sedated…being readied for surgery. According to halachah, I was already divorced…Natas had divorced Daniel and me…but I had held on to shreds of irrational hope, like a drowning sailor holds on to flotsam… All I could see was my marriage to Daniel…and in these moments of agony, that marriage seemed perfect. I didn't want this divorce. Why was this time different from the first time we had gotten divorced? The first time, I had been made of stone. Now, I could feel again. I felt every bit of pain in my heart, my soul, my entire being. I had to die. I had to die. Now.

"*Nu…*" the rabbi said.

I stared at Daniel. He was holding out a piece of paper. My *get.* I had to take it. But I couldn't.

"*Nu…*"

One of the guards pushed my hands forward, curled my fingers around the *get.*

"Hold her up," one of the rabbis shouted. "She's going to faint, and she'll drop the *get.* Don't let her drop the *get.*"

I held onto the *get.* And once again I was divorced from Daniel…forever and ever.

Somehow, I stumbled back to the prison van and climbed in. Through the grid on the window, I could see Daniel. He was hurrying down the street, his long coat billowing behind him. He had to hurry. He had so much to do. He was getting married in two days' time.

"Stop crying," the guard yelled. Once, twice.

Stop crying? I would never stop crying. The *mizbeach*, the altar in the Beit Hamikdash, was crying. How could I stop crying?

That night, I lay on my bed stiller than ever.

The women in my cell stood on Yonit's bed to look out the window. Tzivia's husband had come to Ramle to put on a fireworks display for her birthday.

"Come see," Yonit called me.

"Leave her on her bed, there's no room for all of us to see anyway," Samira said.

I couldn't have gotten up if I had wanted to. Daniel was never going to put on a fireworks display for my birthday. I was no one to him.

The next day, I dragged myself to the learning program. I needed to talk to the Rabbanit. To tell her that I was tired...too tired to do teshuvah any longer. I was worn out, exhausted. I couldn't carry on. I had no strength left in me.

I waited for the davening to end. It was always my job to read out the names of people we had to daven for. But I couldn't do it this time. I could barely breathe.

"I can't do it," I told her. "I can't do teshuvah. I have no strength left in me to carry on." And yet...even as I told the Rabbanit that I had no strength left, part of me, the part of me that was doing everything for my children, wanted to hear that I could keep going.

The Rabbanit held my hand, rubbed it back and forth. "You could be right, Racheli," she said. "Sometimes, a person who has done wrong does feel that she doesn't have the strength to make the first move." She rubbed harder, her soft fingers moving between my fingers. "But you can still do something, Racheli, *motek*. Rav Dessler, *ztz"l*, says that you can still cry out to Hashem. Ask Him to do everything for you."

I stared at the Rabbanit. Ask Hashem to do everything for me? What kind of teshuvah would that be?

Yonit was calling the Rabbanit. A new girl had arrived today. A Russian girl.

The Rabbanit smiled at Yonit. At the new girl. But she kept talking to me. "The normal rules of the universe say that this kind of teshuvah cannot be accepted," the Rabbanit said. "But Hashem's mercy is infinite. Cry out to Hashem. Your cry will be counted as an arousal from below. That will open an opening as small as the eye of a needle. And once you've done that, Hashem will open for you a gateway that wagons can go through."

Cry? I could cry. That was all I did anyway.

***

The children came to visit once a week, but fewer of them were coming. Sometimes Yael was missing, sometimes Avner. Once when Yael didn't come, she sent me a letter with Shimmy. How many times did I read and reread her words: *I remember the letter you wrote me. About the cat on the moon. I save it and it makes me happy when I read it. I have almost forgiven you. I remember how much I loved you. I'm sorry that I don't come so often to visit you. Maybe, maybe I'll come again soon.* I kept the letter because it was a little piece of Yael. Sometimes, one of the younger kids refused to come and visit. There was nothing I could do about the children not coming. The older children made their own decisions. And Daniel said that he couldn't force the younger children to come.

There was always a social worker present to oversee our interaction. Then a new social worker took over my case. Whereas the first social worker had let me do whatever I wanted with the children, Varda was different. She decided that there were important mothering skills that I needed to develop.

"You need to learn how to discipline your kids," she said. "You can't just sit and hug them."

"But I hardly see them," I said. "I can't discipline them. I need to show them that I love them."

Varda ran her fingers through her red hair, lifting it up and showing the gray roots. "Even though you're in prison, you still need to know how to discipline them. Children like to know their limits. It gives them security."

Varda was staring at me, waiting for me to agree with her. When I didn't reply, she continued.

"Children also like routine, schedules...but that we'll leave for another time. Because you can't implement that now."

Routine. Once the children had had a routine. There had been a time to eat, a time to do homework, a time to sleep. Did any of them have a routine now?

Varda was talking again. I had to listen to her.

"You have to be strict with them. Don't just be soft."

I nodded. I managed a smile. I'd been in prison for more than two years. All I wanted was to get out and mother my children. And I knew that to do this, I had to show Varda that I was listening to her and learning to mother in the way that she wanted.

Varda arranged for our next visit to take place in the learning center instead of in the usual meeting room. Instead of low couches and a table, we sat around a table that reminded me of my classroom in high school in Flatbush.

"Now we're playing a game," I told Ahuva, Meir, and Aharon. Yaakov had refused to come this week. "So sit here…and here…and here." I glanced at Varda. She was taking notes.

But the children didn't want to play a board game. They wanted to climb onto my lap. Even twelve-year-old Ahuva. "It's your turn, Meir. Give the dice to Aharon. Don't move his counter. Stop pinching him." My orders came one after the other. There was no time to kiss the children, listen to what had happened to them over the week, ask them about Yaakov. Was he angry with me? I'd been hearing anger in his voice over the last while.

"I want to go home. I don't want to play this dumb game," nine-year-old Meir said. He swiped his hand over the board. All the counters skittered across the table and onto the floor.

Varda was watching me. I wanted to tell Meir that I didn't blame him. Instead, I told him that he was going to have to miss a turn. Which didn't worry him in the least. He wandered to the window and stared out at nothing.

The only person who was pleased with the visit was Varda. The kids left crying, and I went back to my cell crying. Once, long ago, the children had had a routine. Once, long ago, I'd been a mother to them.

***

Around this time, I was moved to a different wing in the prison—the treatment wing. This wing, close to the isolation wing, was for women who had addictions and needed therapy to overcome them. I was moved here because the prison administration had decided that belonging to a cult was an addiction of sorts. Here there were only four women in each cell. Thirty women in total instead of the 150 women in the main wing.

The warden took me to my new cell. Two bunkbeds, two beds each, stood against two walls. And that was where the resemblance to my old cell ended. Someone who loved the outdoors had decorated the cell. Lime green scarves fell in folds across the walls. Dark green pillows with brown tassels hanging from the corners lay on each bed. A woven rug the colors of a forest floor was on the floor. And there, in the corner by the window rocking in a bamboo rocking chair, was a young woman, her hands folded over her enormous belly. Her eyes fluttered open when I dropped my bags onto the floor. She smiled.

"Welcome to our room," she said, tossing her honey curls back from her eyes. "Just because we're in prison doesn't mean that I can't offer you a drink and cookies." She got up and moved toward her closet.

She didn't walk. She seemed to float.

"I'm Shira," she said. "My husband and I are here because of a hit and run accident. I was the driver, he was the passenger. And we drove away from the man we hit and injured." She filled two cardboard cups with orange juice and poured some almonds and dates into an olive-green bowl. "My husband's there," she waved her hand in the direction of the men's prison. "But we have a way to talk every day. Three times, sometimes four or five, so it's not as bad as it could be." She put our snacks on top of a cowhide drum that was next to her chair. "What are you here for?"

What was I going to say to this woman? This expectant mother? I moved to the window. Stared out at the tiny yard. Someone had planted cherry tomatoes in big, empty pickle tins. "So what'd you get?"

"Six years. We divided it between us. Three each." Shira's hazel eyes suddenly widened. "You're the mother who did nothing to stop kids being hurt," she said.

At least she wasn't accusing me. Telling me that I wasn't fit to be a mother. That I should rot in prison.

She put her hands over her belly. "How many kids do you have?" she said.

How many kids do you have? Have. In her eyes, at least, I was still a mother. I didn't answer her.

"This is my first," Shira said. "We waited four years for this child. I guess he, or maybe she, is destined to start life here."

In prison, everything is extreme. There is no middle road. If you feel something, you feel it in every part of yourself. If you don't get along with someone, you hate them with every fiber of your being. And if you like someone, you love them with all your heart. That's how much I grew to love Shira. I became a surrogate mother to her, bringing her milk to ease her heartburn, stuffing pillows under her swollen feet, and reassuring her that this too, three years in prison, would one day come to an end.

In the treatment wing, I could finally breathe a little. There was some freedom to walk around the wing. There was even an adjacent yard. The routine during the week was more or less the same as when I'd been in the main prison wing, but Shabbat was different. I found a small table and put it by the kitchen. The kitchen was next to the shul in the adjacent men's prison, and I could hear them singing. Here I held my Shabbat meals. I would spread out a white tablecloth (really one of my headscarves) and set the table. Shabbat was my light in all the darkness around me. I would sit there for hours on end singing every Shabbat song in the *bentsher* that Abba and Ima had brought me. I would sing so loudly that Neta, who was still in isolation, would hear me. I would read about the *parashah* in the books I had. Imagine that I was sitting at the table with my children. Forget, for those few hours, where I was.

There were various courses offered in the wing, and I took them all. Anything to show that I was changing myself. Anything to show how serious I was about getting back my children. I took anger management classes. Although I'd never been angry, the classes gave me the tools to deal with the anger that the other inmates felt toward me. Instead of telling them that they didn't understand me, I began to say things like, "I understand why you're angry."

Although I had begun speaking to Rotem because that was what was expected from me, although I was taking all these courses so that I would have a good prison report, slowly, slowly, the knowledge and tools that I gained began to change me. The Rabbanit was right. Teshuvah wasn't as easy as flipping a light switch. It was more like gently peeling away layers and layers of dirt that had caked into greasy, flaky scabs over years and years.

The highlights of prison life were the monthly performances that Rabbanit Shlomit arranged for us. Once a month, someone, usually a singer, from the outside would come in. Here was someone from the outside, someone who was willing to come into Neve Tirtza because he cared about us. The performances breathed new life into us. We would sing at the top of our lungs and dance as if it were the day of our release. The stone walls and barbed-wired fences disappeared, and all we smelled in the air was happiness and hope for a different future.

One month, the Rabbanit arranged for Rabbanit Bina Gudlevsky to come bake challah with us. For many of the women, it was the first time they had ever baked challah. For me, it brought back memories of hectic Fridays in the kitchen, little children rushing back and forth between my feet, and Daniel in the living room learning. I didn't need someone to tell me to put in the yeast and the salt in after the flour. I knew all the tricks. As I kneaded the dough, I remembered the Fridays in Migdal Yam when I would get everything ready early and we would drive to the beach for a few hours. I had lost it all. Through bad choice after bad choice. I kneaded and cried. I tried to pray… but there were no words to my prayer. It was just a cry. Would Hashem count my cry as an arousal from below? Could my cry open an opening as small as the eye of a needle? Would Hashem open the gates of teshuvah for me? And would I ever bake challah for my children again?

***

I had been in prison for two years when I invited Ima to an evening that was the product of the drama therapy sessions I had been attending in the prison. Six women each gave a short monologue. Ima told me later that two were riveting. And one, mine, broke her heart. That is…if a shattered heart can be broken again.

The hall quieted down when the first presentation began. A middle-aged woman spoke to her husband. I strained to hear her soft, gentle lilt. "You were so proud of your officer's uniform. I always laundered and ironed it with care, because I thought that if I valued what you valued, you'd value me. But you didn't. After I gave you two sons, I was sure that you'd stop criticizing and yelling at me, but you didn't. Instead, you goaded them to join you, and you taught them also to criticize and yell at me. It was me against the three men in my life. When you retired, I laundered and ironed your uniform, because I knew what it meant to you. I hung it up where everyone would see it and admire it. No one would forget what you'd done. I was sure that this time, this time, you'd thank me. But you didn't. You carried on criticizing and yelling. I couldn't take it anymore, so I took your gun. Now you're buried there, and I'm buried here."

Ima cried for the woman and for what she'd done.

Then a young woman, just scraping out of her teens, spoke to her imaginary mother. "I begged you for a kiss. A hug. For years, I begged. But you didn't kiss me. You told me that it would have been better if I had died. I went to a friend's house when I was five years old. Her mother hugged her and kissed her. She hugged me and kissed me too. It felt so good that I came home and begged you for a kiss. Just one. But you refused. I tried to bury the pain, but I was so hurt and so angry. One day, when I was walking home from high school, I saw you coming toward me. You were smiling, but you weren't smiling at me. I was so hurt and so angry, I pulled out the knife I always carried and I buried it deep, deep inside your chest. And then I saw that it wasn't you. It wasn't you! I had killed someone else's mother."

Ima cried for the girl and for what she'd lost.

Then I took the stage. If you could call a patch on the floor in the prison hall a stage. I didn't have any props. I was dressed all in white. And I held my hands out in front of me, like I was holding a prayer book. I spoke to myself. "You're praying," I said. "Always praying, always davening. Who are you praying to? What are you praying for? Oh…you're praying for forgiveness. You're asking Him to forgive you. So what if He forgives you? So what if the world forgives you? It doesn't matter at all, when you will never, ever forgive yourself."

***

"You can't avoid it any longer," Joanne told me when we met after Pesach. "You have to stand witness against Natas. Next week."

Witness against Natas. A year ago, Joanne had told me that I would have to stand witness against him. But I hadn't been ready. Was I ready now? I had to be.

I sat on the edge of a wooden bench in the courtroom in the district court. I could see Natas, but he wouldn't look at me. I was glad. In my mind, I knew that there was nothing he could do to me. In my heart, there remained no love, no sympathy. And yet…my attachment to him had been so deep, so complete that even as I stood there and told the court what he had done, what had happened to my children, some part of me was still attached to him. How could it be? I didn't know.

I finished speaking and sat down.

Natas's lawyer stood up. She walked up and down past the podium where the judge sat, just once, just enough to make sure that the judge was listening carefully to her. And then she said, "We have nothing to say. Everything that she is saying is not true."

Ask the children, I wanted to scream. Ask the children to show you the signs on their bodies.

Natas was sentenced to thirty years in prison. A week later, Yigal and Eran were sentenced to twenty years each. The pieces of the puzzle were falling together…but there was one piece still left out of place. What would happen to me?

I was sure that I would be released. Released and free to go back to my children. We'd been separated for two years. How many times had I gone through the four steps of teshuvah: I was sorry, so sorry for what I had done. I had abandoned my mission, left behind my sin. I had confessed to Hashem and to the court. I had changed myself to the point that I would never do the same things again. I would never again choose to do nothing.

The days before I traveled to the court for my final sentencing were busy. Joanne had instructed me to write a letter expressing my regret for all that I'd done. I was going to read this letter to the judge. At the same time, I also wrote a twenty-page letter to Hashem, thanking Him in advance for saving me. Full of verses of love, gratitude, and happiness that I had taken from Tehillim. The night before the hearing, I packed up the things in my closet, took down my pictures, gave away the things I would no longer need. Food, shampoo, makeup…I'd buy myself everything new once I was free again. It would soon be Lag ba'Omer, and I was going to celebrate my release in Meron with my children. Of course they would all come with me.

In court, I stood before the judge and read out the letter I had written. I was truly sorry, so sorry. Even a cat protects her kittens, and I had done nothing to stop them from getting hurt. The letters blurred, the words caught in my throat. I could hardly read what I had written. It was so hard to admit that I didn't protect my children. My children were like this because of what I did. I was like David Hamelech…I would have my sin before me always. And finally, finally I sat down.

The judge cleared his throat, slid his glasses down from the top of his head, and began to read out the charges against me. Horror after horror. One after the other. I had done nothing to protect my children. "In view of the charges, in view of the help that you have given to the judiciary system, in view of your regret…" he paused. Cleared his throat again.

I felt my soul soar. I was going to be released. Free. Free after two long years.

The judge took off his glasses and folded them. "You are being sentenced to five years' imprisonment in Neve Tirtza. The time that you have already served counts toward the total."

My soul plummeted to the ground. Shattered into pieces. Five years. It couldn't be. It couldn't be true. Everyone was standing up. Joanne was coming toward me, Abba and Ima, but the guards were pushing me forward. Forward. If I didn't shuffle my feet, I would fall. Tears poured down my face.

"What did you think?" The guard told me when I was sitting in the truck to return to Neve Tirtza. "What did you think...that you'd be going home?" He laughed.

Five years. That meant I was going to sit in prison for another three years. Three years was a long time. I thought of how old the children would be then. Shimmy would be eighteen. And Hillel...Hillel would be eight.

In my cell, I lay on my bed, my face turned to the wall, my back facing the cell.

"You should be dancing," Moriah said. "Five years? All you got was five years. Five years will come to an end. You've already been here for two."

I didn't move. What did Moriah know? She was going home in another six months. Home to her husband and son.

"Remember what the others got...thirty years, twenty years. That's a long time. Five years is nothing."

I heard her opening closets. Slamming the doors shut.

"You can have your shampoo back. But I already ate the chocolate. Do you want me to buy you more, or was it a gift?"

Why couldn't she keep quiet? Leave me alone. I felt my mattress sink as Moriah sat on my bed.

"You didn't really think that you would go free, did you?"

How could I tell her that I did?

Days later, when I was finally able to get out of bed, I stuck up new pictures on the wall next to my bed. What was I going to do with the poster that I had made? *Modeh, v'ozev, v'rucham. Admit to your sin, leave it behind, and you will receive mercy.* Nothing that I had done had helped me. The poster no longer encouraged me. It made me want to give up. Five years was a long time.

Moriah saw me staring at the poster. She snatched it off my bed and crumpled it up. "*Dai*, enough," she said. "You need a new one. Something positive. And I'm going to make it."

Moriah pulled out a piece of paper from under her mattress. Straightened the edge where it had folded over and began to write. Ten minutes later, she handed me my new poster: *Kol mah she'Hashem oseh l'tovah. Everything Hashem does is for good.* I put it up next to the other pictures. I ran my fingers over them. Kever Rochel. Meron. My fingers lingered over the laminated pages. I had plenty of time to look at them. I had three more years to look at them. And when I looked at them, I could pretend that I was there…at Kever Rochel. At Meron.

***

A week later, I still hadn't gone back to the learning program. I was barely making it to my job in the kitchen. And then I heard Shulamit shriek.

"Rabbanit…Rabbanit Shlomit…come, come sit here."

I stopped sifting flour. Watched Shulamit pull up a chair for the Rabbanit, wipe off an orange splatter with a finger that she had quickly licked. "Sit, sit. I'm going to bring you a cup of tea. With cookies…all Badatz, Badatz." She waved her hand at me. "She makes sure everything here is *mehadrin min hamehadrin*. Drives us crazy…all of us."

Shulamit moved across to the other side of the kitchen to fill up the kettle. From across the kitchen, she yelled, "If all religious people were like you… nice…then I'd…I'd make tea for all of them." She kissed her fingers.

I put the sifter down, looked for a towel to wipe my hands. And then the Rabbanit was hugging me.

I put my head on her shoulder.

"Racheli."

She rocked me back and forth gently. Rubbed my back with her palms.

"Racheli, *metukah*, Hashem plucked you out with a pair of tweezers. Brought you here so that you have the time to think. You can't run around from place to place. You have years now to be alone. To think about who you are. Find Racheli. Prepare yourself for your next role in Hashem's world. You will get out of Neve Tirtza, Racheli, and you find a new role to play. You need to prepare yourself for it here."

I lifted my head, stepped back. Slipped my hands into hers. "Prepare myself? Prepare myself for what role? A wife? I have no husband. A mother? You see that my children don't always come to me. Prepare myself for what? What's the point?" I wiped my eyes with the back of my hand. Felt powdery flour against my lids. "I can't change what happened," I said.

The Rabbanit looked at me. "You're right," she said. "You can't change what happened."

I shuddered. All the time I was holding on to the hope that Hashem would wipe out my sins. Make me as white as snow. As white as the thread of wool that the Kohen Hagadol hung up at the entrance of the Kodesh Hakodashim on Yom Kippur. I gritted my teeth. "See, even you're telling me I can't change what happened. And since I can't change it, what's the point of anything? What's the point of becoming a better person…of finding who I am really… so that I never again listen to a mad man?"

The Rabbanit touched my cheek. "You can't change what happened because teshuvah has limitations. That doesn't mean it's all over."

Limitations…I didn't want to hear about the limitations of teshuvah. I wanted to be as white as snow. I wanted everything to go back to what it had been before the madness. I had worked so hard on myself to rid myself of the craziness. I pulled my hands away.

"Listen to me, Racheli," the Rabbanit's voice was firm. "Rav Dessler tells us that after Adam Harishon sinned, he did teshuvah. He had been created to live forever, so when Hashem accepted his teshuvah, He should have made it that Adam Harishon would once more live forever. But it didn't happen. The decree stayed in place. Why, Racheli, why did the decree stay in place?"

Why? It didn't seem fair. Adam Harishon had done teshuvah. And Hashem could do anything. He could make him live forever again. He could make Hillel wake up. Hashem could do anything.

"When Adam Harishon sinned, his body changed. It took on a more physical nature. Reality had changed. This change prevented him from getting eternal life. Even though his repentance was complete, the decree of death could not be lifted. It was part of his new state."

The Rabbanit gripped my shoulders.

"You are now in a new state, Racheli. All of your children are in a new state. Hillel is in a new state. Now you have to create your *tikkun* on the level that you chose for yourself when you sinned. You have to reveal Hashem's glory in the depths of darkness that you created, because decrees cannot be cancelled. You have to fight a long-term battle against the darkness that you created. You will be doing this for the rest of your life."

I began to cry. I couldn't do it. From where was I going to find the strength to do it? I was all alone. I couldn't possibly do it.

"This is the purpose of creation, Racheli. The world was created so that light should come from darkness."

2011

Days flowed into weeks, weeks into months, and then a year was over. Daniel and I were still going to court to try to reach some kind of agreement on custody of the children. Yael and Shimmy were already adults. But the future of the younger children still needed to be decided. Toward the middle of 2011, Daniel and I were once again in the Family Court in Givat Shaul. It was supposed to be routine. Nothing was supposed to be resolved.

I was saying Tehillim, focusing on the words so that my eyes wouldn't wander to where Daniel was sitting. Had he brought the children with him? Were they outside waiting for me? Would I get a glimpse of them?

The judge listened to Joanne, listened to Daniel's lawyer. And then she said, "The children will not be living with the mother until her release. Once she is released, it remains in question whether or not she will be able to care for them physically and emotionally. Therefore this court is removing the children from her custody. The father has sole custody of the children."

My Tehillim slipped out of my hands. I heard it hit the tiles. I wanted to stand up. To shout to the judge that she couldn't do this… I had worked so hard on myself. Attended so many courses. Listened to so many insults without opening my mouth. And it had all been for the children. I had done it all to get the children back. To be allowed to mother again. He couldn't rip that away from me.

The guards were telling me to stand up. I stared at their gray uniforms. The insignia of two crossed rifles. I had to stand up, but I couldn't. One of the guards yanked me to my feet. Held on to my handcuffs and pulled me forward. I began to fall and then my feet jerked forward. Joanne didn't look at me. We hadn't been prepared for this.

That night I didn't sleep. I tossed and turned on the thin mattress even after Moriah yelled at me. I was still awake when the warden unlocked our door at four in the morning to count us. But I didn't get out of my bed. I didn't get out of my bed until the afternoon, when we were allowed to use the phones.

Abba answered immediately. He'd been waiting for me to call. I knew it.

"It's not fair," I shouted. "They can't take the children out of my custody. I've done everything to prove that I am a fit mother!" I was sobbing and shouting.

Moriah pushed a packed of tissues into my hand. I dropped them.

"It's a tough one, Racheli," Abba said. "You've done everything to change, and we're proud of you."

"It didn't help, Abba," I said. "It didn't help at all…they've taken the kids."

I heard Abba sigh. Or maybe he was crying too.

"You feel that Hashem has vented His anger on you to the very limit."

I sobbed harder. Abba knew.

"These feelings are older than you, Racheli," Abba said. "Other people have felt these feelings too. Think of the words in Eichah: *Bring us back to You, Hashem, and we will return. For You have utterly rejected us, You have vented Your anger on us to the limit.*"

I sniffed. Reached down to the floor for the tissues.

"But Hashem hasn't abandoned you. He's vented His anger *ad meod*… up to the limit. But not actually until the very end of the limit. There's one tiny point of holiness left intact. From this tiny point, you can grow, Racheli."

I shook my head. I couldn't speak.

"You'll survive this too," Abba said. His voice was stronger now. "Because whatever challenges Hashem gives you, He also gives you the strength to meet that challenge. And if you succeed here, you'll succeed outside."

I wanted to believe Abba. I had to believe him, because if I didn't believe him, I would have nothing left to live for.

***

In June 2011, I began a six-month course in geriatric care. Was I ever going to use what I was learning? Probably not – I was used to caring for children, not the elderly – but since the course was offered and since I took every course offered, I signed up.

For two afternoons every week, Shira and I joined ten other women in a classroom to learn about the biology, sociology, and psychology of aging; assessing an elderly person's mental health and physical health; and the role of communication in loneliness and remembering the past.

"When an elderly person talks about his past, he isn't just telling you what happened," the instructor said. "He's trying to make sense of his past and in this way come to some sort of closure."

I ran my fingers over the doodles on the desk in front of me. Make sense of the past... I was always trying to make sense of my past. Trying to understand how I could have been so caught up in a holiness that was so completely evil that I couldn't see the real holiness, my beautiful children, around me.

A few months earlier, Shira had given birth to a baby boy. She had moved out of our cell and been given a special room, a nursery of sorts, where she was raising her baby and would continue to raise him until he reached the age of two. But our friendship remained intense, like every relationship in prison. And sharing time together in the geriatrics course intensified it. So when Shira encouraged me to move on to the next part of the course, told me that if I'd looked after my children, I could look after someone old just as well, I agreed to meet one afternoon a week with Rania, a fifty-five-year-old Tunisian inmate who was in prison for life. At Amanda's recommendation, we started by doing crossword puzzles together. Later, I taught Rania to play chess. And still later, I began to ask her the same kind of questions that Rotem was asking me: How do you feel about what happened? What gives you hope?

One afternoon, Shira came to see me in the laundry room. The prison authorities had taken me out of the kitchen. Assigned me to the laundry. It was part of my rehabilitation. I was responsible for the all the laundry in the prison. My parole, a carrot dangled in front of me, was contingent on how successfully I managed this responsibility. The work kept me busy from seven in the morning to five in the afternoon, which meant that I no longer attended the *midrashah*. I missed the daily contact with the Rabbanit, but since I worked alone, I used the quiet time to listen to *shiurim* that the rabbi of the prison would load onto an MP3 player and bring me regularly. Read the *parashah* sheet that two Chabad ladies, Udel and Minky, brought to Neve Tirtza every week.

Being in charge of the laundry also meant that I was able to help Neta, the shawl lady, in an additional way. Neta had been wearing the same layers of clothes for three and a half years. She even showered with them. After a lot of discussion among the prison authorities, Boaz decided that since I had taken care of her skin infection without being negatively influenced by her, I'd also be able to handle more contact with her without being drawn into her craziness. I was instructed to, once a week, help Neta take off all thirty-five layers of her shirts, skirts, shawls, and various rags and launder them. Just as everyone had hoped, Neta agreed...as long as only I would touch her clothes. The clothes smelled sour even after I had washed them with a generous amount of detergent and softener on a long cycle.

All day, I filled the enormous washing machines, poured the detergent into the right compartments, emptied the machines, and tossed the sodden loads into the dryers. When I pulled out the clean, fragrant clothes, I thought about my soul. Could teshuvah really wash away all the stains? Bring my *neshamah* back to its pristine state?

One day, Shira came to visit me in the laundry. She was smiling. She was always smiling. Her hair had grown longer. Her curls were a halo of corkscrews that she kept brushing over the top of her head to the right and then to the left. "You need to meet Chizkiyahu," she said. "Today."

I pulled a load out of the dryer. Watched a single gray sock drift to the floor.

Was Shira for real? Neve Tirtza was one part of a complex of four prisons. Chizkiyahu shared a cell with Shira's husband, Gadi, in one of the men's prisons. Shira had cooked up the idea of bringing Chizkiyahu and me together months ago, back when we were still sharing a cell in the treatment wing. Chizkiyahu was serving twenty years in prison for a car accident, she told me. Reckless driving had killed his wife and daughter. Poor woman. Poor kid. Every time Shira mentioned the idea, I brushed her off. Me? Start a relationship? Get married again?

Shira bent to pick up the sock. Tossed it into the enormous hamper that I'd soon start sorting. "So what do you say?"

Say. What did I have to say? That I was lonely? Miserable about losing Daniel and my kids? Terrified of being alone for the rest of my life? Equally terrified of getting into a relationship that could be all wrong? "I say it's impossible," I said. "Who would want to marry me, anyway?" I dragged the hamper to the table where I folded everything.

"Nothing's impossible," Shira said. She tossed her curls once more. "They don't have the right shampoo for my hair in the prison store," she said. "My hair needs special shampoo. Not this regular Hawaii brand that everyone uses. And he's religious. Super religious."

I grimaced. Super religious? I was done with that.

Shira laughed. Long and loud.

Everyone laughed in prison. I thought of Bruriah. Bruriah whom I'd met in the Russian Compound more than three years ago.

"Don't look so suspicious. Super religious in a good way. Not freaky," she said. "You know the thing…prays three times a day…won't eat the cookies that Gadi's mother brings him." She pulled something out of her pocket. Waved it in front of my face and stuffed it back into the same pocket.

I ignored her. Reached for a handful of socks. Bent my head and smoothed them out one after the other.

"Gadi says that Chizkiyahu…he wasn't always so religious. But he's been here ten years already. Got talking to the prison rabbi."

She was waving something under my nose. The back of a photo. Sure…I was lonely. I was going to leave Neve Tirtza one day and nothing was waiting for me outside. But this idea…this idea was impossible. "Did Gadi…did Gadi tell him about me?" The words popped out of my mouth before I had thought them.

"What do you think they talk about all day? Gemara?" Shira laughed again. Put the photo face down on top of the socks I was folding. "Take a peek," she said.

The tips of my fingers touched the edge of the photo. And then I turned it over. His skin was a warm, golden-brown color. As if he spent his days in the sun. His brown eyes spilled a mixture of sorrow and trust.

"By the way, when you talk to him, tell him to ease up on Gadi. I don't want my Gadi turning religious here. I married a regular guy, and I want to stay married to a regular guy," Shira said.

"Who said I agreed to talk to him?" I said.

"Of course you'll talk to him. Why not?" Shira said. "People make mistakes. Why should two people who made mistakes stay alone for the rest of their lives?"

"It wasn't one mistake, Shira," I said. "It was mistake after mistake after mistake. Why would this guy want to marry someone who made mistakes for five years?"

"Who said anything about marriage?" Shira said. She plucked a stray hair off her sweater.

"Religious singles don't talk to each other unless they're thinking about getting married."

For the first time since she had come into the laundry, Shira's smile wavered. She stared at the curly hair and tugged it straight between two fingers. "Those guys from the American consulate who come to visit you...can you tell them that under your scarf you have curly hair and the prison authorities are forcing you to use Hawaii shampoo instead of shampoo for curly hair?"

"Yeah, sure." Shira was right. She hadn't said anything about marriage. And why...why would Chizkiyahu want to marry me? Why would anyone want to marry me?

"Good. You get me decent shampoo and I set up a call for you. Tomorrow. Here at this time."

Shira picked a pair of socks off the table and headed for the door.

"Give that back," I shouted after her. "Do you know what'll happen to me if something goes missing here?" Boaz, the head warden, had told me that Lilly, who had worked here before me, had lost visitation rights for two months after a warden's shirt had gone missing.

Shira tossed the rolled-up socks over her shoulder without looking back. "I'll tell Gadi to tell him that you agree to talk to him for strictly kosher purposes only. And don't lose the photo," she said.

The next afternoon, Shira burst into the laundry room. "Come quick. Gadi is on the phone near our cell and Chizkiyahu is standing next to him."

Shira grabbed my hand and dragged me past the sacks of dirty laundry. She didn't have to pull too hard... Finally...after years of darkness, there was a tiny flicker of excitement and light inside me.

It was the first of many, many phone calls. Chizkiyahu's voice was deep, soft. His words measured. As if he spent a lot of time thinking about what he wanted to say. The next time we spoke, we used the arrangement that all the prisoners used to communicate between the prisons. It was pretty simple: we decided on a code and set up a time to call. When we both punched in the code at the prearranged time, the prison's communication system automatically connected us. Chizkiyahu had access to a phone at any time of the day. My access was more limited. I used the phone outside my cell. We spoke first thing in the morning, before I ran to the laundry room, at twelve noon when I ran back for a half-hour lunch break, and in the evenings, when I had to stand in line with all the other women who wanted to call their families. For the first time in four years, there was someone who wanted to be in touch with me. I could enjoy talking on the phone instead of getting frustrated that my conversations with the children didn't run as I wanted them to, that they weren't coming to the phone at all. Every phone call felt like a hug. Instead of living ashes, destruction, death...I could begin to think about light, life, and growing.

Since we couldn't see each other, our relationship was built on words. Words and sentences. I suppose it was love at first sound. And yet, because Chizkiyahu had become a man of halachah, if ever I would try to talk about my feelings for him, or get him to tell me about his own feelings, he would stop me. "You're still married to Natas," he would say. "Later, when you get your divorce...then we can talk about such things." And he then would tell me about his childhood or share another insight into the *parashah*. Or make sure I knew what to add into my davening because Rosh Chodesh was coming up. And then it was Rosh Chodesh on Shabbat. Did I know what Musaf to recite? And what about Havdalah? Who made Havdalah for the women in the prison? It wasn't so simple for women to make Havdalah for themselves.

One evening, when Rabbanit Shulamit had brought in a singer, the phone was free for a few hours. I waited for Chizkiyahu's call. "So what do you do all day?" I asked him. My days were full with work in the laundry. How did Chizkiyahu fill his days? And what did he look like?

"I learn."

"What?" I wanted to see him. Photos could lie.

"Gemara."

"What else?" But voices, voices coudn't lie. Could they? And Chizkiyahu's voice was...nice.

"Mostly Gemara. Whenever the material that I'm learning is relevant to practical halachah, I look up the halachah in the *Shulchan Aruch*."

"But don't you learn anything mystical? Anything connected to Kabbalah?"

"No."

Gemara. Abba had learned Gemara. My brothers too. I hadn't heard about Gemara and *Shulchan Aruch* for so many years.

"Doesn't sound very spiritual," I said. And then I bit my lip. Why was I criticizing him? Telling him he wasn't good enough? I mustn't criticize if I wanted this relationship to grow. Men, I'd learned, did not want to be criticized.

Chizkiyahu laughed.

Laughed? He wasn't mad with me? I kept quiet. I had told him something not nice...and he had just laughed.

Footsteps, laughter, shouting. "Off the phone."

"Give someone else a turn." The women were back from the show. I had to say goodbye.

Over the next few days, while I worked in the laundry, I thought about Chizkiyahu and his Gemara. Gemara and the *Shulchan Aruch*. It sounded so different from what I was used to. Daniel had always urged me to work on myself…but I'd never really known what I was supposed to be working on. I had to be nicer. Talk nicely to him. I had to keep the children quiet when he made Kiddush with the Siddur Hakavanot. And what else? I didn't remember. I plugged in the iron. I had a mountain of shirts to iron.

There had been no clear lines to follow. Everything had been blurry. Our move to the Old City had brought so much mysticism into our lives. We'd talked about elevating souls, *tikkunim*, evil forces. I needed to order more detergent… But what had it all been based on? On where the winds of madness blew us. Based on nothing.

I didn't tell anyone in my family about Chizkiyahu, but after we had been talking for about a month, I discussed my new relationship with Rotem. It was something new for me…to be so open about myself. My feelings. And it felt good. So different from when I'd been involved with the Rav. "So what do you think?" I asked her. It was the first time I had directly asked her for her opinion on anything. It felt good to be seeking out advice from someone instead of trying to wing it on my own.

Rotem closed her file. The file she hardly ever wrote in. "In prison, everything is very intense," she said. "Remember how distraught you were when Samira refused to allow you to disconnect the light in the refrigerator for Shabbat? The pages and pages that you showed me you've written about that?"

I nodded.

"Well, this relationship is going to follow the same rules of intensity," Rotem said. "And when things are so intense, you can't think properly. Where are you heading, Racheli? This man, Chizkiyahu, is probably going to be in prison for a good many more years after you get out. Is that what you want… to be married to a man in prison?"

I looked at Rotem. At her silvery-gray curls. "No one else is going to marry me," I said. "And I'm too young…too young to spend the rest of my life alone." I rubbed my palms on my skirt. They were hot, sweaty. "The loneliness will kill me," I said.

Rotem was quiet.

Because she never lectured me. Never told me what to do. Rotem wanted me to think for myself. To learn how to draw my own conclusions. So that it would never happen again. I'd never just follow someone blindly. Well, I had come to my conclusion: I was going to keep talking to Chizkiyahu, keep trying to build something with him, because the alternative, a life alone, was too frightening. And so what if we were two battered souls? We were coming together to build something new. A hopeful beginning after so much destruction.

CHAPTER FIFTEEN

Next Stop

2012

I tossed the shirt with a rip on the shoulder into the mending basket. Later, when I switched off the last machine, I'd take the basket to Gina, a South American seamstress who was responsible for the mending in Neve Tirtza. And I'd give Boaz, the head warden, an exact list of what I had sent. Every single item of clothing had to be accounted for. Missing sock syndrome never struck in Neve Tirtza.

Four o'clock. I sat on a wobbly plastic chair and closed my eyes. The washing machine closest to me began its spin cycle. Screeches of metal on metal filled the laundry room. I put my hands over my ears. I'd told the prison handyman about this. A week ago. But he still hadn't stopped by.

"Racheli!"

My eyes popped open. Boaz.

"Good news," he yelled over the faulty cycle. "Next week, Tuesday, Dr. Aronson is coming to give you the MMPI test."

The MMPI test. Rotem had told me about it: the Minnesota Multiphasic Personality Inventory, a psychometric test used to measure adult personality and psychopathology. I'd been asking for months to take that test, and each time, the prison authorities had pushed me off. And now it was happening.

"Pass that and you'll be out."

Out? They were going to let me out on parole for the last year of my sentencing? I jumped up. The chair skittered backwards and hit a ten kilo bag of detergent.

"We're thinking of a hostel."

A hostel? I wanted to go home…where was home…I couldn't think of that. "I don't want to go to a hostel," I said.

"When you chose to do nothing, you chose to give up your right to choose what you want or don't want to do," Boaz said.

You chose. I knew I'd chosen. I'd spent four years learning not to defend myself. Learning how to say, "I'm so sorry that I didn't protect you." I knew I'd chosen.

"So just be grateful that you might, maybe, if you pass this test, move on, go to a hostel."

Move on. I wanted to move on. But I didn't need to just get out of Neve Tirtza. I needed to get divorced from Natas. And he was still denying that we were married. Eran and Yigal were denying it. And I had no idea who the witnesses had been. I walked to the ironing board where I'd written the list of items to be mended and handed it to Boaz. One step at a time… Would I pass this test?

The following Tuesday evening, a few hours after the grueling test, when it was phone time, I was first in line at the phone. Waiting for Chizkiyahu's call.

"How was it?" he asked. "I davened for you."

It felt good to have Chizkiyahu davening for me. "You must have davened well. I had to answer more than five hundred questions. Yes or no answers. Do I like mechanics magazines? Have a good appetite? Read newspaper articles on crime? That kind of stuff," I said.

"Do you?"

"Do I what? Read newspaper articles on crime?"

Chizkiyahu laughed.

But I hadn't been joking.

He laughed again. That deep chuckle that I knew well. "Do you have a good appetite?"

"I guess so."

"Good. Because after we get married, I'm going to cook up the best chicken with olives that you have ever tasted."

Married? Chizkiyahu was telling me that we were going to get married. Something tingled through me. Suddenly, I felt taller. What was I supposed to say? I didn't know…so I didn't respond to his hint. "They asked me other things too. Whether a person should try to understand his dreams and take a warning from them. Whether I ever think of things too bad to talk about."

"The Gemara speaks about it. Certain dreams should be taken as a warning."

"I had to answer yes or no. There wasn't room for what the Gemara says. And I've never learned Gemara."

"What did you answer?" Chizkiyahu asked.

"No."

"Well, that's not true."

My shoulders were tensing up. I could feel the muscles tightening. "I answered like everyone else who takes that stupid test. I answered what they want to hear. I answered the way normal people would answer."

"Normal people who learn Gemara would answer yes."

Why was he so…so logical? I felt a headache coming. There, behind my right eye, where it always came.

"You can mess up the test results if you lie," Chizkiyahu said. "They have ways of double-checking these things."

Had I messed up? It couldn't be. I'd waited so long to take the test.

"Are you still there, Racheli?"

"I have to go," I said, I glanced behind me. Four women. "There are other people in line." That at least was true.

Later, when I went back to my cell, with the green scarves on the walls, the green rug on the floor, and the green pillows on every bed, I tried not to think of the other questions on the test that I had answered before Dr. Aronson began the second, aural, part of the test*: Once in a while I think of things too bad to talk about. I am sure I get a raw deal from life. I feel that it is certainly best to keep my mouth shut when I'm in trouble.* I'd answered no to all of those questions. Would Dr. Aronson know I was lying?

For the first time since I had begun talking to Chizkiyahu, I tried not to think about him. I was frustrated with him. Angry, even. I had to tell him. I had to speak about my feelings. How many times had Rotem told me that I had to tell people what I was feeling? But I didn't want to tell him. If I told him I was upset with him, he would stop calling me. I missed the Rabbanit. I hardly saw her now that I was busy all day in the laundry. She would tell me what to do. Maybe Chizkiyahu would call again anyway. Even if told him I was angry. I could tell Shira to tell Gadi to tell Chizkiyahu that I wasn't very angry. Just a little. Hurt. Right… I was more hurt than angry. Chizkiyahu was supposed to support me. And he hadn't. He'd told me that I might fail the test. I didn't want to fail the test. I wanted to get out of Neve Tirtza. Get my kids back.

I stood up and walked to Shira's cell. Shira had decorated the nursery the colors of the sky, the earth, and water. I didn't like the color of water. Natas's eyes were the color of water. Shira was sitting in her rocking chair rocking her baby.

"What's up?" she said.

"Nothing." I'd been a mother once. I'd rocked eight babies that way. And then I had lost them. Would I get them back when I got out? Even if I didn't have custody? Was there still a way that I'd see them? What about visitation rights? Would I have a relationship with them, or would I lose even visitation rights?

***

About two weeks after I had taken the test, Boaz called me to his office. The social workers were there. Both of the social workers who had worked with me. Dr. Aronson. Two other people I'd never seen before.

"You have a year plus some left," Boaz said. The sunlight coming through the window hit his shaven head. Made it shine like a low-wattage light bulb.

I didn't need him to tell me. I was counting the days better than he did. Every single day. Besides, Shimmy was counting for me. Waiting for me to come out, to move into a home so he could come and visit. I wanted him to come and live with me. But he'd said that he was going to hold on to his independence.

Boaz started speaking again. About why I was here in Neve Tirtza. About the courses I'd taken. My time in the *midrashah*. My work in the kitchen and the laundry. I didn't need to listen. I knew it all. The shiny spot on his head was moving forward. Dripping yellow light onto his forehead, the bridge of his nose. And then he was speaking about the results of the test. I was listening again.

"You cannot go out on parole," Boaz said.

But I wanted to go on parole. I'd already told him that.

"Given your good record, the prison authorities are thinking about letting you spend the last year in a rehabilitation home…a hostel."

He stopped talking. Looked at me.

Out of Neve Tirtza. Into a hostel. I didn't want to go to a hostel. I'd told him that. The afternoon that he'd come to the laundry.

"In the hostel, you'll start rebuilding a life for yourself."

"Who else goes to this home?"

"Drug addicts," Boaz said. He put his elbows on the table, locked his fingers. Leaned his chin into his hands. "Bayit Tikvah is a hostel, a rehabilitation center, in North Tel Aviv. There'll be courses that you'll have to attend. Every morning, afternoon, and evening. After two months, if you're doing well, you'll be able to work in the afternoons."

Work in the afternoon. If anyone would employ me. Did people really employ former inmates?

"When do I go?" I asked.

"They have to find an opening. Before Pesach or after, depending on space."

***

One morning, a few days before Pesach, the warden told me I had ten minutes to pack my things. No time to say goodbye to anyone. Not even Shira. No time to ask her to get a message to Chizkiyahu to tell him that I'd left. And who was going to launder Neta's clothes? I was released like Yosef Hatzaddik – in a flash.

The hostel was a beautiful six-bedroom villa surrounded by a lush garden. Seven women. A mixture of former prisoners like me and drug addicts. With as many counselors. By the end of the first day, I wondered if I'd made the right decision…if the right decision had been made for me. I'd made myself a niche in Neve Tirtza… I'd been in charge of the laundry, I'd listened to *shiurim* all day, made beautiful Shabbat *seudot* every week. I had used the phone regularly, talked with whomever I wanted. But now that I was in Bayit Tikvah, the identity that I had built for myself over four years, the niche I'd made for myself, were both gone. And no one wanted to hear about religion.

"I can't eat here," I told Yaarah, the head counselor, half an hour after I climbed out of the prison van. "I can't use your dishes. Nothing is kosher here."

"Kosher?" Yaarah ran her tongue over her very white, very straight teeth. Skipped over the little chip on her eye tooth. "You need to learn how to let go of things," she said. "Your obsession with these kinds of things is what got you into trouble."

She turned away, got busy welcoming a blonde woman in a tank top and shorts.

"No phone calls for six weeks," Yaarah told us at the orientation meeting.

I clenched my teeth. I'd had more freedom in prison. No phone calls was for former drug addicts, to make sure that they wouldn't get in touch with any of their pals. I wasn't a drug addict. The rule made sure that I couldn't talk to Chizkiyahu…the one ray of light that was left to me when I came out of Neve Tirtza.

"Here's your schedule," Yaarah said, handing out a pink sheet with a flowery border.

I scanned the schedule. Morning, afternoon, and evening. Every waking hour of the first two months was devoted to some type of course or therapy. That was why Boaz had told me that my weekly meetings with Rotem were over. I had no time to meet her. The schedule included a rotation of housekeeping chores. Every single day of the week, including Shabbat, every girl had been assigned a list of housekeeping chores. I looked around the living room. It was spotless. We'd be scrubbing and scouring a spotless house.

"Cognitive behavioral therapy…that's CBT," Yaarah looked around. "CBT will address the connection between thoughts and behaviors and how they both lead to your motivations to use drugs." She smiled at us. Looked at each and every one of us.

Stared deep into our eyes. As if she could read our thoughts. But of course she couldn't read our thoughts. Mind reading wasn't something that happened these days. Maybe once. In the times of the Baal Shem Tov. But it didn't happen today.

Yaarah continued speaking. I looked at the girls I'd be spending the next year with. Some of the women I knew because we'd been together in the treatment wing in Neve Tirtza. But I didn't know them well. They'd had their own routines to follow. Hudi had kicked off her thongs and was picking at the skin around her toes. The woman with a tank top – I hadn't heard her name – had folded her schedule into a fan and was fanning her neck. Rita, an Italian girl whose breath smelled of garlic and pasta, had closed her eyes. Her head lolled to the left.

Yaarah stood up, put her hand on Rita's shoulder.

Rita's eyes fluttered open.

"By understanding your negative thought patterns and their consequences, you can choose healthier thoughts that'll lead to healthier behaviors," Yaarah said.

Negative thought patterns. Sure, I had negative thought patterns. Sure they had led me to places I wished I'd never seen. But I'd already worked so hard to change. I didn't want to go to any more courses. I wanted to talk to Chizkiyahu. Chizkiyahu helped me to think healthy thoughts. Good thoughts.

"You'll have motivational interviewing and twelve-step group meetings, but we'll speak more about those when we get closer to them," Yaarah said, with a brilliant smile. "Sleeping arrangements are posted on the noticeboard in the kitchen. And by the way, my hugs come for free."

We all drifted toward the kitchen to find out who we'd be rooming with. Valentina Borgovsky. Russian.

Someone pushed against me. The woman with the tank top and shorts. Peered over my shoulder and then poked me in the back. "We're roommates," she said.

Classes began the next morning. Accompanied by a counselor, we bused to the center where our classes were held. During the afternoon class, I went to the bathroom. An Ethiopian cleaning lady was bent over a bucket squeezing out the water from a floor cloth into a bucket half-filled with murky water. I asked her if I could use her phone, and I called Chizkiyahu. It was the first of many times that I broke the rules at the hostel.

***

It took two more days for Yaarah to realize that if she didn't allow me to go buy a couple of pots and basic food supplies, I was going to starve. But that wasn't enough for me. Shabbat was coming, and I wanted to bake challah. Finding time on Friday was going to be hard. We had classes in the morning and in the afternoon. On top of that, I tried to do the cleaning chores that were assigned to me for Shabbat on Friday so that I'd still have some type of Shabbat feeling. I prepared the challah dough Thursday night, hid it under the blankets of the bed in an empty room, and woke up at five the following morning to bake it. They say that the sense of smell is closely linked with memory, probably more so than any of our other senses. As the aroma of baking challah wafted through the prison kitchen, I remembered all those times that I had baked challah with my kids in the Old City.

And then Yaarah walked into the kitchen.

I'd broken another rule. Cooking was not allowed outside of the set meal preparation times. I braced myself.

But Yaarah just sniffed the air. "Do you have enough for all of us?" she asked. And then she gave me one of her hugs.

That Shabbat was probably the loneliest I'd ever experienced. I made Kiddush over the music on the radio and handed out my challah while the counsellors busied themselves with their cell phones and the residents wished they had one. The entire meal lasted twenty minutes. There was no singing, no sharing of insights into the *parashah*. I missed the specialness, the holiness of Shabbat. On Shabbat, I was never sad, never sank into depressing thoughts. But now I had nothing. What would keep me going from week to week? And as if that weren't enough, Yaarah announced that it was time for another class. I followed everyone into the living room, sitting on the edge of the couch so that I wouldn't fall asleep. She was saying something about reflective listening. I would listen to her. Even though I didn't want to be here. Not on Shabbat.

The lecturer, a young woman with pink lipstick on her teeth, was saying something about reflective listening. What was that? Should I listen? But I didn't want to be here. Not on Shabbat. Besides, I'd attended enough courses.

"The first step is understanding what someone is telling you," the lecturer said. "Hear the feelings behind the words."

She looked around.

I tried to nod.

"The second step is to offer the idea back to the speaker. Check that you understood correctly what he or she was trying to tell you."

Reflective listening. Why hadn't I known about this when Shimmy came back from Natas's yeshiva? I closed my eyes tight against the memory. Closed them so tight that I fell asleep. I woke up when the lecturer caressed my cheek.

"You fell asleep, Racheli," she said. "That's not a good sign. Think about why that happened. There's obviously a large gap between your goal and your current behavior."

I wanted to tell her that I fell asleep because I'd woken up at five in the morning to bake challah. I wanted to tell her that she was right: there was a huge gap between my goal and where I was now. I wanted my children back. Would she hear me? I didn't know. But I did know that I had to be good. Show that I was taking in everything they wanted to teach me…and so I just nodded. And thought about the kids.

During the four years that I had been in prison, the children had been coming to see me regularly. True, sometimes one or another of the children didn't come, but the others did. We had also been speaking on the phone regularly. During the two years I had been in the treatment wing and had had unlimited access to the phone, I had called them several times a day, always hoping to catch at least some of them. This regular contact, especially the visits, had been our bonding time, as imperfect as it had sometimes been. But once I was in Bayit Tikvah, everything changed.

Daniel wouldn't allow the younger children to come visit because the hostel was totally secular. Phone calls were limited to a measly five minutes at seven in the evening. In short, my connection with my children was almost severed. For four years, I had worked toward coming out of prison and getting the kids back. Now that I was finally out, I was seeing the kids less than ever before. The shock and pain were almost unbearable. That Friday night, when I sat through a lecture on reflective hearing instead of singing Shabbat songs with my family, it became clearer and clearer that in a year's time, when I left Bayit Tikvah, I would have nothing familiar left to return to.

***

It was late one night about a month after the program had started. Too late. Yaarah had turned off the lights at ten o'clock at the main switch like she always did, but enough orange light filtered into the room from the street lamps outside.

Tina, as Valentina liked to be called, had come to Israel from the Ukraine with her mother.

"Fifteen years old," Tina said. "I was fifteen when I came. And that isn't the right age to pick up and leave your peer group."

She unwrapped a chocolate wrapped in gold foil and bit into it. Closed her eyes and chewed. "Good chocolate feels like velvet in your mouth," she said. She held out the box of chocolate.

I shook my head.

"Fifteen. Not surprising I was drawn to drugs."

She crumpled up the foil. Opened a second one.

"Ferrero Roche...you sure you don't want one?"

"Not kosher," I said. Was Tina Jewish?

Tina hiked up the strap of her tank top. She had nothing else in her wardrobe. "So tell me," Tina said. "You're really still religious, after everything that happened?"

I nodded.

She chewed thoughtfully. Made soft clucking sounds with her tongue as it smoothed the chocolate against her palate.

"I think," she said. "I think that you should run far, far away from religion. It's better that way."

I stood up. Stared out the window. The branches of a jacaranda tree scrape-scraped against the window pane in the breeze. Tomorrow, the ground below would be covered with lilac blossoms. And we would crush them underfoot as we hurried to make the bus. Tina couldn't understand. I could never reject Hashem, run far away from the Torah. I'd always loved Hashem. Never stopped loving Him. Hashem had never abandoned me. Never would. Why should I abandon Him?

***

Two months after the program at the hostel had started, we all began looking for work. Instead of rushing off to class, we spent the first two hours of the morning poring over the newspapers that one of the counselors brought in and calling prospective jobs. *Haaretz*, *Maariv*, *Yedioth Tel Aviv*, *Zman Tel Aviv*, and *Ha'ir*. There were always more copies of *Ha'ir* than of the other papers because it was distributed for free. I opened the papers, circled one or two job postings, and called none. I didn't want to work in any of these places. I wanted to work among religious people.

"What are you looking for?" Anat, one of the two social workers at the hostel, asked me one day when I sat watching the jacaranda blossoms drift to the ground instead of punching numbers into one of the cell phones that the hostel provided us with.

"Any job," I said, because that was what we had been told to look for in the employment preparation course that the hostel had given us. "I'm not looking for a university position."

Anat didn't smile. She rarely did. "You need to be more specific," she said. "What are you good at?" She pushed her hands into the pockets of her jeans and rocked back and forth on the balls of her feet.

I wanted to tell her that I was good with kids. But who would give me job babysitting their kids? I wanted to tell her that I could cook well, fast, for crowds. But I didn't want to cook. I'd spent too many years cooking for the wrong thing. I shrugged.

Anat brought over a paper, spread it open on the wooden windowsill and began to run her finger down the list of jobs. Housecleaner. Waitress. Petrol pump attendant. Aide to old man. She looked up.

I shook my head. I waited for Anat to tell me that I was unmotivated. That the years in prison had taken away my drive to improve myself. But she didn't.

"Tomorrow," she said. "Tomorrow, we'll look again."

The next morning, when Anat came in, she was waving a newsletter at me. She hurried toward me and pointed to its name: *Meida Bnei Brak.* "This is what you want, right?" she said. "You want to work in a place where everyone wears black, and men walk on one side of the street and women on the other. Let's go outside."

We sat on a bench under an enormous palm tree. Anat flipped to the last pages, bent the newsletter open to make the pages stay flat, and handed me a pen. "Read," she said. "And don't tell anyone that I brought you this newsletter, and don't ask me what I had to do to get it."

I began reading the ads. No to an aide in a kindergarten. No babysitting. And yes…yes to working as a cashier in a store…a spice and nut store.

Two hours later, Anat drove me to Bnei Brak. We parked in a backstreet and walked to the center of Rechov Rabbi Akiva.

It was the middle of the day, and the store was empty except for a young mother choosing vanilla pods with one hand and rocking a baby carriage with the other. It smelled of citrus, mixed with something pleasantly leathery and earthy.

"I want to see Nachman," I said to the Breslover Chassid with an enormous white *kippah* sitting behind a metal bin divided into compartments filled with roasted peanuts, walnuts, almonds, cashews, macadamias, pumpkin seeds…

He put his finger on one of the lines of the book he was studying to mark his place and glanced up.

"I'm Nachman," he said. His long, gray *peyot* waved back and forth.

"I need a job." I wasn't supposed to say that. I was supposed to begin by telling him why I was suitable for this job. What I could contribute to his business.

He stood up. Pointed to the large glass jars behind him. "The pink peppercorns are from Madagascar. Those long, red pepper grow in Cambodia. Turmeric and cinnamon sticks come from Sri Lanka. Saffron is from Kozani in Greece. All Badatz." He rubbed the tip of his nose between his thumb and finger. "Got it?"

I nodded. He was talking about spices, so why did I get this feeling of compassion, optimism, and hope?

"Minimum wage. You're the cashier. When there's no one here, you dust the shelves, sweep the floor. And tell anyone who'll listen a little bit about the spices. They enjoy the flavor more if it comes from across the world."

That was all? Did I have the job?

Anat put her hand on my arm.

I turned to face her. She nodded at me.

Right. I had to tell Nachman. He was already looking into his book again. But I had to tell him that I was an ex-prisoner. The words came out in a rush, tripped off my tongue as fast as children pouring out of school at the end of the day. Who I was...what I had done...where I'd been...where I was now.

Nachman put his elbows on the metal bin and leaned forward, as if he was telling me that I hadn't frightened him off with my revelation. He picked up a watermelon seed and cracked it between his teeth, chewed slowly. "Fine," he said. "I'll give you a second chance. Hashem gives us second chances all the time. Besides, Rebbe Nachman teaches us that we must never despair! Never! If we fall, we have to keep trying to get up."

I smiled. Those were the first inspiring words I'd heard since I had left Neve Tirtza.

"You start tomorrow. And remember, the rub for the meat is a blend of pink Himalaya salt, coffee, and star anise. Recommend it to everyone. It's my specialty."

Anat put her arm through mine as we walked out. "Nice guy," she said.

She was smiling. I could hear it in her voice. She didn't actually curl her lips into a smile, but that was because she never smiled.

The next day, I began working at Nachman's Spices and Nuts from three in the afternoon to ten at night. Sometimes, when I thought about all that had happened, my eyes would fill with tears. I'd blink hard, tell myself that it was the smell of Nachman's meat rub. And sometimes, Nachman would shout out from behind the metal nut bin, "Rebbe Nachman says that it's forbidden to despair. You just keep on praying and everything will be okay."

The best part of the job was Nachman's phone. He let me use it whenever I wanted to call the kids and Chizkiyahu. My past was shattered, the future unknown, the present overwhelming. But Chizkiyahu was the wind under my wings.

***

About two months after I started work, the hostel organized a full-day trip to the marina in Ashdod for residents and one guest. I invited Yael. She was eighteen years old now. In charge of herself. I wasn't sure where she was living or what she was doing. It would be the first time I was seeing her since I'd left Neve Tirtza, but with the entire hostel team coming along, I knew that there would be plenty of advice available if I needed it.

We strolled along the promenade at the marina, lagging behind everyone else. Determined fishermen dangled their lines into the harbor where hundreds of boats and yachts were berthed. A strong sea breeze tossed Yael's long hair over her eyes. My hand automatically reached up to push it back.

Yael pulled back, startled.

Something inside me cringed. It was a natural, motherly gesture. Full of the love that I wanted to give her. The love that I wished I had given her.

Above us, seagulls circled quietly. Swooped into the waves.

We caught up with the others, climbed into the yacht. Settled on a bench.

"She looks like you," Tina's mother said.

Her arm was linked through Tina's, pulling her close.

I wanted to do the same. Pull Yael close to me, close enough for her to feel that I would never, ever leave her again.

The yacht motored out. Picked up speed. The wind was stronger now. The prow of the boat cut through the gentle waves, sending up salty spray. My lips tasted of salt. And then the boat hit a wave that was bigger than the others. The prow reared up and crashed down. Yael yelped, grabbed my hand. And my heart soared.

***

"Tomorrow morning, when we leave the hostel to go to class, I'm going to forget my bus pass in the room and I'll have to come back to get it," I told Tina.

She was doing sit-ups on a thin rubber mat in the middle of our bedroom floor. Up and down. Up and down. She stayed up, curled her chest up even further and then slowly she lowered herself to the floor. "How do you plan in advance to forget something?"

She was breathless. But she put her legs straight up in the air and began to curl her abdomen up again and again.

I had to tell her. Make sure that she'd convince Yaarah that I was responsible enough to hurry after them on the next bus. Finally, Tina lay still. Stretched out her hands behind her head, pointed her toes toward the floor.

"It's got something to do with your brother," she said. "The brother you call every night."

"How do you know?"

"You're talking to Tina. You know how many phony phone calls I've made in my years? Hundreds. No one's eyes shine like stars after they speak to their brother." She rolled over onto her stomach. "So you go right ahead and forget your bus card. I'll cover for you if you tell me his name."

"Never."

Tina straightened her arms and pushed herself up. She threw her head back. "I'll still cover for you. Because I'm a nice person."

The next morning, I took longer getting dressed, putting on my makeup. My hand was shaking so much that I couldn't outline the bow in my upper lip. I used a tissue to wipe off the lip liner and tried again. I should have bought a new outfit for this meeting. The first time I'd be seeing Chizkiyahu. A new outfit…ha! I could just imagine going through the stores on Rabbi Akiva with Yaarah in tow. I ran down the stairs only as Yaarah was chasing everyone out of the hostel.

"Too bad about breakfast," Yaarah said. "I packed you some fruit." She held out a plastic bag full of apricots and plums.

"*Metukah*!" I blew her a kiss and took the bag. I wanted to skip out the door. Race over the jacaranda blossoms on the paved path that led to the gate. But I sauntered along slowly, just like we all always did. Where was Tina? I turned my head. There coming out the door last. Oh, how I wished I didn't have to hide this. How I wished I could have shouted to all the women, "Here he is…see him…this is the man…this is the man I'm going to marry." And then I'd stand beside Chizkiyahu, and everyone would take photos, and I'd send them to Abba and Ima…to the whole world…because I was going to marry him, wasn't I? It didn't matter that I'd never seen him. I knew him. Knew him better than I'd ever known Daniel. Because we spoke, really spoke.

"Racheli…"

Rita was calling me. No! I didn't want to speak to her now. I couldn't. Someone else was yelling behind me.

"*Ciao*, Rita, *come va*?"

It was Tina. Her thongs slap-slapping on the sidewalk as she hurried toward us.

"Rita, teach me some more Italian," she said, nudging Rita forward. "When I leave this hostel, my mom and I are going to Rome, Venice, Pisa! *Si, si, certamente*!"

I was the first at the bus stop. And he was there. Like he had said he would be. Chizkiyahu was a minimum-security prisoner, and that meant he was granted home leave once a month. From Friday to Sunday. He had told me he would be here, at the bus stop outside the hostel. That had to be him. There on the seat, his arms on his knees, his head bent over an open book on his lap. A Gemara. He didn't look up.

I heard the bus roaring toward us. I reached into my bag, shouted that I'd left behind my bus pass. Tried to turn around to go back to the house, but my feet were molded into the sidewalk.

"We're going to stay with Rita's aunt in Rome," Tina told Yaarah. She nudged her toward the bus. But Yaarah wasn't moving.

"Racheli…"

"She'll come on the next bus. Let's go…I'm not waiting in this sun. Do you know what Mediterranean sun does to Russian skin?" Tina boarded the bus.

Yaarah looked at Tina's back. Looked at me. "Hurry," she said. The doors of the bus whooshed closed behind her.

My heart was beating fast, too fast, pumping that mixture of fear and excitement through my body. I was finally going to meet Chizkiyahu face to face for the first time. Were any of the other counselors going to suddenly appear? I turned around slowly. Would I like what I was going to see?

Chizkiyahu looked up. He had the same gentle eyes that he had in the photo. He would never hurt anyone. Not me and not my children. Did he like me? Like what he saw? He had to like it. He had to. Because I liked what I saw. I liked it very much.

Ten minutes later, I was on the next bus, traveling toward my classroom. My stomach roiled with the same feelings of fear and excitement. Would Yaarah suspect something was up? Had Tina spilled the beans? I didn't want to get into trouble. I wanted to obey all the rules in the hostel. Not jeopardize my chances of getting out. But there was a stronger emotion coming through. Riding over the fear. Racing in my blood…joy…excitement… I was sure that I was going to marry Chizkiyahu. And I knew that at some point soon, very soon, I would have to tell my family. Tell them that I was getting married… to a man who was in prison for another ten years.

***

I had three months left in the hostel when Joanne and Rabbi Moshe Levi, the *toen rabbani* who had been trying since my arrest to sort out my marital status, came to visit me.

Yaarah, who'd gotten used to me and my kashrut requirements, brought some plastic cups and a bottle of water to the study that served as an office and closed the door behind her.

"Natas is still denying that your marriage took place," Rabbi Levi told me. "But whatever exactly happened in that ceremony in the Ramot forest was enough to make your marriage to him binding. Without a kosher *get* from Natas, you will never be able to remarry."

I stared out the window behind Rabbi Levi. The branches of a tall date palm waved lazily in the cold sea breeze.

"Eran has come before the *beit din* and told them that there was never a wedding, that he was never a witness."

Joanne had told me already. She had been in the *beit din* when Eran had told over his lies. I stared at the palm branches scratching the gray sky. It was going to rain early this year. It couldn't be…it couldn't be that there was no way to get a divorce from Natas. *Agunah*. Could words soak up the pain surrounding them? *Agunah*. The word was too heavy for my tongue. Full of shards of broken hearts.

Rabbi Levi took off his glasses and scratched his forehead with the tortoiseshell arm. "You have one more chance," he said. "Write a letter to the Rabbanut. Tell them that everything you said against Natas until now was false."

False? I stared at Rabbi Levi. It couldn't be! What was he saying?

Rabbi Levi pointed at me with his glasses. "There is someone in the Rabbanut who is willing to go to Natas with this letter and convince him that this letter will stand up in a court of law...that with this letter, his thirty-year sentence will be shortened."

I stared at Rabbi Levi.

"When he sees this letter – the devil, the Satan that he is – he will maybe, maybe...pray hard, Racheli...he will maybe give you a *get*."

Rabbi Levi arched his eyebrows. Lifted his eyes to the ceiling. So high that I saw only the whites of his eyes.

"Write it now," he said. He pushed a sheet of paper and a pen toward me.

Could I do it? Write that everything I'd said in court was false? Write that I was retracting? I stared out the window. The fronds of the palm tree were still swaying. Would Chizkiyahu tell me it was another lie? I had to call him.

Rabbi Levi looked at his watch. "Write," he said.

I picked up the pen. It was easier than I had imagined. I was writing my own letter to freedom.

Two weeks later, together with Yaarah, I traveled to the Rabbanut in Jerusalem. On a bus. It was a cold day. Did it get this cold in Jerusalem in winter? I couldn't remember. The wind rolled across the barren fields, threw itself at the sides of the bus. Sharp, skinny rods of rain bounced off the windows. The aroma of orange zest stung from my nose. The old lady across the aisle was peeling a clementine. I lifted my hand to check that the loose butterfly backing of my earring was still in place. I took it off and clamped it closed with my front teeth. On this ride to the Rabbanut, my hands were free. No handcuffs. This time, there was no van. No guards and no tears. I wasn't a prisoner. I was a free person. I didn't have to think of the time I'd been to the Rabbanut to meet Daniel for a *get*. Those weren't good thoughts.

We got off the bus at the central bus station and caught another bus to the *beit din* offices. It was pointless trying to open my umbrella in the blustery wind. A white van sped past, too close. Dirty water splashed against my legs.

And then, finally, Yaarah and I were sitting on a wooden bench at the back of a room in the *beit din*. I didn't look at the table at the front of the room. Three rabbis were almost hidden behind an enormous pile of books. Through the windows, I could see the heavy sky. Yaarah reached for my hand. Gave it a quick squeeze.

"How do you feel?" she asked.

I stared at her. At the chip in her eye tooth that made her Yaarah.

"Nervous…excited…sad…angry." I looked away. Tried to count the specks in the yellow and brown floor tiles.

Yaarah nodded.

But she couldn't understand. No one could understand. Even I could barely understand. Of course I was nervous. I hadn't seen Natas for almost five years. Since we had all been arrested. And of course I was excited. Soon I'd be free to marry Chizkiyahu. Yaarah didn't know about Chizkiyahu. No one except for Shira, Rotem, and Tina knew about him. Any romantic interest was forbidden at the hostel.

Suddenly I heard that familiar rattle…shackles against a stone floor.

"Move aside. No talking to the prisoner." Two guards shouted at the same time. Took Natas to the front of the room. He was wearing the orange prison pants and shirt. I knew that thick, canvas fabric that rubbed against your skin even though you wore it on top of your clothes.

Suddenly it wasn't just cool. It was cold. I hugged myself, rubbed my arms with my palms.

What was Yaarah whispering to me? The head of the *beit din* had told me to move forward. To stand next to Natas.

I tried to stand up. My legs were shaking. Yaarah put her hand under my elbow. Heaved me to my feet. I wasn't afraid. He couldn't do anything to me. Nothing. Never again. But the memories…the awful memories flew at me. Hit me in the belly. Natas at the head of our table with a staff in his hands; Natas in an inflatable boat; Aharon in a suitcase; Hillel eating peas. My feet wouldn't move. They had melted into the yellow tiles. Yaarah pushed me gently. Stop. I had to stop thinking or I would faint.

I stepped forward. I wouldn't look at him. No, I wouldn't look at him. But my head turned toward him. He was nothing. A sob rushed into my throat. Nothing. Daniel and I had made him who he was. We had built our own destruction.

"Come here," the rabbi in the middle called. His long, thin beard lay on his chest divided into two neat halves.

Natas shuffled over. The rabbi tapped at the *get*. The tap was a loud bang in the silent *beit din*. Natas signed. The rabbi rolled the *get* up and handed it back to Natas. "Go back. Give it to her." He beckoned me forward.

I held out my hand. And Natas put the *get* in my open palm. No one needed to tell me to hold on tight. I wasn't letting go of this *get*. And then – before the guards could hustle him away – in the heavy silence of the *beit din*, I heard my own voice. For the first time ever, I spoke my mind to Natas. "You are an evil man. And you know that everything – every single word I said about you – you know it's all true." My voice shattered the silence that hung heavily in the room.

"Keep quiet," one of the guards shouted.

I wasn't supposed to talk to Natas. No one was allowed to talk to a prisoner. I knew the rules. I'd lived them. But I wasn't finished. I took a deep breath and shouted: "Hashem will pay you back for everything you did to me and my children."

The second guard glared at me, shoved Natas in the back. "Move," he yelled. "You're not on a joy ride." He was angry. Spittle flew from his lips. He wiped it away with the back of his hand.

"Take her out, take her out," one of the rabbis shouted.

I was already walking out, the *get* in my hand. I had been sucked in. My whole essence had been sucked in. Now I was finally free of him. But I had paid such a heavy price.

***

During the last week of my stay in the hostel, a short while before Pesach, I was allowed to move into the attic. The attic was set aside for women who were about to graduate from the hostel. For the first time in five years, I was alone. A spiraling metal staircase in the attic led to the roof. I spent every spare minute that I had on the roof, standing close to the white balustrade, gazing into the distance, into my future. The tall buildings of northern Tel Aviv partially blocked the view of the ocean, but I could still make it out, between a building whose walls reflected the sunlight like enormous mirrors and a building whose floors tapered upward like a flame. My tears, the endless rivers of tears that I had cried over the last five years, had filled up this ocean, I was sure. But now, when I stood on the porch and looked out to sea, breathed in the warm, salty breeze, I smelled freedom. All that stood between me and freedom was one more court hearing in Neve Tirtza.

A few days later, I traveled by train to Ramle and walked from the train station to Neve Tirtza. Alone. I had traveled to so many different courts over the last five years with guards in prison vans and trucks. With bars and handcuffs and shackles, but to this hearing, I traveled on a regular train, walked down the streets, by myself.

I walked past the green shelter outside the kiosk where visitors waited to be let into the prison. The stone floor was covered with empty sunflower seeds, mashed into pulp a hundred times by impatient feet. I walked up the brown-red steps. Ran my fingers along the dark blue handrails while I waited outside the dark blue gate to be buzzed in.

The courtroom was near the prison offices. I looked for women I knew as the guard walked me through the prison, but saw no one. Had so much changed in so short a time? The panel of judges was waiting. I recognized no one. It was a sign, I decided, a sign that I no longer belonged here.

The judges whispered amongst themselves, looked up things in the prison computer system. One of the judges, a man with a frame of white hair around a large bald patch, finally looked up. "You have finished sitting out your sentence," he said. "You are now a free person. Free to choose to do anything. We hope you chose to stay on the right path."

Five minutes. It had taken five minutes to get the release papers for which I had waited five years. The guard walked me through the corridors again. But I wanted to run. Run into my new life.

I stepped out of Neve Tirtza. Blinked in the sunlight. It couldn't be…but it was! My family – Abba, Ima, Shimmy, Yael, Avner, my brothers, Gila, and even Faygie from New York – had all come to surprise me. Yael closed my fingers over a bunch of ribbons. Purple and red balloons danced back and forth above our heads. Who was I going to hug and kiss first? Never again, never again would I let go of any of them. I jiggled the ribbons. The balloons bobbed madly. We hugged tight, in a circle of love. Ima pushed a packet of tissues into my hand. Ima, Ima always thought of everything.

"She needs to say a *berachah*," Yossi said. "Now, when the joy is the greatest. *Hagomel*, Racheli, *hagomel*."

Dov grabbed Yossi's shoulder. "No *hagomel*. The *berachah* is only for someone who was imprisoned for murder charges."

"It depends on shackles and chains," Abba said. "And Racheli was in shackles and chains."

"She needs a minyan," Dov said.

I looked at my family. Dear Abba and my brothers. Words of Torah flew between them. I wanted to call Chizkiyahu. He would know the halachah. But I hadn't told anyone about him. What were they going to say?

I linked my arm through Yael's. Reached for Shimmy's hand. "To the ocean," I said. "Please, please, take me to the ocean."

The ocean wasn't far away. On the beach, I took off my shoes. The sand rose between my toes. Rough grains rubbed against the soft skin. I walked forward toward the waves. The sand became wet and hard under my feet. The waves rolled forward, broke into gentle bubbles and foam on the sand. There, in the waves, I could hear my cry. The water was whispering to me, echoing back the verse in Tehillim that had kept me going all these lonely years: *Hashem, he'elita min she'ol nafshi, chiyitani mi'yardi bor. Thank You, Hashem, for lifting me up from the grave, for keeping me alive and saving me from going under.*

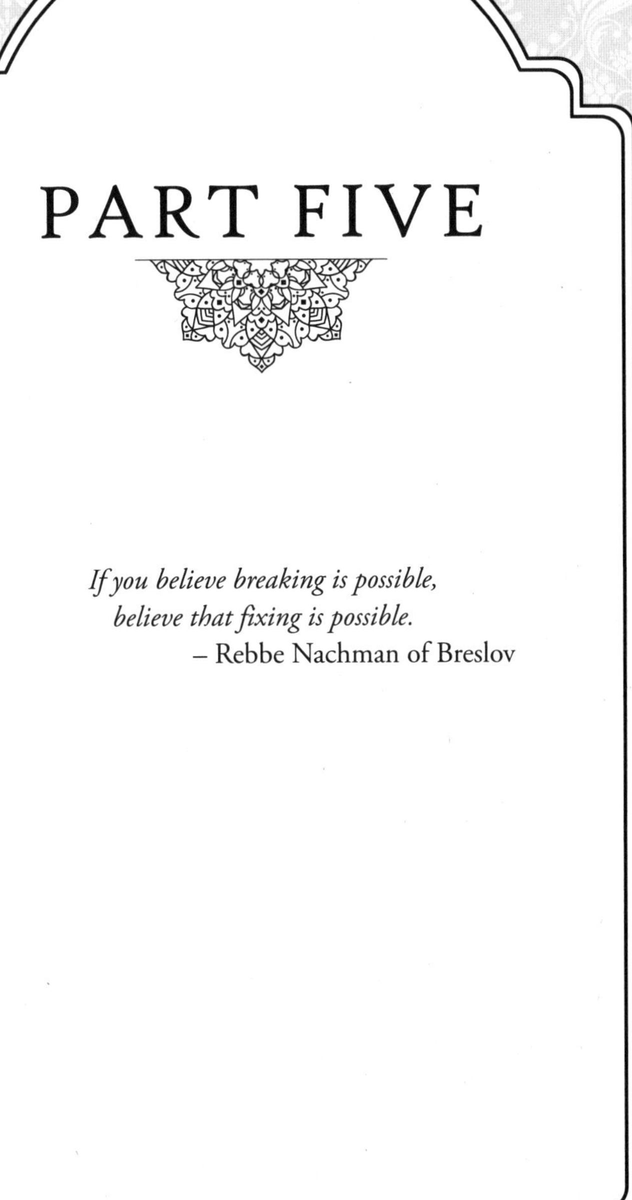

PART FIVE

If you believe breaking is possible,
believe that fixing is possible.
– Rebbe Nachman of Breslov

CHAPTER SIXTEEN

Free to Marry

April 2013

It was a shack. But it was close to Hillel's home, and that was all that mattered. And rent was cheap. The two rooms were part of a house that was older than the State of Israel. The grandparents of the present owners, wealthy Lebanese business magnates, had fled Lebanon in 1943 when France agreed to transfer power to the Lebanese government. When the wheel of fortune turned and they lost their wealth, they divided up their spacious home into six smaller ones. Mine was the smallest.

Every morning when I woke up in my two-room shack, I told myself that home was where the heart was. Much of the furniture and appliances that we had had in our home in the Old City had been sold to cover the bills that I had run up over the years in prison to pay the fees of Joanne and Rotem. Ima had packed my clothes and some of my kitchen utensils in boxes and put them in storage in Ayin Yaffa, but I hadn't yet opened the boxes. The rest had gone to Daniel…to the new home that he had set up with his new wife.

I was brave that first week in my new home. Full of determination to make it work. Full of the heady energy that comes with freedom. The exuberance that only someone who has been in prison can know. My home was going be the pot of gold at the end of the rainbow. The living room was an explosion of color. Purple and blue scarves hung from every nail on the walls. The couch, a wicker relic that I had dragged home on one of my first nights, was filled with pillows of different sizes and colors. Two rugs, one brown and one green, covered the cracked floor tiles.

On one of the first afternoons in my new home, Yael came to help me paint a rainbow onto the wall behind the couch. Her hand flew over the wall lightly as she sketched the outline of a rainbow arching above a sea of clouds. Then we painted it together with paints that I had bought in the hobby store on Kanfei Nesharim, close to the family court I'd been to too many times to count. Before the paint dried, I flicked gold glitter onto the paint. When we stepped back to admire our artwork, the glitter caught the light like thousands of sparkling diamonds. When had Yael developed into such an artist? Another piece of her growing up that I'd missed. A wave of sadness was coming toward me, going to drown me. But I could be stronger, couldn't I? I had to be, if I wanted to have a second chance. "Nice work, Yael," I said cheerily. "Thanks for the help."

Yael was rinsing the paint brushes at the kitchen sink. She looked up. Stopped rubbing the bristles, but didn't turn off the faucet. Her eyes shrank into their sockets. Became as old and weary as eyes that had lived through a war.

What had I done wrong? I took a step forward and then stopped. Could I go to her? Should I ignore her sudden flash of pain? Our relationship was still so fragile, the wet wings of a newborn butterfly. One wrong move and I'd scour off the iridescent colors that were emerging. I swallowed. I was alone. No Rotem, no Yaarah to help me. And then the hours and hours of therapy kicked in. I could talk about her feelings. "Yael…"

She looked at me. She was struggling…struggling to make her lips curve into a smile.

What was I going to say? My lips trembled. I pressed them together.

"It's okay, Ima," Yael said, rubbing her eyes with her fingers, still holding the half-washed brushes. "It's just…just that…" And then the tears came. Flowed down the cheeks that she had streaked with green and blue paint. "You never said thank you to me before."

I'd never said thank you to her before? Hashem, help me… How much more pain could my broken heart bear? How much had I made my children suffer? How much had Yael done for me? How many meals had she cooked, how many children had she bathed, how many errands had she run…and I'd never thanked her.

I stumbled toward my daughter, pulled her close to me. So close that I could feel the hammering of her heart. Pressed her head against my shoulder. "Thank you, Yael. Thank you for all the times you did things for me and I never thanked you."

Yael didn't pull away. And then I knew that maybe, maybe she was right. Maybe it was going to be okay. A new kind of okay. An okay in the darkness that I had created. But still an okay. When did my baby grow up and become big enough to comfort me?

***

Every morning, I spent an hour with Hillel, bathing him, dressing him, singing to him. None of the staff wanted me in his home. They blamed me for what had become of him. But I went. Hillel was eight years old now. He'd grown, and he was heavy, but I quickly got used to lifting him alone. Every evening, I pulled his heavy limbs out of his day clothes and into pajamas. Slipped him out of his chair and into his bed. None of the staff wanted me in his home. But I went because I was his mother. Sometimes, Shimmy, Yael, or Avner would come with me. When I was busy with Hillel's clothes, straightening his bedsheets, I would catch them stroking his face. A witness. I became a witness to their pain. I had thought that nothing could be harder than bearing the pain of my destruction, but when I became a witness to the pain of my children, the part of me that had begun to bloom, to rise up out of the ashes, plummeted down.

And things just got worse. Two weeks after I had moved into my new home, Joanne called me. Yael, Shimmy, and Avner had built their own lives and were living with friends. Yael and Avner were sure that they didn't want to come and live in what I called home. Shimmy was wavering. And the younger ones…I had lost custody, and now that my sentence was completed, I also lost the right to have them come to visit me. Joanne was doing everything she could to get me some sort of visitation rights. I was sure that I would get visitation rights. I was their mother. I had completed my sentence. But then Joanne called me and told me that things didn't look good. It was very likely that I wouldn't get permission to see the children, and that any relationship I wanted to build with them would have to wait until they turned eighteen.

For five years, I had held on to the hope that I'd be able to salvage something of my life. If not my marriage, my children. And now I realized that my home had no substance. It had never been more than morning mist on a summer day. The fact that I had nothing was screaming in my face.

***

"It's not fair," I said to Rotem. As soon as I had left the hostel, I had started seeing her again, this time in her home office. To make sure that I'd reenter society in a healthy way. I leaned toward her across her desk. "I didn't hurt them…I spent five years in jail…I've changed…Joanne told them that I've changed, she *told* them…and it counts for nothing."

Rotem filled my tea cup with jasmine tea. "I hear you, Racheli."

I didn't like jasmine tea. I stood up. Walked to the window of her home office. Sat on the thick pillow that filled the wide sill. "Five years of my life counts toward a big zero. Tell me…" I jumped off the pillow. "Tell me… where was Daniel when I was living in Natas's house? Where was he? He was my husband. He was their father. He loved us. Where was he? Why didn't he come to see what was happening to us? Three months. For three months, we were there, and he didn't come." I was panting. Or was I sobbing? Was there anything left inside of me to cry out?

"Six years – we were in that circle for six years – why didn't *anyone* think that something was strange? Why didn't any of the teachers in the schools of the older kids wonder where they were? Why didn't anyone ask? Once? Why didn't my family stop me? Why? Why?"

"Your family asked you. You told them it was all okay."

I stared at Rotem. She was supposed to be on my side.

"You're finally angry, Racheli," she said.

She was wrong. I was never angry. I didn't get angry.

"It's okay to be angry," she said.

Angry. Something inside me burst into red fire. Crackled. Spat. Rotem was right. I was angry. Did I know how to feel angry? I'd never been angry with Daniel. Never been angry with Natas. But I was angry now, raging, furious.

"He brought those crazy rabbis into our lives – Tzefanyah and Natas – he brought them in. Why couldn't we have stayed in Migdal Yam?" I saw us in our yard planting flowers. I saw us at the beach digging for shells to put on our sandcastle, I saw us on an evening walk…and all the layers of hope and light that I had carefully applied to my heart since I'd walked out of Neve Tirtza and Bayit Tikvah ripped off. Again, I felt the tragedy of my loss. How many times, how many times did I have to feel this? My anger was roaring. I had to make it roar redder, so red that it would burn away the pain. I wanted to scream, shriek. No words could contain my anger. Instead I stumbled back to the window seat, fell against the cushion, and put my hands over my face. Who was moaning? I could hear the moan of the angel of death.

After a long time, I heard the clink of a teaspoon against china. Rotem was stirring her tea. "You're out of prison, and you can finally say that you are angry. You can finally say what you feel without thinking about what the prison authorities or the counselors will say," Rotem said.

But it wasn't that simple. Not at all. There was one more question that I wanted to scream out. Why? Why had Hashem let this happen to me? I loved Hashem, wanted to do the best for Him. Why had He let it happen? It wasn't fair! But I didn't ask that question. Because four years of Neve Tirtza and one year of Bayit Tikvah had given me the answer, pounding it time and time again into my brain, into my soul. Hashem had let this happen because I had chosen wrongly.

"It'll take years of therapy – of following a healthy path – before you can rid yourself of everything that the evil cult of Natas put inside you. Excise the anger you feel. Vent the misery. It takes more than a couple of pills and a good night's sleep to wash it all away," Rotem said. "It takes more, even, than an ocean of tears. You have to fight back, Racheli. Against depression, pain, anger. You have to keep climbing up, even when you fall again."

It was the longest speech that Rotem had ever given me.

I didn't want to go home when my hour with Rotem was over. I didn't want to go anywhere. When I left her house, I began walking. The sky turned from mauve to gray to black. My feet hurt. My new shoes had rubbed blisters onto my heels. There was a deserted playground. I took off my shoes. Pulled myself up the ladder and crawled into a green plastic tunnel. I woke up with my phone ringing. It was Chizkiyahu. He would want to talk about our wedding. We were going to get married in June, right after Shavuot when he was on home leave from the prison for the weekend. But I wanted to talk about my anger. What was this new emotion? What was I going to do with it? I couldn't live like this. Chizkiyahu had to help me. I turned onto my knees and crawled out of the tunnel. How long had I slept for? I was so stiff.

"We need to book a hall," Chizkiyahu said. "It's hard to find a hall for after *sefirat ha'omer*."

I moved down the ladder, and my feet hit the rubber. I stretched up on my toes. Bent my head forward and to the sides. I didn't answer. A hall. I had to find a hall… But I was angry. How could I find a hall if I was angry? And first, first, I had to tell my family that I was getting married.

I heard Chizkiyahu inhale. He was trying to be patient.

"Shall I book a hall?" he said. "Are you too busy…with Hillel? Setting up the apartment? Looking for a dress?"

I could tell him about my anger. Our relationship was built on words. He always listened. But no, not now, not now when he was so excited. I could tell him, but not now. "You find a hall," I said. "I'll…I'll manage the rest… photographer, band…what else?" I had to leave my anger behind, there in the green, plastic tunnel. Because I had something in my life. I had Chizkiyahu. I knew that we could come together to rebuild our lives and serve Hashem in a kosher way. I wanted so much to start again and get a second chance at life. "I need to find a dress. And a *sheitel.*" I was going to find a beautiful *sheitel.* With a hint of auburn. Because my hair was still auburn.

I didn't want to put my shoes on. I'd walk home barefoot. "Chizkiyahu, when you buy me flowers, I like bold colors – purple, orange, red – enormous blooms. Nothing white and fragile. I want something that is…" What was it? I searched for the right word while Chizkiyahu waited. "Something that is bursting with life and hope," I said.

***

The next day, when I went to Hillel as usual in the evening, as I neared his door, I heard voices – one voice – someone was learning. And it sounded like Abba. I pushed open the door, Abba was sitting on one side of Hillel's wheelchair, learning from his Gemara. Ima was on the other side knitting. As if they were sitting on the porch in Ayin Yaffa enjoying time with their grandson. I breathed in. Smelled the pine-scented floor cleaner that was used in Hillel's home. It should have been the peppery smell of Champion.

"Hi!" Did Ima and Abba come often? There was so much I needed to learn about. So much had gone on without me.

I kissed Ima. She still smelled of roses. Kissed Abba.

"You look surprised," Ima said. "Why wouldn't I want to visit my grandson?"

I took out the tube of hand cream that I had bought for Hillel. His hands were a tiny bit dry. Squeezed a dab into my palm. "What're you knitting, Ima?"

"A hat. Every summer, I knit a winter hat for Hillel. This year the in color is mustard."

Another thing I didn't know. How many times had Ima and Abba come to visit Hillel, and I'd never thanked them. "It's nice…nice that you come to visit."

Ima's knitting needles clack-clacked.

How many evenings had I sat on the porch, listened to the crickets, and watched Ima knitting? I adjusted the pillow under Hillel's head.

Abba closed his Gemara. "How's the new place?" Abba asked. "Shimmy moved in yet?"

Shimmy had finally decided that he was moving in with me. "Most of his stuff's there – not that he has much. Next week," I said.

"When are you going to unpack the boxes I saved for you?" Ima said.

"Soon." I didn't want those boxes. I didn't want one thing out of them. I wanted nothing that would remind me of my life in the cult.

"Soon?"

Ima never left stuff lying around. I capped the hand cream. Took a deep breath. "Ima, remember when you caught flu when I was in second grade… fourth grade? Which was it?"

"Third."

"Remember how you never again wore the brown sweater with beige pockets that you'd been wearing on the day you crawled into bed with a fever?"

Ima nodded. She'd stuffed that sweater into one of the bags that we always sent to the clothing *gemach* before Pesach.

"Well, everything that I have from that time…those years that I was busy with Natas and the craziness…all those things…Ima…I never want to see those things again."

Ima kept quiet. Pulled at the ball of mustard-colored wool. Unraveled a long strand.

I'd said it. Told her what I was really feeling. "Not a single thing." I liked the sound of my strong voice. I'd been strong about that. I could be strong about other things too.

"There's good stuff there. Kitchen utensils that you could use." Ima sighed. "I wish you were rolling in money and could afford to buy yourself matching everything, at Ikea."

"She wants a new start, Rita," Abba said. "I can understand that."

A new start. Chizkiyahu was a new start. I'd told them about the boxes. I could tell them about Chizkiyahu too. I looked at the floor. "I'm getting married," I said. Was that my voice? Had I really said that?

I heard Ima's knitting needles hit the floor. I looked up. Abba's eyes were wide.

"His name is Chizkiyahu, and he learns just like you, Abba. He has soft, gentle eyes." What else did I know about Chizkiyahu? I knew that together we would grow. That we were going to bring out the best in each other. But all I told them was that he was in prison.

"You're not doing it," Ima was clutching the arms of her chair. "I won't let you. You almost destroyed your life once. You can't do it again," Ima shouted.

"Stop shouting, Rina. The staff will come running. Did you tell Rotem?" Abba asked. "You did tell her, didn't you? Why didn't she talk some sense into you? That's what you pay her for."

Of course I'd told Rotem. Many times. And she'd never given her blessing. My eyes were burning. I was hurting Ima and Abba. Hurting them again. And this time, unlike all the times I'd hurt them when I was in the circle, I could feel their pain. But they couldn't feel mine. "I'm all alone, Ima. I have no one. This way…this way at least I'll have a husband. Someone who loves me."

"You're not alone. And we love you," Abba said.

His voice was dead. Because he knew that he'd lost the battle before it began.

Ima leaned forward in the chair. Her foot kicked her knitting across the floor. But she didn't notice it.

"You've come so far…so far…you're putting a new life together…you can't ruin it before you've started. You can't tie yourself to someone who…who's in prison! And what's he there for? Are you really crazy?"

"I have nothing." I stared at Ima. At Abba. "No one else is going to marry me…ever. I can't live alone, and he's good to me. I *need* Chizkiyahu."

"You don't need a husband who's in prison," Ima said.

"I'm going to marry him."

"Marry him and you'll be alone, Racheli," Abba said. "All alone. Because Ima and I are having nothing to do with this madness. And we'll make sure that Yossi and Dov – everyone – they won't have anything to do with it either." Abba stood up. Picked up Ima's knitting. Waited for Ima to get up.

Ima heaved herself out of the chair. And they walked out of Hillel's room together.

I moved to Hillel's side. They wouldn't do it. They wouldn't leave me alone, would they? This was my first step toward a stable future. I was putting down the first stone in my new foundation. Why couldn't they see it?

***

Our wedding was held on the first Thursday afternoon after Shavuot. This way we took the most advantage of every second that Chizkiyahu had on home leave. I'd been to the Kotel earlier in the day, drove almost onto the plaza in a fancy car that Chizkiyahu's brother had rented. Fifty guests gathered in a tiny hall right on the edge of the Jerusalem Forest. The smell of pine trees and flowers growing in the surrounding gardens wafted into the hall. Chizkiyahu's parents came; they were happy that he was rebuilding his life. Yael and Shimmy came, together with some of their friends. Hillel came with his aide. Netanel and Yemima from Migdal Yam; the Chabad ladies, Udel and Minky, who brought the *parashah* sheet every week to Neve Tirtza; Shira with her baby; Nachman from the nut and spice shop. But no one else from my family. They were no longer talking to me.

We were already under the chuppah when I saw Abba making his way through the gathered guests. Slowly, as if he wasn't sure that he should be here. Abba. He stepped up onto the dais, stood in front of me, and lifted his hands. I felt the weight of his hands on my *sheitel*. Felt them trembling.

"Racheli, you need to rebuild," he said. "And even if this isn't the husband I want for you, I need to bless you…to daven that you'll build a home of Torah."

I had been right. Partially. Abba hadn't left me alone.

***

We'd been married almost three days when we both realized how difficult it was going to be to build a new home. We hardly had any time. Home leave lasted seventy-two hours, and seventy-one and a half of those hours had already flown by. So it was only natural that as we were standing beside the bus stop at the entrance to Jerusalem waiting for Chizkiyahu's bus, the bus that would take him back to Ramle, I'd talk to him about what had been weighing on my mind. About my anger. Before he was gone for another long month.

"It's not fair," I said. I handed him a bottle of iced tea that I had prepared before we left.

Chizkiyahu took the bottle. "Tell me," he said. "Tell me what's not fair."

It had been simmering. This new feeling. This stranger in my heart. Smothered by the preparations for the wedding. Doused by the excitement and joy I felt in my new marriage. But now, now that there was a listening ear, it began to glow with soft orange hues. "It's not fair that I got five years. Not fair that Daniel gets the kids."

Chizkiyahu shook the bottle. Watched the sprigs of mint dancing against the ice cubes.

"I want to see my kids. Talk to them. Hug them. I haven't seen the little ones for a year – not since I left Neve Tirtza."

Chizkiyahu was looking at me. He was listening. But he wasn't nodding.

"Is that normal?" My voice was loud. A woman with an enormous black backpack turned to stare at me.

Chizkiyahu didn't answer.

This wasn't the time to bring this up. Not when he was about to leave. But…but I wanted him to understand me. To tell me I was right. "Is that normal? I spent five years away from them. I want my kids. And it isn't fair. None of it is fair!"

"Why?" Chizkiyahu's voice was low.

She was staring at me, the backpack woman who looked like a turtle. I walked toward the outlook over Lifta Valley. Checked that Chizkiyahu had followed me. We should be hiking down there together, peeping into the ruins of the old stone houses, instead of waiting for the 433 bus that would take Chizkiyahu back to prison. "Why what?" I asked.

"Why isn't it fair that you got five years?"

I stared at him. He hadn't said that.

"Something went wrong, Racheli. Very wrong. You went to prison to make sure that it won't happen again. That's fair."

My back sank against the rails. This couldn't be happening. Chizkiyahu was my support. I loved him. He was my prop in my new life. He wasn't saying these things.

"Prison hurts, Racheli. Every single minute in prison hurts badly. And that's good. Because without that pain, people won't ever make any changes. They'll just keep saying that it wasn't their fault. That others made them do whatever it is they're in prison for. I know all about it. You can feel angry now that you're in a safe place. That's okay. But don't let your anger become a slippery slope. Don't let your anger whizz you back to where you can say that you didn't have a choice."

Suddenly, over Chizkiyahu's shoulder, I noticed the 433 bus to Ramle. The doors of the bus banged shut behind the last passenger. "Quick!" I yelled. "Your bus!" I ran toward the bus. Hammered on the door. The driver had to open up. Chizkiyahu had to be on this bus to get back on time.

Chizkiyahu was beside me. The door swung open. This wasn't the way I wanted to say goodbye. A second later, he was on the bus, waving goodbye.

I stared after the bus. I could make it till next month. I was strong enough, wasn't I?

I glanced at my watch. Eleven o'clock. I had to run if I was going to get to work on time. Work was looking after Mrs. Badenheim, an elderly lady who needed an aide. Thanks to the course on geriatric care that I had taken in Neve Tirtza, I had been able to find a job as a caregiver for the elderly. I pushed Mrs. B. to the park around the corner from her home and read to her until her eyelids drooped and finally closed. Tiny blue capillaries crisscrossed her paper-thin lids like streams and rivulets leading to an estuary. I called Rabbanit Shlomit. I'd been talking to her at least weekly since I'd left Bayit Tikvah.

"He doesn't understand me," I said as soon as she answered.

The Rabbanit laughed.

I imagined the angular line of her chin softening with her smile. But I didn't laugh.

"Well, that's the first step to getting it right," she said.

I brushed a fly that was buzzing around Mrs. B.'s head. "He doesn't understand me," I repeated.

And then the Rabbanit answered. The longer I poured out my heart, the more I realized that she was right: Chizkiyahu was all logic. Once, when I had tried talking to him about what had happened, he'd stopped me. *I don't want to talk about it,* he said. *I can't understand how such a thing could have happened.* It wouldn't have happened to Chizkiyahu. He was too much of a straight thinker. And I was all emotion. Opposite ends of the spectrum. It would take time and patience to learn each other's language.

"Speak to him, Racheli. Work hard at articulating your thoughts. Chizkiyahu has all the time in the world to listen to you."

Mrs. B. let out small sigh. The white bristly hairs that dotted the underside of her bottom lip quivered.

"And Racheli, one more thing. You should be happy that Chizkiyahu's in prison. You need space to grow. Time to get to know yourself. You wouldn't be able to do that if Chizkiyahu were at home with you all the time at this point."

Was that right? I needed time to get to know myself? I put my hand over Mrs. B.'s hand, just to let her know that I was there. And I remembered some of the Rabbanit's first words to me: *Who is Racheli? You need to find her.* Find her. I'd been trying to find myself since I'd woken up in Neve Tirtza. And now the Rabbanit was telling me that I still had a way to go! *Hashem, how much more do You want from me? How much longer must I search?* I closed my eyes. What did Racheli want? A family. Closeness to Hashem. I laughed. But it was a bark, really. A strange sound that jumped out of my belly and made Mrs. B. jerk. I hadn't changed that much over the years. A family. To be a beacon to the Jewish people. That was what I'd dreamt of for Daniel and me when we first went to Migdal Yam. I thought of all those wonderful stories of great women – I'd heard them on the *shiurim* that the rabbi of the prison had put on my MP3, read about them in the books he'd brought me – and a wave of sadness surged through me. Where…where in Hashem's plan for the world was I? What role was I supposed to play? Hashem had given me a family. Had entrusted me with His children. I was supposed to look after them to raise them to be good Jews. But look what I had done! A complete lack of *hakarat hatov.* Could there be a greater lack of gratitude?

Tears were trickling out of my eyes. There was a packet of tissues somewhere. Where was it?

"Why are you crying?" Mrs. B. had woken up. She was looking at me.

I couldn't find the tissues. I ran a finger under my eyes, carefully, so that my mascara wouldn't smudge. "Why shouldn't I be crying?" The anger was there, always there these days, a smoky mass weighing on my chest.

"You're crying because you don't know. You don't know what I know," she said. "When you get old, you realize these things." She nodded. The bristles under her lower lip caught the sunlight and glistened.

"Every person in the world has a unique job that no one else can do. It was worth Hashem creating the entire universe just for any one of us to be here," Mrs. B said. She pulled her hand out from under mine and began rubbing the back of my hand. Her skin was dry and soft. "Some of us do this, some do that, some sit in a wheelchair and sleep in the park. Different jobs with one goal: to realize that whatever you're doing, you're doing it for Hashem."

For Hashem. I didn't want to think about what I'd done for Hashem. Besides, it was hot in the park, and I wanted to go back into the air conditioning. But Mrs. B. wanted to be outside for a little longer. So I waited. I had to get used to waiting. In my new life with Chizkiyahu, I'd be doing a lot of waiting.

***

When I called the Rabbanit the next time, I was working in a flower store where the pay was better. It was easier to get up in the mornings, knowing that I'd spend my day in a cloud of color and fragrance. I stepped back to view my arrangement. Red roses in the center, yellow hypericum, lilac sweet peas, and orange pansies filled in the gaps. Three weeks had gone by, and I was getting ready for Chizkiyahu's home leave. I'd spoken to Chizkiyahu the previous night and he'd told me that when he came home, he wanted quiet – none of Shimmy's friends hanging around smoking. I hadn't answered.

"He needs to know that our home is Shimmy's home too," I said. "I don't want to tell Shimmy that he can't bring his friends over when Chizkiyahu is back."

"So how are you going to tell him?" Rabbanit Shlomit asked.

I didn't answer.

"Quiet?" she asked. "You're going to have to do it, Racheli, because no one else is going to tell him for you. What's holding you back?"

I fitted in another red rose. It was a sunrise bouquet. I'd caught the colors of a new day.

What was holding me back? I closed my eyes. Imagined myself talking to Chizkiyahu. What was I feeling? Fear. "I'm afraid," I said. "I'm too scared to tell him what I want..."

I heard the Rabbanit sigh. A soft whoosh of air. "Everything you learned in prison was theory," she said. "Now you have put to it all into practice. And this is where you start. Don't be afraid to stand up for what you believe in. What will happen if you refuse to tell Shimmy not to bring his friends?"

I didn't know. Maybe Chizkiyahu would get angry with me. I didn't want him to get angry with me. He was all I had. But…but I had to stand up for Shimmy. I had to tell Chizkiyahu that it was Shimmy's home too. I picked up a block of florist's sponge. Blues. This time I'd work with blue flowers. I could do it. I could tell Chizkiyahu.

But I didn't. Not until Chizkiyahu came home and smelled the cigarette butts that were on the windowsill in an empty can of tuna. I hadn't noticed them.

"The boys are out," I said. "They'll come back later tonight." I held my breath.

Chizkiyahu walked toward the flower arrangement in the center of the kitchen table. The blue one. I'd bought it for us. Hyacinths, tulips, irises, and hydrangeas – every shade of blue, indigo, and violet. He bent his head to smell the flowers. "You did a beautiful job," he said. "All different colors, shapes, and sizes. What are they called?"

It was over. I could breathe again. "Tulips." I pointed to the bright blue blooms.

But Chizkiyahu wasn't looking at the flowers. He was looking at me.

"No one has ever said no to me," he said.

I stared at him. I didn't want to argue. I opened the fridge. I took out the tray of lasagna I had made the previous night. Slipped it into the oven.

"Say something," Chizkiyahu said. "You have to react to what I said. To tell me what you're thinking."

I stared at him. He really wanted to know what I was thinking. It was important to him. I felt something inside me opening up. Chizkiyahu loved me. He loved me just because I was me. And that knowledge gave me the courage to answer. "No one ever said no to you? Well, I never said no to anyone," I said.

Chizkiyahu laughed. It was a loud sound that rolled around the room, got right into the corners where the dust gathered, and made me feel safe. I smiled. All the theory that I'd learned in prison and in the hostel – all those hours of lectures and workshops – I was finally putting it all into practice.

After we ate, I put a plate of strawberries on the table between us. I wanted to eat them whole, to savor the burst of sweet and tart that came with every bite.

Chizkiyahu didn't reach for one. "Did you check them?"

"I rinsed them in soapy water. Like I always do," I said. I chose a juicy strawberry. Twisted off the leafy top.

Chizkiyahu didn't reach for the strawberries. "Checking strawberries for bugs is a big thing these days."

It was? I picked up another strawberry, turned it around. Viewed it from all angles. It looked fine.

"Some people cut off the tops, brush them and rinse them in soapy water three times."

I wanted to eat strawberries. Fresh. Whole. I could tell Chizkiyahu that. "I'm not sure I want to do any of that."

"So you can peel them."

Peel them? Who peeled strawberries? No one I knew peeled strawberries. Everyone knew that rinsing was fine. I'd said no once today. Nothing had happened. I could do it again. "I'm not going to do that either."

Chizkiyahu pushed the box toward me. "That's okay, but I can't eat them. I don't need desert after your lasagna. It was great." He stood up, started at the rainbow on the wall. "Is there anything else you don't want to check? I need to know what I can eat and what I can't eat when I come home."

I didn't want any more strawberries. Shimmy and his friends could eat them. I snapped the box shut. "All these halachas…they're crazy. Too strict. I never checked strawberries."

Chizkiyahu was quiet.

Was he mad at me? I should have just told him that I'd check the stupid strawberries. I didn't want Chizkiyahu to stop eating at home. I knew about checking flour, rice, beans. So big deal…I'd check strawberries too…or never buy them again. Chizkiyahu was looking at me.

"Racheli, Yiddishkeit is about halachah. It's not about doing something vague that feels right, that gives you a spiritual high."

Touché. A French word. Rina, in the hostel, had used it a lot. But she was Italian. Never mind. Touché means you've hit the nail on the head. Hit a sore spot. *Yiddishkeit is about halachah.* We hadn't thought much about halachah in the cult. We'd been too busy with angels and evil spirits.

***

About a year after I'd come out of prison and married Chizkiyahu, Ayelet's third daughter, Sara Bracha, got married in Jerusalem. It made sense. Her *chatan* was the youngest in an enormous Israeli family. My family had watched me trying to put together a life, and they had began talking to me again. So it was good to see them. Faygie had come from the States. Yossi and Dov were there with their families. And I was there with Shimmy and Yael. I didn't have to think about the other children.

"Two peas in a pod," Gila said as soon as she saw us. She didn't let go of Yael's hand. "You remind me of your mother. Back when I used to come visit you on Migdal Yam."

Yael smiled. "You took us for rides on your bike. Remember, Ima?" she turned me.

"You loved it." I said. Something inside me twisted. She had some happy memories.

Yael wandered off to find her cousins. And I was left alone with Gila.

"I should have visited you more often," Gila said.

Visited me. She meant in Neve Tirtza. That was Gila. Straight to the point. I waited for her to continue.

"But it was hard for me to visit."

I waited. No one wanted to hear how it had been hard for me. I'd learned that.

"When I visited, I wanted to talk about what had happened. About the cult. I wanted to understand where the Racheli I knew had gone. But you kept talking about the kids and the kids and...well, I got frustrated."

I nodded. "It's okay, Gila."

We spoke a little more. Skirted around the things that Gila really wanted to talk about, and then we drifted apart to talk to others.

After the first course, before the dancing started, I went outside to call Chizkiyahu. We spoke a few times every day. A stone path wound around flower beds and ended in front of a pond with a large fountain in the middle. Chizkiyahu didn't answer. I would try again later. I turned around ready to go back inside. But then I saw Gila. She had followed me outside.

Suddenly, all the memories came flooding back. Gila naming my kitten. Taking me for hikes around Long Island. Coming to watch the kids so I could rest after a bris. Visiting me in the hospital after I gave birth. Visiting me in Neve Tirtza. I walked toward her. And I hugged her. Her hair smelled of lemon and mint.

"Pretty soon, you'll be making a wedding like this for Yael," she said. The clasp of her bracelet had snagged onto the lace of my top.

"I can do that," I said. "I planned my own wedding in three weeks."

"The wedding I didn't come to."

Gila fiddled with the clasp, tried to release it without tearing the lace.

"It's okay, Gila," I said. "I missed you all, but it was a happy wedding. Shimmy brought his friends, and the dancing was great."

Finally, Gila unhooked the clasp. She stepped back.

"You look like Racheli," she said. "Your face isn't stiff and frozen like some cardboard cutout. Like it was when I told you, all those years ago on Migdal Yam, that Daniel should fix his own tea."

"Maybe…maybe if I had listened, it would have been different," I said. "But it's too late. Too late for maybes."

"You owe me," Gila said. "You need to help me understand. Don't talk to me about the kids."

I looked away. Into the night. Then I nodded. "Let's walk," I said. "To the other side of this fountain." I linked my arm through hers.

"You're wondering how I can close the door on what happened, right?" I asked Gila.

"I'm wondering," she said.

I sat down on a seat carved into the rocks. Pulled my legs up under my chin.

Gila sighed. "You're asking me to give you my blessing for a new start. I'm not sure I can do that yet," she said.

I picked up a loose stone. Threw it into the fountain. I heard the little plop, but I couldn't see the ripples.

"When you reach such a low level, you make excuses, give reasons… because without excuses and reasons, you'd never survive…you'd die from the pain or go insane."

I looked at Gila. To see if she was following.

"At that low level, you realize that you have two choices: you can keep those excuses and reasons pinned to your sin, or you can grow and strip them away, layer by layer. If you strip them away, you have to acknowledge your sin…acknowledge that everything happened because of the bad choices you made. And the pain that comes with realizing that is almost unbearable. So you develop a coping mechanism…" I stopped.

"Don't stop," Gila said.

I stared into the darkness. Were the words I needed there? "Every time I think of what happened, I feel the pain again. But I can't live with such a painful truth, so I don't go there too often. If I did…I'd die." I swallowed. "I used to have a lot of guilt. Today, I don't have that. I've worked to forgive myself. I feel sorry, I feel the pain, and I can beg for forgiveness. But I don't feel guilty."

"You don't feel guilty? How can you not feel guilty?"

I heard the tinge of anger in Gila's voice. "A person feels guilty when he surrounds himself with excuses," I said. "I stripped away those excuses. I can see the sin without making excuses for it. When I get to the real heavenly court, the Beit Din shel Maalah, I want to be cleansed."

I slid my feet down the rock and stood up. "I hear the music starting," I said. "Let's go dance…together."

Epilogue

Jerusalem, 2018

Every morning I go to visit Hillel and take him through his morning routine. This morning, I'm in a good mood. For two reasons. One, it's the morning of Hillel's bar mitzvah, and, two, I've just heard that I've been accepted into a course to learn how to be a fitness trainer. A good choice given my background as an aerobics instructor.

"Hi, Tehilla," I say, waving to the nurse on Hillel's floor.

She smiles. It's a reserved smile, but it's a smile. She never used to smile at me.

"In two weeks, I'm starting to learn how to become a fitness trainer," I tell her.

"You are?"

Tehilla's eyes are wide. She can't believe that I'm going to do something useful.

"Now, that's the first clever thing you've ever done," she says.

I keep quiet. Because she's probably right. But then my years of therapy kick in. I've done other good things too in my life. Many. But I can't tell her. Not when Hillel is in the room.

Tehilla puts down the tray of medications she's carrying, and I know that she's going to say something to me. Something she's been thinking of for a long time.

"You know, we hated you even before you came to visit Hillel," she said. "We hated you for putting him in this place. This is a home for kids who were born with challenges. Not one for normal kids who've been abused." She takes a breath. "You came here with your hands and feet handcuffed. All dressed in white. You came here to visit him, and we all thought: *How could you?*" She takes another breath. "And now I see that you're an okay person. Maybe even nice. *Maksim*! Good luck with your course."

An okay person, maybe even nice. I want to be better than okay, better than nice. But I don't answer Tehilla. She's come a long way from hating me. I'm happy she's shared her thoughts. Maybe now I'm accepted in Hillel's home. I hurry down the corridor, past the pictures of animals, children playing in a field, flowers in bloom. I go to Hillel and help his aide to get him ready for the ambulance ride to the Kotel.

I've organized a grand affair at the Kotel for Hillel's bar mitzvah. We are at Shaar Ashpot. Chizkiyahu, me, Hillel, and his aide. I'm happy I arranged for the Old City Train to bring our guests from Shaar Yafo. They won't have to fight against the blustery wind.

I rub Hillel's hands to keep them warm. Pull the hat that he is wearing a little lower on his head. He's had his hair cut for his bar mitzvah. His light brown *peyot* twist into two long curls that almost reach his shoulders. I stroke his cheek. The beginning of a short mustache covers his upper lip. Does he feel me? Does he hear me when I wish him mazal tov?

And then I spot the yellow train. There's Yael, cradling her newborn, her eldest daughter holding on to her skirt. There's Shimmy helping his wife to tuck their baby into the stroller. Old friends from Migdal Yam. Tikvah. They hurry toward us. There's a mixture of sadness and joy in the air. I can feel it in the wind stinging my face.

I hug my friends and family.

Yaeli strokes Hillel's cheek. "He's moving his lips," she tells her daughter. "He's thanking you for coming."

And then the music starts. Shofar blasts. The deep drumming of a darabukka. The piercing lilt of a clarinet. And we walk toward the Kotel. Slowly up the slope. Chizkiyahu pushes Hillel. I clap and dance alongside the wheelchair. The entourage sings and claps. And all along the way, the tourists part to let us through. Everyone is trying to smile, but that undercurrent of sadness is still there. Strangers come forward to take Hillel's hand. One man, about forty years old, tall, with dark eyes that are too shiny, is talking to himself. "Klal Yisrael needs *yeshuot*, salvation," he whispers. Maybe he's not talking to himself. Maybe he's talking to Hashem.

Suddenly we're at the Kotel.

I hurry to the partition and peep over. Someone wraps tefillin around Hillel's arm. Puts tefillin on his head. The Torah is read. The candies thrown. And then we're heading to the lavish lunch party that I've set up for us in a hall nearby. I wonder if I'll stumble over the speech that I prepared. I've rehearsed it a hundred times.

Yaeli catches up with me and gives me a hug. She squeezes my arm. "Ima," she says, "Hillel's *neshamah* was listening."

In the hall, I check on Hillel and make sure that the guests all have a seat. Then I go to wash my hands. Dina is already there, adjusting her snood in the mirror.

"How'dyou do it, Racheli?" she asks without turning around.

"Phone calls," I says. "I booked the train, booked the hall, booked the caterer."

"Not the bar mitzvah, Racheli. How'd you get to be normal again?"

I move closed to her. "You really want to know, Dina?"

Dina nods. "Sure, I want to know. I'm your friend, aren't I? Always was."

"Think of the yellow train," I tell her. "We're all on a journey. And sometimes, we make choices that take us to places we wish we had never seen. When we do, it's up to us to change direction."

"How'd you do that? Change direction?"

I close my eyes. It's easier to think this way. "Looking back, it's hard to understand why I didn't act differently. Why did I let those awful things happen? A mother's instinct is to protect her children and her family." I stop and open my eyes. My breath is caught in my throat. "You want to know how it started, Dina? Cults work by isolating you. Once you're out of contact with anyone normal, they can control you. You stop thinking for yourself and adopt the norms of the cult. Pretty simple, really."

My thoughts are clear now. And the words come more easily.

"When you stop thinking for yourself, when you adopt the norms of the cult, then tragedy is born. You make the wrong choices again and again. And again. Until those wrong choices become normal. Then you plummet down to places lower than your worst nightmare. Only you don't realize that you're there…until the fire breaks out and everything turns to ashes. You wake up and then you feel like your *neshamah*, your soul, has died. But it's worse than death, because even though your *neshamah* is dead, your heart is still pumping blood through your body, and your body is still alive. From this place of death, you have to fight to remain connected to Hashem. You have to believe that you can do teshuvah and that Hashem will forgive you. Even though you know that you will never forgive yourself. Even though you know that the results of your bad choices will always be before you, it's your choice, once again, to climb out of the ashes or remain in them forever."

Glossary

agunah. Woman whose husband has deserted her or has disappeared; she may not remarry until she gives proof of his death or obtains a bill of divorce.

aliyah. Immigration of Jews to Israel.

Badatz. Acronym for *beit din tzedek*, major court of justice. Used to refer to a rabbinical group that oversees supervision of kosher foods (with the Badatz supervision being particularly stringent).

beit din. Rabbinical court.

Beit Din shel Maalah. The heavenly court (that judges people's deeds at the end of their lives).

Beit Hamikdash. The Holy Temple in Jerusalem.

bentsh. To bless (give thanks after a meal).

bentsher. Booklet with blessings to be recited after eating bread.

berachah (pl. *berachot*). Blessing.

bris. Jewish ritual circumcision.

bubby. Grandmother.

cheder. Jewish boys' elementary school, where boys are taught about the Torah.

Chol Hamoed. Intermediate semi-holidays during the week-long Passover and Sukkot festivals.

daven. Pray.

derech. Way.

din. Law.

divrei Torah. Words of Torah.

Edot Hamizrach. The Sephardic (originating from the Iberian Peninsula) arrangement of the prayer service.

Eichah. Book of Lamentations.

frum. Prioritizing mitzvah observance.

gan. Kindergarten or preschool. Literally: garden.

gemach. Acronym for *gemilut chasadim* (the performance of kind deeds); a resource set up to benefit others, usually involving lending or giving away needed items or services.

Gemara. Talmud, the Oral Law (codified in writing around 500 CE).

get. Bill of divorce given by a Jewish man to his wife.

geulah. Redemption.

geveret. Mrs.

gilgul (pl. *gilgulim*). Reincarnation.

hakarat hatov. Gratitude.

halachah. Jewish religious law.

Hashem. God. Literally: the Name.

Hatzalah. Volunteer emergency medical service.

Havdalah. Short ceremony that signals the end of Shabbat.

hechsher (pl. *hechsherim*). Certification that a product is kosher for consumption or use.

hillula. Anniversary of the death of a Torah scholar, marked with festive celebration.

kallah. Bride.

kashrut. Jewish religious laws concerning suitability of food and ritual objects.

kavanot. Intentions. Specifically, a mindset of sincere, heartfelt religious feelings.

kefitzat haderech. Miraculous travel between two distant places in a short time. Literally: shortening of the way.

kameya. Amulet that provides spiritual protection.

kever. Gravesite.

Kiddush. Ceremonial blessings said over wine on Shabbat and festivals.

kinnot. Dirges, sad poems lamenting the destruction of the Holy Temple in Jerusalem or marking other calamities in Jewish communal life, recited as part of the observance of Tisha b'Av.

kippah. Yarmulke; a round head covering worn by observant Jewish boys and men.

kittel. A white cotton robe worn by religious Jewish men on some festivals.

kivrei tzaddikim. Burial spots of righteous Jews.

Kodesh Hakodashim. Holy of Holies in the Temple.

Kohanim. Priests.

Kohen Hagadol. High Priest.

kollel, kollelim. Institute, institutes for full-time, advanced study of the Talmud by married Jewish men.

korban tamid. Sacrifice that was brought in the Temple twice a day.

Kotel. Last remaining enclosing wall of the Holy Temple in the Old City of Jerusalem. Also called the Western Wall.

Lag ba'Omer. Minor holiday on the thirty-third day of the forty-nine-day *omer* count between Passover and Shavuot. Literally: thirty-third of the *omer*. The holiday is often celebrated with festive bonfires and a pilgrimage to the gravesite in Meron of Rabbi Shimon bar Yochai, author of the mystical book the *Zohar* (basis of the Kabbalah).

malachim. Angels.

mashgichah. Supervisor (female).

mehadrin min hamehadrin. The most stringent of the stringent (in matters of Jewish law).

metukah. Sweetie, sweet girl.

middah (pl. *middot*). Trait or attribute.

midrashah. Study institute.

mikveh. Ritual purification bath.

minhag. Tradition or custom.

Mitzrayim. Egypt.

mitzvah (pl. mitzvot). Commandment of Jewish law.

mizbeach. Altar used to offer sacrifices.

modeh ani. I thank. Short prayer of thanksgiving recited upon awakening.

motek. Sweet boy.

Musaf. Additional prayer service recited after the morning prayer service on Shabbat and festivals.

neitz. The moment when the sun rises above the horizon.

neshamah. Soul.

netilat yadayim. Hand-washing ritual in which water is poured from a special cup three times, intermittently, over each hand.

neviim. Prophets.

nu. Vernacular for "so," or "hurry up."

nusach. Exact text of the prayers.

parashah. Weekly portion of the Torah.

peyot. Sidelocks worn by fervently observant Jewish boys and men in observance of the biblical commandment not to cut the corners of one's beard (Leviticus 19:27). Literally: corners.

rasha. Evil person.

rav. Rabbi.

ruach hakodesh. Divine inspiration.

sandek. Person who holds the baby during a bris (considered a great honor).

Sefer Tehillim. Book of Psalms.

sefirat ha'omer. The counting of the forty-nine-day period between the holidays of Passover (recalling the Exodus from Egypt) and Shavuot (commemorating the giving of the Torah at Mount Sinai).

seudah (pl. *seudot*). Festive meal.

Seudah Shlishit. Third festive meal eaten toward the end of Shabbat.

Shabbat. The Sabbath, a weekly day of cessation from weekday activities, devoted to prayer and festive meals.

Shacharit. Morning prayer service.

shaliach. Messenger.

shamir. Supernatural worm that could cut through stone, iron, and diamond.

sharav. Oppressively hot, dry, eastern wind filled with sand.

Shavuot. Festival at the end of the *omer* (seven weeks after Passover) to celebrate the giving of the Torah.

sheitel. Wig worn by some observant Jewish married women in fulfillment of the law requiring a married woman to cover her hair.

sheva berachot. Seven blessings recited over wine at a wedding. Literally: seven blessings.

shiurim. Lectures.

shuckeling. Swaying movement during prayer.

shul. Synagogue.

Shulchan Aruch. The Code of Jewish Law compiled by Rabbi Joseph Karo in 1563.

siddur. Prayer book.

Sukkot. Festival of Tabernacles.

taanit dibbur. Abstention from any speech that is not related to Torah for an entire day. Literally: fast [of] speech.

tachrichim. White linen burial shrouds.

tamei. Ritually impure.

teshuvah. Repentance. Literally: return to the Source.

tikkun (pl. *tikkunim*). Rectification.

Tisha b'Av. The Ninth of Av, a day of intense mourning over the destruction of the Temple and other Jewish national calamities.

toen rabbani. Rabbinical advisor who assists petitioners in a *beit din* or rabbinical court hearing.

tzaddik (pl. *tzaddikim*). Righteous man.

tzaddikah. Righteous woman.

tzanua. Modest and refined.

tzedakah. Charity. Literally: justice.

tzitzit. Ritual fringes worn on a four-cornered garment by observant Jewish boys and men in fulfillment of the biblical commandment (Numbers 15:38, Deuteronomy 22:12).

yeshiva. Institute for full-time study of the Talmud by unmarried Jewish men and boys.

yeshuot. Salvation.

Yiddishkeit. Judaism.

yishuv (pl. *yishuvim*). Settlement.

zechut. Merit.

zivug. Predestined marriage partner.

ztz"l. Acronym for *zecher tzaddik li'vracha*, may the remembrance of the righteous be a blessing.